CW00833745

Perfect Charity

Women Religious Living the Spirit of Vatican II

Edited by

Mary Ryllis Clark, Heather O'Connor
and Valerie Krips

Morning Star Publishing

Published in Australia by
Morning Star Publishing
P. O. Box 51
Northcote Vic. 3070
Australia

ISBN 9781925208399

Copyright © Mary Ryllis Clark, Heather O'Connor and Valerie Krips

All rights reserved. Other than for the purposes and subject to the conditions prescribed under the *Copyright Act*, no part of this publication may be reproduced, stored in a retrieval system, or transmitted in any form or by any means, electronic, mechanical, photocopying, recording or otherwise, without the prior permission of the publisher.

Cataloguing-in-Publication entry is available from the National Library of Australia http:/catalogue.nla.gov.au/.

First published 2014
Book design by John Healy
Printed in Australia

In memory of Carol Hogan who lived and died with grace

Contents

There is a diversity of gifts. Wherefore, each one must stand firm in the vocation to which she has been called, since the mission of those called to the religious state in the Church is one thing; the mission of secular Institutes is another thing; the temporal and apostolic mission of the laity not especially consecrated to God in an Institute, is quite another. *Renovationis Causam*

Let them know quite clearly, at the same time, that they will be unable to accomplish so great a task unless the members have so thorough a grounding in matters divine and human that they will be truly leaven in the world, for the strengthening and increase of the Body of Christ. Superiors therefore should devote great care to the formation, especially the spiritual formation, and also to the promotion of their higher studies. *Perfectae Caritatis*

Foreword

Rachael Kohn

I am often asked who is the most impressive person you have interviewed for The Spirit of Things?[1] Immediately my mind turns to the many women religious I have met over the years. They are rarely household names, and usually not media stars, but they are women of remarkably broad achievement, and often possessed of a quiet dignity that belies the challenging paths they have trod.

One such woman is Maria Casey rsj, whom I met in Sydney in the period leading up to the canonisation of Mary MacKillop, where as Postulator she was in charge of examining the medical cases that were candidates for the required 'miracle cures'. A huge responsibility fraught with 'deception and bribery' required meticulous documentation, which her legal mind, as a canon lawyer, enabled her to carry out.

Yet typical of the women religious I have met over the years, Maria's biography reveals that her highly authoritative position was not inevitable, but arrived at through the steady accumulation of greater responsibilities in a life of service. From schoolteacher to running schools and overseeing their restructures and amalgamations, to pursuing further degrees, including training in canon law in Canada, to assuming the role of Director of the Marriage Tribunal in the Ballarat Diocese, the responsibilities and opportunities kept presenting themselves. Later, when the canonisation of Australia's first saint had been achieved, Maria would apply her considerable skills to oversee almost every aspect of the huge multi-media celebration.

In the past women religious could choose to retreat from the world in holy matrimony to God, but in modern times they have rarely shrunk from responding to society's needs. Through the most tumultuous times in the Church, as a consequence of Vatican II, they founded schools and hospitals, have entered the fray in solidarity with civil rights activists, have travelled to impoverished countries serving in alien cultures and they have walked the corridors of the university in search of answers to the theological and ecclesial questions of the day.

1 Rachael created The Spirit of Things in 1997 and it has been broadcast weekly since then.

Many of these themes appear in the life of Veronica Lawson rsm, whose considerable scholarly achievements led to her election as the first woman President of the Australian Catholic Biblical Association. Yet, her scholarship combined with a keen social justice commitment also resulted in a strong focus on the feminist reading of the scriptures leading to an increased participation and authority of women in the church. At the same time, such 'first world' concerns of a highly educated woman were balanced by assisting the people of Timor Leste in the areas of housing, hospital care and refugee assistance.

This combination of higher education and social justice has also meant that women religious are ready to involve themselves in some of the newer areas of concern, such as the environment. Patricia Powell rsm, who worked in Dubbo in a ministry of support and advocacy for the local Indigenous community, became greatly sensitised to the issue of land care and ecology. That led her to spearhead programmes that nurtured an 'ecological conversion,' which would in effect see all aspects of life, from the cosmos, societies, communities and families, as interconnected in a delicate web of life.

Many of these Australian initiatives have their parallel in America, where women religious have, arguably, made a greater impact on the public debates about human rights, feminism and ecology. Formidable scholar on science and religion, Professor of Theology at Fordham University, New York, Elizabeth Johnson, and prolific writer and social activist Joan Chittister in Erie, Pennsylvania, both guests on The Spirit of Things, come to mind, and both have caused a stir in the Vatican. In Australia, women religious have not on the whole attracted the ire of the Vatican with their outspokenness. On the contrary, they largely focused on quietly pursuing higher education and providing an array of social services, which have benefitted generations of Australians.

In all the cameo portraits of women religious in Australia gathered in this book it is evident that a complete reversal of the idea that the duty-bound life of women under religious vows is somehow insular or hemmed in. In fact, their vows have been a springboard to serving in a variety of different capacities, which enlarged their skills and widened their knowledge and understanding of the world. Such experience has a flow-on effect to the way in which their theology has developed and enveloped the changing world in which they live. And because it is inevitable that their theology is grounded in their lives, this fascinating collection of biographies demonstrates that women religious are at the forefront of future developments in the faith and the church. They are a truly impressive and inspiring bunch of women!

Introduction

It suddenly came over me as I sat looking at this vast assembly of almost three thousand people...that it has about it an air of artificiality and that the main reason for this is that there is not a single woman in the whole company. Up and down the nave you look and into the transepts, nothing but men. It is an abstracted body, incomplete, a torso of true catholicity, speaking more of an outmoded past than of the living present. Let us hope that the world will see something of Rome's strong women at Vatican III.

Douglas Horton, *Vatican Diary*[1]

In this book women talk frankly about a revolution. It was, from the point of view of most of the world, a largely unremarked one. It affected the life of women who lived a paradox: they had left the world as most of us know it in order to come closer to it. These women are Catholic religious, nuns, who lived through a change of historical as well as personal significance. And they are Australian. In their stories we read of experiences that have universal and particular resonance, of leaving behind traditions, many of which were hundreds of years old. Some of these traditions were beloved, and parting with them was more than painful: for some of them it was loss, plain and simple. For others, it was a renewal. What their stories reveal is the power of overcoming difficult change, of a fruitful forgetting that remembers even as it forgets.

They did this - forgetting and putting away, making anew - in large part because they were told to do so, but even before the orders came from Rome, they were getting ready, they were responding to their time and its changes with eagerness and anxiety in equal measure. Australia is far distant from the Europe in which many of their orders were founded, orders that sent the early sisters out to a young country that could scarcely be imagined, on the other side of the earth. As much as distance is a tyranny, it is also a freedom. The stories you will read in these pages reveal women who, whether active or contemplative nuns, have a spirit of freedom within them, which surely helped them to come to terms with the demands that Rome would make of them in the 1960s. These women went forward into the new world which was offered them in a spirit like their founders', and

1 Douglas Horton, 'Vatican Diary' in Carmel McEnroy, *Guests in their own House: the Women of Vatican II*. New York, Crossroad Publishing Company, 1996, 12,13.

like that of the women who took the long journey from Europe to establish their orders in Australia. They went forward in excitement equal to that of their precedessors: with exhilaration, and in joy and, because they are sensible people, with a little fear too. What they made of it is remarkable, and a story which reveals not just what these religious women were made of, but what made their local, their very Australian experience, special.

In the final stages of Vatican II in November 1965, the Council Fathers produced a document called *Perfectae Caritatis* – perfect charity – a decree on the up-to-date renewal of religious life. None of the women were consulted in the preparation of this document even though they numbered approximately eighty per cent of all Catholic religious worldwide, a fact that puts our opening quotation into context. Nevertheless the wholehearted and serious manner in which women's religious orders responded to *Perfectae Caritatis*, as they did to all the council documents that affected them, is one of the most remarkable events in the history of the Catholic church.

Few who grew up after the Second World War in Australia would have failed to notice Catholic nuns. Women clad from head to toe in black moved mysteriously from convents to the local parish schools, were seen visiting the sick, and were glimpsed occasionally at public celebrations of Catholic life. But even the most devout Catholics had little idea of how nuns lived behind their convent walls.

Vocations to the religious life, a public path to the perfection in which 'many are called but few are chosen' were highly revered. Nuns lived a semi-monastic life, whether the order was strictly enclosed or active; enclosure and the requirement to wear habits was made compulsory by Pope Boniface VIII in 1298: active female congregations with simple vows were not recognised formally by Rome as true religious until 1900. The Code of Canon Law in 1917 further imposed a high level of uniformity on the women's orders, so that by the early 1960s constitutions, spiritual formation and the daily routine did not vary greatly from one religious order to the next.

Women entering religious life did so accepting that the life would be austere, and would demand sacrifices not asked others. Their vocation 'surely had something to do with that never ending God-quest that leads us all on different paths,' as Veronica Lawson, one of the women we interviewed, remarks. That nuns' vows required them to remain chaste and to act in obedience to their superiors was commonly understood, but the specific details of their lives remained opaque.

Even those who visited them in the convent may not have noticed, for example, that while the nuns might provide beautiful afternoon teas in the parlour, they did not take a cup of tea or eat a cake themselves, since eating with seculars was forbidden. Some of the institutes did not permit attendance at family funerals, and when they did it was understood that the nun should seek accommodation in a nearby convent, rather than stay overnight with her family. Nor was it unusual for personal letters, whether going in or out, to be read by those in charge. Sisters were discouraged from forming friendships within their communities; for the small number living the life of a contemplative within the enclosure this meant 'a total rejection of any relationship, except with Jesus, and no opportunity for human development, except through prayer' as Carol Hogan, one of the contemplatives among those we interviewed remarks.

Presents could not be exchanged, and visits to the practitioners such as the dentist had to be in the company of another sister. Deirdre Browne recounts that when she was studying music at the Conservatorium at Melbourne University in 1960, the other students found her 'a bit of a pain' since if none of the sisters was available to escort her home, she had to ask a student to accompany her.

Within the convent there was no television, no personal access to phones and limited reading material. The few nuns able to drive were those who learned to do so before entering the convent. Ringing bells marked long hours of silence, seating for meals was regimented, and every minute of the day was organized around prayer, physical work in maintaining buildings and grounds, supervision of boarders in the case of schools, and care of elderly or sick nuns, as well as the work that constituted the corporate mission of the congregation; study and preparation for the next day's work were also fitted in. Recreation was communal and usually limited to an hour a day and permission was required for any variation to the daily routine.

In 1962 Cardinal Léon Joseph Suenens wrote that nuns were 'out of touch with the world as it is'; they were 'an anachronism'. Acknowledging that 'what one can only call the anti-feminist tradition has had a long inning' he also felt that the nuns themselves were partly to blame. They had long held positions of authority and responsibility in the worlds of health and education but, he wrote, that as 'a nun she will not allow herself to claim even a few of the rights that women have managed to obtain bit by bit from man in the world'.[2]

His comments were prophetic. Three years later, in 1965, the Decree on the Up-to-Date Renewal of Religious Life, *Perfectae Caritatis,* revolutionised the lives of nuns. It demanded a return to the scriptures, to the 'spirit and aims of the founder', a proper understanding of and adaptation to 'the changed conditions of the times' and an accompanying inner 'spiritual renewal'. Each congregation was asked to revise its 'constitutions, directories, books of customs, of prayers, of ceremonies' and bring them into line with Council thinking. Any distinction between members, such as lay sisters and choir nuns, was to be abolished and systems of authority reviewed. The religious habit was to be 'simple and modest' and 'suited to the times and place and to the needs of the apostolate'. Appropriate training and support for individuals was considered essential and it was emphasised that 'successful renewal and adaptation depended on the cooperation of all'. To ensure that action would be taken every institute had to hold renewal chapters within three years of the Council.

Much has been written about the nature and the pace of change, economic, social and cultural, affecting all sections of society following the Second World War. All non-government and voluntary agencies, all churches and the communities that supported them, religious and secular, and all work places associated with them were transformed almost beyond recognition in the space of a few decades. Nuns in Australia were not immune to the maelstrom of social change that raged around them. In every major city in Australia Saturday morning lectures on the Council documents, presented by scholars and theologians, many who had been in Rome, were arranged for women and men religious by Church authorities. In the mid-1960s women were, for the first time, able to study theology. Many religious enrolled in courses overseas with their communities' support and encouragement since theological study for women was not yet available in Australia. Embarking on diplomas, degrees, masters degrees and doctorates, nuns took up studies in scripture and canon law, psychology, pastoral studies, human and faith development. They also learned new approaches to spirituality in which

2 Cardinal Léon Suenens, *The Nun in the World,* London, Burns & Oates, 1962, 51.

retreats became directed rather than preached, and a spiritual director might take the place of a Father confessor.

The habit became a metaphor for the changes. Many women saw it as symbolic of their religious commitment and were loathe to abandon it, while others thought the change in their outward appearance to be liberating and equally symbolic of changes within.

The women we interviewed who entered before Vatican II emphasised how extraordinary it was to take part in the conversations that followed the changes. Women who were not consulted on anything were suddenly consulted on everything.

Neither the adaptation to the changing sociological circumstances nor the renewal of religious life was easily achieved: both involved unrelenting challenge, work, discussion, prayer and study, against backgrounds which might include conflict as well as excitement and exhilaration, joy as well as sorrow, all achieved through new processes of decision-making: discernment. At the same time, the numbers of women in religious life declined as some women left the convent, and fewer younger women entered. The women remaining were less likely to be supported by the lay sisters who had previously borne the load of domestic work. Boarding facilities in convent schools across Australia rapidly decreased, partly as the result of the loss of domestic labour, and with that fading an icon of Australia's educational history all but disappeared in a little more than a decade.

The introduction of state aid to Catholic schools and the subsequent development of a Catholic education system that began in the late 1960s marked a paradigm shift. Funds began to flow from the Commonwealth Government and the States and many nuns were released from classroom teaching. With the funding came increased accountability, exercised through the burgeoning Catholic Education Offices at national, state and diocesan levels, effectively shifting much of the day-to-day control away from the religious.

The opportunity for self-determination, and consideration of where the individual's talents lay, arrived at through discernment - 'the recognition of the divine in one's personal life'- became part of the women's post-Vatican II vocabulary.[3] Returning to their founders' originating vision, the women were able to direct their work to the needs of their contemporary worlds.

---

3 Greg Dening, *Church Alive – Pilgrimages in Faith 1956-2006*. Sydney, UNSW Press, 2006, 85.

Women had founded five of the orders whose members we interviewed, and their journeys to foundation were frequently long, arduous, and sustained in the face of considerable obstacles, of which hierarchical obstruction was by no means the least. The Presentation Sisters' Nano Nagle, the Mercy Sisters' Catherine McAuley, the Sisters of Charity's Mary Aikenhead, the Josephites' Mary MacKillop and the Loretos' Mary Ward were all strong, radical, independent and inspirational women who, before Vatican II, had scarcely rated a mention in the novitiate of the orders they had founded. In her interview Maria Casey remarked that some of her peers in the Josephite novitiate complained that they had learned little of their founder. Returning to the originary vision of the founder was a breath of life, a renewal of spirit. Maria, originally trained as a primary school teacher, remarks that 'we have a lot of sisters now in individual ministries who are right out at the edges...we know that they're with the people who are marginalised, who are suffering, and that is truly Mary MacKillop territory…there is still that urge to go out to the edges, or the margins, to where the need is'.

Each of the women we have interviewed has arrived at a different destination. Whether it is Stancea Vichie, working to combat human trafficking, Anna Warlow sustaining parishes without priests, Clare Condon winning the 2013 Australian Human Rights Medal for the work of the Good Samaritans under her leadership, Maria Casey acting as procurator for the cause of Mary MacKillop, Josephite Anne Derwin spending 25 years in leadership roles or Patricia Powell, playing a key role in transforming the Mercy convent in Bathurst into an ecological learning centre.

Biblical scholar Veronica Lawson has made a major contribution to the intellectual and reflective life of Catholics in Australia; similarly Deirdre Browne has had a significant impact through music and liturgy. Libby Rogerson has focussed on social justice; Brigid Arthur has espoused the cause of asylum seekers. Maryanne Confoy teaches theology and ministry while Bernadette Keating establishes structures for Presentation Sisters Victoria for a future without nuns. Carol Hogan became a feminist theologian and Joanna Bagot, as a mature modern post-Vatican II woman, entered the Benedictine order at Jamberoo in New South Wales. Each of the women encompass the spirit of *Perfectae Caritatis.*

The women we interviewed were chosen not so much because of what they undertake but because of how they managed the journey from the 'normal' of religious life as it was at the time of the Council to the 'new normal', as

Sandra Schneiders has called it, that is in place now. For us they represent the women of Vatican II in Australia who rediscovered the vision of their founders, the courage of the pioneering early sisters of their congregations and the deep meaning of the gospels. They embody the 'new' holiness Pope John XXIII hoped the Council would offer. We invited them to share their experiences to honour lives that seem to us remarkable. We thank them for their generosity, openness and trust.

The Apostolic Orders

The Missionary Sisters of Service

The Missionary Sisters of Service, one of a handful of orders established in Australia, was founded by Father John Corcoran Wallis, a diocesan priest who was ordained in 1932 for the Archdiocese of Hobart. As a young priest he noted the difficulties faced by those living on the margins of society, the isolated, forgotten and disadvantaged. To serve this need, he founded an order of women who, going into the 'highways and byways', could offer care, support, and education in faith to people 'round their kitchen tables'. Four mature-aged Tasmanian women formed the nucleus of the new order, and on 8 July 1944 they commenced their lives together in Launceston, receiving official recognition as a religious congregation in 1951. The sisters acquired a caravan in the 1950s to help with their extensive travels around Tasmania; they became widely known in the state as the Caravan Sisters. A photograph of their caravan began to appear on their newsletters and brochures and in 1955 they took the caravan to Melbourne as part of the Catholic Life Exhibition; unsurprisingly it caused something of a sensation. From Tasmania, the MSS spread into New South Wales, Queensland, South Australia and Victoria. Outside Australia, the sisters have worked in Timor Leste and Papua New Guinea, while one sister currently lives and works in Singapore. In 2010 the sisters set up the John Wallis Foundation to continue their mission 'beyond their life-span'.

Stancea Vichie mss

Stancea Vichie was born in 1948 and entered The Missionary Sisters of Service in 1968. She took her final vows in 1976.

Born in Brisbane in 1948, Stancea grew up in Bundaberg. She is descended from Irish, English and Croatian immigrants. They all came to Australia within a 50-year period between 1835-1885, and with the exception of one family, all settled in Queensland. Stancea's father was a fitter and turner, recruited into the RAAF during the Second World War; later he worked in the sugar industry. Her mother was a dressmaker who made costumes for dance and theatre; during the war she made uniforms for American servicemen in Brisbane.

An active community and parish life in Bundaberg gave Stancea a strong sense of belonging. Educated by the Sisters of Mercy, she was the oldest of five children, and left school upon completing Year 10. Her membership of the Young Christian Students (YCS) while she was at school was an early influence leading to active membership in the Young Christian Workers (YCW) after she completed school. Working in a lawyer's office, she was restless. 'My big goal was to travel, especially to Europe. I was saving my little wages like mad…I wanted to travel, I wanted to do things and was getting totally bored with work. I knew there was something more for me. I always knew I was going to leave Bundaberg'. She travelled around parts of Australia and also went to Fiji and the Solomon Islands; she thinks of these early ventures as a precursor of what was to come later in her life.

During her primary school years she learned of the Missionary Sisters of Service (MSS) through publicity provided by the Marist Fathers in their publication *Harvest:*

> When I was about ten they were doing a picture story of the different religious orders. I remember one – the caravan was on the cover - about a couple of women in ordinary grey dresses. They had cars and they were going out and actually being in people's homes and staying with them. They were not teaching in schools or nursing in a hospital. I remember having this warm glow and thinking 'that looks great! Very adventurous! That looks terrific!' I kept the magazine in my wardrobe and probably didn't think too much more about it, although there were times when sister asked the class, 'Now who's going to be a nun?' and I always put up my hand.

A cousin of Stancea's had joined the Caravan Sisters, but left the novitiate after 18 months with them. When she came back to Queensland she brought brochures about the congregation. Stancea found them really interesting but 'a year or so later I left school and pushed it out of my head'.

The possibility of becoming a nun was raised with her by the YCW chaplain, but Stancea was much more interested in travelling, although, as she said to him it 'is very funny that you ask me that, as there's something been happening within me and I haven't wanted to even look at it or talk about it to anybody'. She 'didn't want to commit myself because marriage was an option for me. There was someone in my life who was a real possibility for me…then some months later our chaplain said he had made an appointment for me to see the sister who was the leader of the Missionary Sisters of Service as she was coming up to Brisbane…I didn't want to commit myself…I was in a total stage of yes – no, yes, no…a total state of resistance'.

She was clear that if she did become a nun, she did not want to join an order focused on teaching or nursing; 'I just knew that I was meant to be with a group that was free, to be mobile, to go where the need was, outside of an institutional framework'. She met Sister Teresa Morse, then leader of the MSS who impressed Stancea as a woman with a sense of dignity: 'she wasn't remote from me. She treated me like a human being. I could engage with her. Maybe I had an expectation that she might be a bit removed being leader'.

It was another twelve months before Stancea felt ready to commit to religious life. She left Bundaberg for the novitiate in Tasmania at the age of 20 in 1968, three years after the conclusion of the Second Vatican Council. There were 50 women in the order and although much was changing for religious the dimensions of those changes were in some ways less for the MSS, whose recent foundation anticipated some of the freedoms and expression of mission adopted by other orders after Vatican II. 'At one level,' she said, 'we were less affected because of the way in which we had been able to carry out our mission. On the other hand, daily life within the MSS house up until the latter part of the 1960s was more structured in terms of having an order of day and this began to change after the Council. In terms of our understanding of mission, we began to develop a broader and richer perspective which came from the Council, looking in the world for 'the signs of the times', and entering into that world with its joys, griefs and anxieties'.

Of her novitiate experience she wondered, 'What have I come to?' Very soon I thought I would leave. It wasn't what I expected. I was ready to save the world! When I discovered that I needed to do a bit of study, I was quite thrown. During the first six weeks it didn't appeal to me at all and I was leaving!' However, after 'that initial six weeks, we went out to spend a week with two of our sisters who lived at Ellendale in the Derwent Valley':

> We went with them in their work through the villages and farms in the Valley. That experience was a turning point for me. I began to commit myself in a new way to the call to mission with the MSS and realised that I needed a sound formation that required time. A really important aspect of the third year of our formation was spending most of the year involved in pastoral work with our sisters in rural parishes throughout Tasmania.

The other excitement for her was study undertaken with John Wallis, the founder of the order, whom she found to be widely read in the new theological work associated with Vatican II. A year or two before joining the MSS, Stancea had already begun to read the Vatican II documents:

> I started to read them from page one and it was heavy going. I just didn't have the language to cope with it. This changed when I had the opportunity to understand the vision of Vatican II as it was being opened up to us in the novitiate studies. I remember the feeling of exhilaration as we studied 'The Church in the Modern World' and the other documents; in fact our whole congregation was being challenged to live the vision of the Council because of John Wallis and other great people.

The theology and other reading that the MSS sisters took as the basis of their spiritual lives rested on the insistence of John Wallis that it be based firmly in the scriptures. He introduced them to a wide range of theological and scriptural reading, as well as Church history, encouraging their independent study and providing a sound basis for their understanding of the importance of Vatican II.

The Catholic Church in Tasmania was then under the leadership of Archbishop Guilford Young, who had been present at all the Council sessions. He was another man who, in Stancea's view, was ahead of his time in creating a church community that was 'very alive and on fire…great work was done on liturgical renewal. Priority was given to opportunities to hear some of the Australian and overseas theologians and scripture scholars who were committed to Vatican II. There was a lot of ferment around that. I couldn't have been in a better place at the time. A lot of other places caught up with Hobart after that I think'.

The calibre of women who have been the order's own leaders matches that of John Wallis. The four Stancea has experienced have all provided positive leadership: 'I've been fortunate in that I've had very good relationships with our leaders…so my overall experience of leadership in the congregation has been very positive'.

In her early formation Stancea was schooled into a quiet time each day, a time for contemplation: 'that is the other thing that has always been at the heart of who we are as MSS: it's been that contemplative base…John used to talk about it in terms of apostolic contemplatives and contemplative apostles'. He encouraged them to see they could not provide the support needed by the people they served unless their lives were based on a deep contemplation and understanding of the Scriptures. The ethos of the congregation relied on trusting that, as mature women, they would find their own 'rhythm of the day': prayer, quiet time, reading and contemplation while they were travelling away from their home base. 'There are times, to be sure, when I might fall by the wayside in some shape or form but basically there's a sense that I'm trusted, I'm a mature adult and I need to find the way. This is in contemplation, in prayer, in relationships, in everything really'.

At the end of her initial formation, the MSS leader suggested to Stancea that she might go to university in Hobart, to undertake an arts degree, something she had never imagined; in fact, she did not sleep the night it was mentioned to her:

> My family existed in something of an Irish sub-culture in Bundaberg in Queensland. Many of the priests and sisters were Irish. The sisters worked very hard to give us an education that would equip us to enter the work force, especially in areas that had previously been denied to Catholics. Generally speaking, young women from my part of the world just didn't go to university. That was for people with money. I was the first person in my family to have this opportunity. The time at university was a great experience. I had no background of studying at that level and I found it hard at first but slowly I found my way. History and psychology were my two majors. I discovered I had a real passion for history. What was really interesting, and challenging, was the people I met there. I will be forever grateful for that opportunity.

After completing her university studies, Stancea worked in adult faith formation, firstly in a parish, then in the Catholic Education Office in

Hobart. These experiences challenged her to find ways to unfold the vision of Vatican II continually with catechists, parish councils and family groups, work which was a strong commitment for the MSS.

Among the influences in Stancea's life were Action for World Development (AWD), and the Asia Bureau, organisations raising awareness about justice and peace issues in the world. The material they presented in their newsletters and workshops 'opened up a picture of the structures and systems which were causing poverty and oppression of so many people in the world'. This began 'to influence my thinking and the way I was living my life more and more during the 1970s. The questions that were often there: why is this happening, what are the causes? The old YCW training of 'see, judge, act' came in handy there too!' As a result Stancea and another sister began to 'put together a small Justice and Peace newsletter and send it off to the whole community. Year by year, we were all being transformed by the growing awareness of the massive inequalities which were in the world, something which was so at odds with the central message of Jesus'.

At the beginning of 1981, she joined the MSS team based at Whyalla in South Australia, the first of many experiences working in rural and outback regions. It was here, and across a vast area, that she met farming communities on the Eyre Peninsula, graziers along the Oodnadatta Track, the Stuart Highway, and the Flinders Ranges. She met railway workers along the line to the West Australian border, and came into contact with a diverse cultural mix in the opal mining areas, as well as encountering Aboriginal communities and a wide variety of people on the way, right through to Uluru in Central Australia[1]. 'These were extraordinary times of learning to trust in some of the most isolated parts of this country, going from place to place, not always knowing what the next day would bring. The hospitality of the people was such a gift. It felt again like a total immersion in the stories of the missionary journeys of the disciples as told in the gospels'.

The 1980s was a time when the sisters were beginning to move away from a pattern of work made up of responding to diocesan requests. They began to diversify in what they undertook, often accompanied by re-training or upgrading their qualifications. They began to work in retreats and spiritual direction as well as personal and spiritual development and industrial

1 Other MSS sisters worked in twos or threes in Parkes (NSW), or Toowoomba (QLD), until about 1969. After their first chapter following the Vatican Council more sisters lived alone as pastoral workers. One of their sisters assumed responsibility for running a parish without a priest.

chaplaincy. They worked with refugees, and Aboriginal people, and undertook pastoral leadership in parishes, and provided a more sustained presence in small towns from Weipa in the Gulf Country to Beaconsfield in Tasmania.

Stancea moved to Melbourne in 1987 to become part of the MSS leadership team. Some years later, a further paradigm shift in her life's work grew out of an opportunity to study overseas at the Maryknoll School of Theology, New York, with its concentration on liberation theology:

> I always had a great love for being with people from different cultures. Maryknoll was a great place to be.[2] The people who studied with me were from Latin America, Asia, Africa, some from the US. I was the only Australian there. The people who came into the dining room each day, apart from the students, were working in all those places. We used to sit there for hours talking. My main area of learning was in the dining room!

When she finished her studies at Maryknoll, Stancea traveled to Peru, staying initially with two Franciscan nuns from the US. On her second day in the country she learned that Irene McCormack, an Australian Josephite nun, had been killed the night before in Huasahuasi, a small village in the mountains. A day or two after Irene's death, Stancea attended a memorial Eucharist for Irene at the little church in El Pacifico, at which the Australian Josephites working in Peru were present. Recounting her thoughts she says,

> I couldn't believe I was there. There was a picture of Mary MacKillop hanging on the outside of the church. There were too many people for us to use the church. I thought to myself, here am I standing here, a woman from one of our Australian foundations has been killed – one of the great Josephites; I'm standing here a member of another Australian-founded community and asking myself, how did I get to be here for this amazingly powerful moment?

She woke the next morning, 'feeling great anger at what was happening, especially to poorer people, I got out of that bed and thought, I am going! I am going to the mountains. I don't want to be killed. I don't want to be a martyr but I'm going. I was so inspired by seeing the people getting on with life within a context of such insecurity'. She had received an invitation from a nursing sister from New Zealand who was working among the Aymara people in the region around Lake Titicaca high up in the Andes. Peru was in the grip of an extremely difficult political situation, poverty was endemic

2 The Maryknoll School of Theology, famous for its liberation theologians, closed in 1995.

and there was a cholera outbreak. The experience helped her understand 'what it meant to channel anger felt about injustice and oppression into a loving creative response'.

That experience in Peru, followed by a time of travelling in part of the Middle East and South East Asia on her way home, left Stancea with a deep sense of what solidarity meant, even when she was no longer a physical presence with the people she had met:

> The experience took me back into the heart of what we, as MSS, believe community means for us – that is, communion of mind and heart. That's what it is for us. It's not about living under the same roof. It's about being deeply connected to one another no matter where we are or with whom we live…It was this sense which developed even more for me, that is being in communion of mind and heart with the people I had been amongst – the family afraid of being kidnapped in Mindanao in the Philippines, the woman who hoped the Sendero Luminoso would not enter her village in Peru to kill the village leaders as they had done in the village where Irene McCormack was, the Palestinian man who stopped to help Israelis whose car had broken down on the road from Jericho to Jerusalem; often, I simply sat with the chaos and beauty of it all.

When she returned to Australia later in 1991, Stancea continued her work on the MSS leadership team, followed by re-election for a further six years. In early 2000, she was able to gain access to visit asylum seekers inside the Maribyrnong Detention Centre in Melbourne.

> The years spent being with people who were detained was such a significant time in my life. I so often found that simply sitting there with a person who has fled violence, and who has no certainty of when they might be released from detention, was often a time of 'wordless presence'. The centre was a microcosm of our suffering world, with people from many cultures, all desperate to find a peaceful life. I constantly questioned the policy of mandatory detention and worked with others to lobby for change, seeing first hand the trauma that could result from such a policy, especially with children.

After her period on the MSS leadership team expired in early 1999, Stancea began to work with the East Timor Human Rights Centre in Fitzroy. Soon she began to work with the Australian Council for Overseas Aid Human Rights (ACFOA) whose office was in the same building. Its Director was Pat Walsh, a long time advocate for the people of East Timor. Within weeks, Pat called a meeting regarding a solidarity visit to East Timor prior to the independence ballot that was to take place on 30 August 1999. The idea was to go to East

Timor to support human rights workers through a presence on the ground, since the workers were the constant target of the Indonesian military. Stancea recalled clearly being asked 'Would you go?' by Pat. Without thinking she said 'Yes. Here again, the words came: I don't particularly want to be a martyr! I was very aware of the situation in East Timor and had been part of a group which wrote letters of support to people there.' Her first night in Dili:

> brought me in touch with stories of the trauma being faced by the people. Later that evening as a military helicopter flew overhead, the young man whose family owned the small house where I was staying quietly left the room, went around the house, and closed the wooden windows on each room. He was such a sign of the divine, protecting and keeping watch. I spent time with people who had fled the mountains in fear of their lives, and those who waited for rice each day. I returned to Australia on 30 June, two months to the day before the independence ballot – on 30 August 1999.

During the next year or so, Stancea also worked with an ecumenical team to develop a conference in Melbourne with the theme 'Religion and Culture in Asia Pacific: Violence or Healing', which provided a further opportunity to make links with human rights advocates and interfaith networks.

By the end of 2000, the ACFOA Human Rights Centre and work on the conference came to an end. Where to now? Since she had been visiting the Maribyrnong Detention Centre all that year, the next call was clearly to be with asylum seekers who were trying to exist in the community with very little support. At about this time, Stancea came into contact with Grant Mitchell, who had been working for a year at the Hotham Mission Asylum Seeker Project under the auspices of the Uniting Church. Stancea joined him in this venture. It was an opportunity to grow a small organization with little resources, largely reliant on part-time and volunteer work, into a thriving centre that provided both material aid and advocacy on behalf of asylum seekers who were living in the community without rights or entitlements.

> It has always been about the people whose faces I look into and see suffering, yet so often a great resilience too. Just as Jesus did in being with the people most ignored and cast out, it challenges me to walk with people in such a way that I stand in solidarity with them as they find their voice and make the decisions they need for their lives. This spirit is one with the gift that we MSS sisters try to live, that of being with people in their ordinary everyday lives, allowing ourselves to be transformed by being with them.

If there is one aspect of their lives that women religious tend to discount, it is the power and influence they have when acting as advocates for social change, standing up in public on behalf of those who lack the resources or opportunities to do so themselves. To Stancea and others like her, it may seem no more than 'doing what ought to be done'. But without advocates with skills and passion refugees, the poor, and those who are marginalised by society, remain condemned to rely on charity rather than on justice to tackle the cause of their hardships. Stancea is one of many women religious who took on the role of advocacy, borne out of the day-to-day work she undertook as her mission with asylum seekers and women who have been trafficked into Australia.

Whilst at the Hotham Mission Asylum Seeker Project, Stancea and the team began to present to politicians and immigration workers community based housing and support alternatives to placing asylum seekers in detention centres. The lobbying of the team was based in the grassroots experience of the generosity of people in the community who were supporting the work of the project. 'Eventually, we invited the Minister for Immigration to visit some of our housing work in one of the leafy wealthy eastern suburbs of Melbourne, housing that had been donated to us for a year by a church group'. Families with children and single men were living in the complex.

> Even with minimal financial support [because] of the wonderful companioning by our volunteers, it was working well. It is possible to house asylum seekers in the community. You do not have to have them in detention. We just kept advocating for services for the people, and continued lobbying the various Ministers for Immigration to soften the harsh policies.

Asked if she felt uncomfortable lobbying politicians, she answered with some enthusiasm 'No – not at all!'

> When I have been to politicians with others in Canberra or elsewhere, my companions and I have been well prepared and have spoken the truth that honours justice for those who have been denied a voice. I always remember some years ago in Parliament House in Canberra, a worker for one of the politicians we were to visit, said to us, "Don't you women ever underestimate the clout you've got in this place". I think we ought to use our 'clout' as much as possible.

Building on her work with asylum seekers, Stancea moved on in 2008 to work with the team at the Good Shepherd Social Justice Network as well as involving herself with ACRATH (Australian Catholic Religious Against

Trafficking in Humans). ACRATH was based at the Good Shepherd Convent in Melbourne, where the two groups worked together for the elimination of human trafficking in Australia and beyond. Six years earlier, during her weekly visits to the detention centre, Stancea had met some groups of women who had been trafficked into the sex industry and were placed in detention before being sent back to their home country. At that time, no programme of support for these women existed. It was during the next year, in 2003, that a government inquiry found that the women would no longer be detained, and would have basic support if they would agree to interviews with Australian Federal Police.

The intensive lobbying and public education by ACRATH and other groups had its outcome in the gradual improvement of support for women who had been trafficked, but still remains linked to the criminal justice system. Through the generosity of numbers of lawyers, the women are able to access pro-bono legal advice.[3]

> Over numbers of years, some of us in ACRATH have been accompanying young women who have been trafficked, being with them to listen, and offer friendship and to walk with them in the healing process after the trauma they have been through. Again, this experience of being with a person who has been trafficked, makes our voices as advocates even more powerful. We are privileged to be with people who have suffered so greatly.

ACRATH members have been lobbying in Canberra since 2004. The numbers of politicians and staffers in various government departments visited in these trips have grown greatly over the years; 'A wonderful group of younger and older women who are not part of religious communities have been joining ACRATH each year. This is important because in years to come there will be few of us (i.e. religious) sitting round the table; there are other women involved now.' When asked what sustains her, she says 'this is an exciting yet chaotic time to be in the world, and isn't so much coming from women!'

---

3 The women have 45 days to consider how to proceed. This period can be extended a further 45 days if necessary, and if they are prepared to give evidence about the traffickers. While the sex industry is the most common destination for trafficked women, advocates like Stancea believe they are also being exploited in the hospitality and agricultural industries. There is also evidence of men, particularly from China, being trafficked into the construction industries.

Stancea has had 'a rich life – it's been very interesting. What a gift! And it's continuing to be exciting and rich too. A lot of religious women in their 80s and beyond are still so vibrant and alive, aren't they? They are my models for when and if I reach that age'. Her spirituality, she says, like that of other MSS sisters 'has been very much shaped by the land of this ancient continent, Australia. Over the years, it has been a gift to be with Aboriginal people, to grow in reverence of their spirituality in which they are one with the land, and to marvel at the deeply spiritual presence they have brought to this land over tens of thousands of years'. The influence of the land upon her is clear:

> One of the strongest experiences of land shaping my spirituality was formed in the times of working in the outback opal-mining town of Coober Pedy. The time of quiet each day was often spent at 'Boot Hill', the cemetery on the outskirts of Coober Pedy. I would look out across the horizon, no trees, or anything else in sight apart from very small saltbush, just experiencing the emptiness and aloneness of it all, sensing a presence which drew me into the mystery of it all. The time of working in the desert areas brought alive for me the scriptures which speak of deserts coming to life – the greening of the vegetation on the sandhills, and the brilliant red of the Sturt Desert Pea as it snaked along the red earth after the rains.

But what sustains her ultimately

> Is the presence of God in the risen Christ who keeps inviting me to be alert to the signs of the reign of God…even in the dark times, the flicker of this flame of invitation is never quite extinguished, and hope is found even in the unspectacular moments if I am able to recognise the love which is there. All this is possible only if I remain faithful to time apart each day for silence. Relationships through the support of my community, family, and friends, are at the heart of life. Wandering in the bush is one of the most profound places of sustenance for me. Sharing meals, laughter, and conversations bring new energy when I listen to the stories of others. Music often moves me deeply as I listen to an orchestra, or play an instrument at home. Reading is central to my life and takes me to new places I could not have envisaged.

The order was founded to meet the needs of a unique section of the Catholic community, people in remote and rural communities who are cut off from many of the pastoral supports provided by the church in the towns and cities. The sisters' adaptability and flexibility in response to these needs leads them into uncharted waters even to this day. The MSS are concerned to ensure that their vision and spirit should continue to find expression beyond, as they put it, their 'life-span'. In 2010 the sisters inaugurated the John Wallis

Foundation, named in honour of their Founder. The Foundation's original Board consisted of seven laypeople and three sisters. Today, Foundation Regional Groups have been established around Australia where the sisters are still present, or have worked in the past. These groups, in touch with the local people, are the 'eyes and ears' of the Foundation. The Foundation Board and Regional Groups form partnerships with others to reach out to the geographically or socially isolated, to young people, and groups who work for justice.

The Sisters of the Good Samaritan

Affectionately known as the Good Sams, the Congregation of the Sisters of the Good Samaritan of the Order of Saint Benedict was the first order of religious women founded in Australia. It was the realisation of a dream long held by John Bede Polding, Australia's first Catholic archbishop. Polding, a Benedictine monk from Downside Abbey in England, was appointed Vicar Apostolic of New Holland and Van Diemen's Land in 1834. Before leaving England, he recruited Irish Sisters of Charity to work with the poor of Sydney, especially destitute women. In 1848 they took over the running of a women's refuge which they renamed the House of the Good Shepherd. When they transferred their resources to establishing a free hospital in Sydney, Polding recruited five women willing to take on the women's refuge and commit their lives to God in a new religious congregation.

The women began their training in February 1857 as Sisters of the Good Shepherd under the guidance of Sister Scholastica Gibbons, superior of the Sisters of Charity, but known by the early Good Sams as Mother Foundress. Their rule, drawn up by Polding, combined Benedictine spirituality with practical charity responding to the needs of nineteenth century Sydney. Its emphasis was simplicity of life and compassionate service. Apart from running the women's refuge, the sisters visited people who were sick, impoverished and in prison. In 1866, when a revised rule was submitted for approval in Rome, Polding changed the name of the congregation to Sisters of the Good Samaritan to avoid confusion with the French Sisters of the Good Shepherd already established in Melbourne.

By this stage there were 40 Good Samaritan Sisters and their work had expanded to include caring for orphans and teaching in schools. As their numbers increased, the Good Sams spread to every state and territory, focusing increasingly on education. In 1948 a group of sisters went to Japan at the invitation of the Bishop of Nagasaki. In the 1990s they also went to Kiribati and the Philippines and more recently to Timor Leste.

After the Second Vatican Council the sisters reconnected strongly with their original charism and extended their support to indigenous people, the elderly, homeless, prisoners and people with disabilities. Their ministry also includes catechetics, parish work and spiritual direction.

Anna Warlow sgs

Anna Warlow was born in 1947 and entered the Sisters of the Good Samaritan in 1973. She made her final vows in 1980.

Anna Warlow doesn't believe in doing things alone. She is someone for whom collaboration is all-important and it was therefore not surprising that she did not want to meet to talk about her life's work in adult faith development alone. Instead we met at the home of her friends Terry and Michael Gleeson in Redhill, a Canberra suburb of comfortable houses and wide, leafy streets. Apart from the Gleesons, Anna was accompanied by her friend, Loreto sister Margaret (Marg) Finlay and by another Canberra friend, Jane Scroope. Anna was in Canberra to attend a dinner for recipients of Medals of the Order of Australia and had invited Marg as her guest. The two had flown from Perth where Marg lives but for Anna the journey also involved a long drive from her home in the mid-west of Western Australia. Sitting in Terry and Michael's beautiful sitting room around a table laden with cakes and coffee seemed more like a social occasion than an interview about Anna's life and work until Jane Scroope started to weep.

Rather than talk about herself, Anna had invited Jane as someone who was a living example of her work in action. As Jane told her story and talked about the transformation she had experienced after doing a retreat with Anna more than 25 years before, her tears began. It was the mid-1980s and Jane and her husband, both practising Catholics, were looking for ways of deepening their faith. Jane in particular felt her religious education was lacking.

> I was in Years 9 and 10 in a little school in Tumut when Vatican II was happening and I remember one of the nuns coming in one day and saying, 'I don't know what we're going to do for religion today because we're told that the old stuff's gone and the new stuff's on'. And she had nothing to say…and I remember thinking, how peculiar.

Jane and her husband, she explained, had joined the Teams of Our Lady, 'hoping to develop our spirituality outside just Sunday mass and the sacraments'. Twice their group had tried self-directed retreats and found them unsatisfactory. It happened that a member of the Teams of Our Lady group worked as a secretary with Anna Warlow, principal of St Francis of Assisi, a parish school in Calwell, Canberra, and told her about the group.

'Anna sent marvellous material for us to use in our study topics,' said Jane, 'I especially recall a series called *God is Sea* aimed at helping people find an image of God other than that of an old man in the sky. Another thing which had a great impact on us was a Jesuit publication, *God of Surprises*'.[1]

Jane approached Anna about giving a retreat to the group and Anna agreed.

> Anna led us on a spiritual journey. From the start she told us we were the future of the Church, that we could sustain our own spiritual lives. She showed us things we had never dreamed about – like Aladdin on his magical carpet ride. She gave us faith life tools for bringing up our children, for happiness, for caring for body, mind and spirit. It was liberating.

Jane's tears in describing this time were a piercing reminder of so many people's yearning for what Irish priest and writer Daniel O'Leary, whom Anna Warlow greatly admires, describes as 'light in their darkness, hope in their despair, courage in their fear'. To emphasise this point, Anna gave us copies of O'Leary's article from which she quoted. After decades in clerical ministry, Daniel O'Leary wrote that he came to understand that rather than information about the Church and its doctrine, people wanted the experience of God. This insight into the true meaning of Incarnation became the motivational driving force of his ministry as it is of Anna's.[2]

As a religious, Anna's inner journey had always been of fundamental importance, but a catalyst for change in her life came in 1981 when she was principal of St Bede's Catholic School in Canberra. One of her teachers posed the question at a staff meeting: 'So much is done for curriculum development in this diocese and we're well served with that, but there's nothing for faith development and we're not getting it in parishes – why?' Anna explained that it was because of this question 'we're doing what we're doing today'.

Anna had entered the Sisters of the Good Samaritans in 1973 as, she said, 'an older woman'. She was 26. Growing up in Wollongong, she had attended the Good Samaritan school, St Mary's Star of the Sea College, and after university, taught at the Josephite Teachers Training College in Sydney. 'It was there that I started to explore the next stage of my life,' she said.

> I was drawn to the Good Sams. There was something about their simplicity and their extraordinary ability to cope, and their prayer life was strong. The other

1 Gerard W. Hughes, *God of Surprises*. London, Darton, Longman & Todd, 1985.

2 Daniel O'Leary, 'A Delight in Company', published in *The Tablet*, 18 April 2009, 10.

> thing was that there was a real option for those on the margin. Right from the beginning there was the education of women, on whatever were the needs of the time, but always a focus on people who are struggling. Our sisters visited families who were most needy in all the school communities. That was the core of it.

Looking back at her experience of the novitiate, Anna recalled a rich sense of community prayers and personal prayer. 'Community prayer, liturgical prayer, has always been essential to me and we had good solid stuff, no pious practices. There was also a big emphasis on the Good Samaritan story. We're founded on that parable - to go and do the same. Our simplicity of life, our social justice emphasis, also comes through our Benedictine tradition and scripture has always been the key. All this was strong for me.'

Anna's first placement as a young nun was to St James parish school at Forest Lodge in inner city Sydney. 'I was terrified about the whole business,' she recalled. 'There was one old sister in the community, Gertrude Ford, who had taught my mother and she's someone who was unremarkable to the outside world, she just said to me, "lovey, don't worry about anything. Just pray well, teach well, and visit the poor after school," and that stuck with me.'

During these post-Vatican II years the Good Samaritans 'just went along with change,' said Anna, 'it was just part of who you were. The Good Sams always encouraged theological study…we got together in groups…we had a lot of stuff'. Looking back, she recalled 'wonderful seminars' organised for the religious of the Sydney Diocese by Mary Shanahan, principal of Sancta Sophia College at Sydney University, and Roger Pryke, the University chaplain. 'One of our own sisters, Pauline Fitzwalter, was part of this movement too', she said. 'It was great, it gave you energy but very few priests did it. That was the change…there was the journey.'

For fifteen years Anna worked in a number of Good Samaritan primary schools, both as teacher and principal. This, she thought, would be the pattern of her life until she heard the question about faith development asked at the staff meeting and saw there was a need that was not being met. As a member of the Catholic Principals' Association executive she engaged with interested colleagues in researching avenues to respond. She and three other school principals decided to study the Jesuit Colloquium programme and they introduced a version of it to staff in Catholic schools in the Canberra/Goulburn Diocese. 'The Colloquium was an opportunity to bring staff together,' she said. 'It took off like wildfire. It wasn't about church doctrine or teaching religious education, but all to do with their own lives, of finding a personal journey of faith, of exploring such questions as "Who am I?" "What's my image of God?" Above all, it was listening to and telling life stories.'

Through this work, and also through her contact with the school parents, Anna became increasingly aware that 'lay people were starting to seek out ways of living their spirituality'. It was a popular time for groups, she recalled, such as parents and friends associations and mothers' clubs. 'I thought that there was an opportunity to gather the parents and explore spirituality with them.' As well as meeting with small groups, she started to hold reflection days for people seeking more than mass on Sundays. It was clear to her that unless Catholics lived in a parish alive with the spirit of Vatican II, or had taken the initiative to seek out means of deepening their own knowledge and understanding, that for many of them faith had not developed and matured since their school days. 'They were looking to explore stuff after *Humanae Vitae*...there was a sense they wanted to be free of the oppression but had no forum in which to talk about it.'[3]

This was the time that Anna met Jane Scroope, whose group continues to meet regularly, although no longer as part of the Teams of Our Lady. 'This is partly because we didn't want it to be just married couples. We wanted it to be more inclusive. Anna helped us realise that church is not about Sundays and sacraments. It's about the way you live your life,' said Jane. 'We couldn't manage if we didn't have this group in Canberra supporting us,' added Anna. 'They fundraise for us they pray with us, they do all kinds of things. They come over and do work with us, and that to me is church.'

In the early 1980s, the effect of Anna's work with staff in school communities in the Canberra diocese was such that, when one of the parents at her school, Peter Tannock, was appointed as Director of the Catholic Education Commission in Western Australia in 1985, he invited Anna to Perth to set up an adult faith programme for staff in Catholic schools. Anna went with the full support of her then Superior-General, Helen Lombard, and her congregation.

3 *Humanae Vitae* (Of Human Life) is an encyclical letter written by Pope Paul VI in 1968 subtitled *On the Regulation of Birth*. It was widely anticipated among Catholics that it would allow artificial forms of birth control but did not. The subsequent controversy following *Humanae Vitae* continues.

Peter Tannock asked Anna to work throughout the state but she told him it would be crazy to entrust one person with such an enterprise, that he needed a team of people 'alive with what you want to do'. She organised a meeting of Catholic principals and formed a core group of seven that included Loreto Sister Margaret Finlay and Marist brother Bill Tarrant. Marg Finlay believes the time the team spent reflecting and praying together was critical to the success of their faith formation weekends across West Australia. The group in turn trained others and, in time, teams were formed to continue the work.

Anna said of her work in West Australia that

> What we were trying to put in place was the concept of the Church as being the people of God. There were people falling off the edges all the time because they just were becoming disillusioned with the institution. They were intelligent women and men who were very professional in their teaching lives, and had degree after degree, but many still had the faith life of a seven-year-old. What we did allowed people to think, to claim their faith, rather than have it put on like a helmet. They started to appreciate this and ask questions…We were giving people a forum and little groups started to form, and then offshoot groups and every group we worked with never just came for a weekend. It wasn't just fluffy, feel-good kind of stuff, it was really looking at the scriptures and how they impinged upon our life, on family life, work life, and then they would go away and put some of it into practice. And then we'd meet again and go deeper.

After two successful years in Perth with the programme well established, Anna, Marg Finlay and Bill Tarrant were all moved to New South Wales by their various orders and given different tasks. The spiritual and intellectual needs of adult Catholics that Anna had first encountered in Canberra and again in the West were just as urgent in eastern Australia and, as word of their work had preceded them, the three found themselves regularly called on to give faith formation sessions to the laity at weekends. They consulted the leaders of their orders about ways of meeting these needs more effectively. Their leaders in turn raised the issue with the Conference of Leaders of Religious Institutes in New South Wales. A process of discussion and discernment between the leaders of religious congregations highlighted the different levels of knowledge and faith practice between the laity and religious.

Whereas before the Vatican Council the difference between knowledge and faith practice of laity and religious had been accepted as the norm, the Council document *Lumen Gentium,* the 'Dogmatic Constitution on the Church', held possibilities that went well beyond external changes such as the mass said in English and the inclusion of women as readers. Priests like Daniel O'Leary saw themselves as midwives at the birth of a new way of being Catholic. He writes about his priestly role as 'helping people understand that the inner conversion of their hearts was what Jesus was after, not just the improved religious observation or increased church attendance that we often mistake for inner transformation'.

In Perth, Anna had been able to explore the implications of *Lumen Gentium* further with Marg and Bill. In New South Wales they took their reflections to another level when the leaders of their three congregations approved their collaborative ministry as a spiritual formation team. It was an enterprise they knew from past experience would not succeed unless they themselves practised what they preached.

Anna, Marg and Bill went away together for a week to think about how to develop their work. In the West their focus had mainly been on the staff of schools; this time they wanted to be available to a wider circle. 'That was the key for us,' explained Anna. 'We wanted to be ready to explore where the church was moving, and when it wasn't moving to make it move to where we were and to be church, and not to wait for someone else to tell us what to do.'

Similar inter-congregational teams had been tried before but had not worked; however, the three were determined to succeed. They took the constitutions of their religious orders with them and began by getting to know each other's spiritualities more profoundly. Marg's was Ignatian-based while for Bill the emphasis was Marian.[4] For Anna it was the Benedictine spirituality of the Good Samaritans.

'We put our cards on the table', said Anna. 'We asked ourselves questions like: where do I come from? What are my values?' 'And we got on with each other,' adds Marg, 'we were good friends - that was really significant'. Thus the three were well prepared when the new fast-growing diocese of Parramatta offered them full-time work as a team in faith formation. Several programmes were developed, one of specific significance, Wellspring, used

4 Mariology is the veneration of Mary, the mother of Jesus, and the study of her place within the theology of the Catholic Church. The Marist Brothers were founded by St Marcellin Champagnat in France in 1817, a man with a particular devotion to Mary.

the Gospel story of the woman at the well. 'It's a story about conversion/ change/action,' said Anna.

The spiritual formation team offered courses, retreats and days of reflection all grounded in scripture and scholarship presented through the prism of Anna, Marg and Bill's life experiences and accumulated faith understanding. They covered a range of topics and occasionally invited experts in their field such as Christologist Kees Bijman msc, to contribute. People attending were given time to reflect, to talk and exchange ideas and experiences. Creative ways of praying through ritual and liturgy were explored, and participants were assured that they had within them the capacity to make the liturgy happen. 'It's not something that comes from outside,' said Anna. 'Unless it comes from within, it's not going to nurture you.'

Repeatedly the team found themselves listening to life stories that moved them deeply. Many times, particularly in remote rural areas, they heard the distress in the voices of women who had struggled to comply with the Church's teaching on contraception. 'The emotion just rose in them as they started to speak about their lives: how they would go to confession and tell Father they had five children and couldn't afford any more and he would say there was nothing he could do,' said Anna. She devised a ritual to support and heal these women and free them from the pain they clearly still felt. The results were absolutely extraordinary, she claims. 'I remember one woman in particular who said it was concrete in her heart to go on the pill after five children. We were running a weeklong retreat and you could see her face changing as the days went by. At one stage she came up to us and said, "I would never have thought I would have the capacity to let go of the anguish I have lived with all these years".'

Catholics who have grown up in the post-Vatican II years might wonder at the apparent passivity of such faith, but the pain of going against the rules, even eating meat on Fridays, imposed a heavy weight on the hearts of the devout. [5] The novels of Graeme Greene reveal the depths of despair felt by practising Catholics of this era caught up in situations, particularly of sexual sin, which cut them off from the Eucharist. One of Anna's great gifts to the people she encountered through her work was to explore with them the concept of primacy of conscience and help them to a mature understanding

5 Before Vatican II Catholics were required to abstain from eating meat on Fridays as a form of penance in memory of the crucifixion of Christ on the cross on Good Friday.

of divine mercy, compassion and forgiveness. Her friend Marg claims Anna is so effective in groups because 'her capacity to process things and engage with people is brilliant'.

On one occasion Anna and Marg were invited to run the annual spiritual gathering of women in a vast rural diocese, parts of which had recently experienced severe flooding. Two hundred and fifty women came and six local priests. 'The conversations were alive,' recalled Anna, 'but these guys just sat and watched and did not engage with the women because they were afraid'. The vicar of the diocese came up to Anna at the end of the weekend and told her, 'This has been wonderful, but the sad thing is that these women will go back to their own places and won't be able to put one thing in place because of the situation in their parishes'.

One particular Bishop in the diocese, however, understood the parochial landscape. He had a plan to keep the sacramental life of parishes alive without priests and engaged the spiritual formation team to support this process. They covered long distances to meet and work with local communities and frequently found people determined to hold on to their faith. For example, at one time when they met with a group at the back of the local pub, one woman stood up and said that because of the lack of a priest, she had taken up theological studies to support local Catholics since she couldn't bear the thought that faith could die. Another man explained that the consecrated hosts were parachuted into his paddock. 'I can't tolerate them flying Jesus in from Port Pirie,' he said, adding, 'that woman over there,' pointing to the one who was studying theology, 'she's the one who ought to be the leader of what we're doing out here'.

The team would do their best to encourage the laity in remote areas and elsewhere to have the confidence to hold their own liturgies, maintain their sacramental life as far as they were able, to nurture their inner lives and to love and support each other. From the time she first started this work, Anna taught scriptural based tools such as *lectio divina* – praying with the scriptures. Whenever possible she encouraged people to set up reading or prayer groups, to keep in contact with each other and form networks. She acknowledged that it's so much easier in cities where like-minded people can meet in each other's homes, or in local cafes or restaurants.

In 2004, Anna Warlow went to live and work in the mid-west where the wheat belt of Western Australia meets the desert; where life is hard when rain is scarce. When she arrived the area was in the midst of drought.[6] She took up her ministry, at the request of both her congregation's leadership team, and the local Bishop, to support a number of parishes without priests and to train the people in sustaining themselves liturgically and communally. Her years in the mid-west have demonstrated the impact a woman of faith, inner strength and imagination can have: she keeps the sacramental life of this remote community alive, supporting local people on every level, however bleak their circumstances. 'At first it was confronting,' she said. 'Adult faith education was limited. People were still doing the same thing, thinking the same way as they had for years. When I started to develop these simple little processes to try and get them to talk about what they did to keep the community alive, their response was negative. They didn't appear to make the connections between their contributions in life and faith to building community'.

On the surface it was all 'Yes, Sister, that's wonderful, Sister, we'll do that, Sister' but underneath, said Anna, there was resistance. 'The face was there but it was like a mask and they were all the time pulling the stuffing out of the pillow.' The drought was bad, affecting everybody. In Anna's first three years, there were five suicides in the district. People, she felt, didn't see how much they already contributed to the community through agencies such as Red Cross or recognise their own resilience. Anna struggled to imagine ways of raising their self-esteem.

Initially Anna shared the ministry with Loreto sister Ellen Moran. They were housed in a dilapidated church building badly in need of attention. To Anna's delight, Jane Scroope and her husband, and Terry and Michael Gleeson came from Canberra to help. They scrubbed, washed and painted walls, refurbished the kitchen, stripped and repainted the tired furniture and started an open garden. Renamed St Paul's House of Welcome, the property was transformed and so, in the years to come, was the community.

When Anna first went to the mid-west, she found herself serving a mixed community of white and Aboriginal people. Many of the white people were not only conservative in their views but also strongly racist. One Sunday after leading the liturgy she was hit on her shoulder by a man with a rolled up newspaper who demanded to know whether she was there for the

6 Anna Warlow has asked us not to include details of the places where she works to protect people's privacy.

Church or as a social worker for the Aboriginal people because if she was there for the latter, she wasn't needed or wanted. The same evening two of the Aboriginal women came to see Anna and Ellen Moran. One of them was a local Elder. The four women sat and wept together, and the Elder said, 'You know, Sister Anna, I've been thinking. That's the kind of stuff that happens to us all the time. We're used to it but we never thought they'd do it to you – but anyway, now you're one of us, aren't you?' 'That was a key moment for me,' said Anna. 'In that really painful time when I felt rejected by the white community, not all of them, but a core group, this woman turned the whole story round'.

Until then, Anna was seriously considering whether to stay in the west, but the Elder's words reinforced the importance of the Indigenous community and how vital was her connection, especially to the isolated older women in the area, black and white. Some years after the incident, Anna received a letter of apology from the man who attacked her. He wrote: 'I realise that you have suffered intolerance for the last nine years and yet you have still stayed kind to us'. She was astonished and grateful.

Anna is the sister of lyric baritone Anthony Warlow and his influence has made her well aware of the potency of music. It is therefore not surprising that one of the most successful agents for change she has introduced is song. Inspired by the Choir of Hard Knocks in Melbourne,[7] she formed a choir called 'Crowing in the Midwest' which has been an extraordinarily effective means of building community. Members range in age from eight to 80, are of mixed races, mixed faiths or no faith at all, most with almost no musical experience. 'We are an absolutely ragtag mob,' said Anna, 'but everyone is so proud of the choir. The underdogs and those on the edge are absolutely rapt in it and talk about it all the time'. In 2008, Jen Charadia, a friend of Anna's from the Catholic Education Office in Wollongong, took some pre-recorded backing tracks and made a CD with the choir. The wonder of it, she said, was to see 'a community divided standing shoulder to shoulder and singing together in harmony'.

Anna has introduced a number of initiatives that have made a difference locally, including establishing a bank in partnership with the WA government. Developing leaders in the community, especially the

7 The Choir of Hard Knocks was formed by Jonathan Welch in Melbourne in 2006, for homeless and disadvantaged people; Welch was inspired by the Montreal Homeless Men's Choir in Montreal, Canada.

Indigenous community, is an important part of her work especially among the young. Education is the key and much of her time and energy is spent keeping primary children at school and then encouraging them through scholarships to continue their education at Nagle College in Geraldton or Clondarf College in Perth. 'The kids won't stay there without someone like Anna in the background,' said Jane Scroope, whose prayer group in Canberra also supports Good Samaritan Rural Outreach. 'She puts an enormous amount of work into supporting their families.' Jane's prayer group contributed to a scholarship for a young Aboriginal woman studying nursing at the university in Broome.

In 2010 Anna and Ellen Moran received the 2010 Australia Day Community Award for their 'outstanding work'. When Ellen retired in 2012, Anna did not continue her work on her own. 'I have an Aboriginal elder who comes with me,' she said. 'I have been training her for some years and working with her. She's very much a part of who I am. I also work with a retired nurse, now in her seventies.' Together the three women form a team offering retreats and visiting other women in remote rural areas, some of whom live vast distances from their nearest neighbours.

Anna finds her focus with the Indigenous women relies less and less on Sunday liturgies and more and more upon helping them reconnect with their own spirituality with a gospel dimension. 'They're not a mass people,' she said. 'We use rituals incorporating symbols. The women tell stories and yarn around the scripture of their culture. We give them the freedom to be who they're meant to be, not as we want them to be'. Many white people have found it difficult 'because the Aboriginals are starting to find their feet', said Anna. The institutional Church, she thinks, can learn much about the appropriate inclusion of our Aboriginal sisters and brothers.

> I'm learning from people I'd never thought I'd learn from. When I started out with Marg and Bill, we were confident in what we wanted to share, we knew how we wanted to do it, not because we had all the answers, but we knew there was something there that was going to engage people. Now it's the other side of the coin.

Anna believes strongly that the future of the Church in Australia lies in small groups. This allows flexibility with prayer, a closer sharing of the ups and downs of life and friendship based on a common faith, in gatherings of people into freedom where all learn from each other.

Those of her friends and colleagues, such as Marg in Perth, Jen Charadia in Wollongong, Jane in Canberra and her Good Samaritan friend and colleague in the west, Val Deakin, believe in the importance of Anna's work and support her in every way they can. [8] They see her as a woman of great courage and resourcefulness. The practical spirituality of the Good Samaritans is her rock, people like Daniel O'Leary, the great American activist Dorothy Day, and the man of courage, Oscar Romero, whom she calls 'the prophets of the time' are her inspiration, while it is her friends who keep her spirits up. It was also her friends who nominated her for the Medal of the Order of Australia that she was awarded in 2011 for her service to the Catholic Church. It is a public acknowledgement of a woman who has given so many people the experience of being valued for who they are, together with the tools for personal enrichment.

8 Val Deakin is a Good Samaritan sister living and working in Geraldton in Western Australia. In 2013 she was awarded the OAM for her service to the Aboriginal communities in WA and the Northern Territory.

Clare Condon sgs

Clare Condon was born in 1948 and entered the Sisters of the Good Samaritans in 1969. She made her final vows in 1978.

When Clare Condon completes her time as congregational leader of the Good Samaritan Sisters in 2017, she dreams of embarking on a doctorate on the life and work of John Bede Polding, the Benedictine monk who founded the first Australian order of women religious in Australia in 1857. Upon reading Polding's letters Clare was 'surprised by the number of times he refers to Indigenous Australians'. His concern for them and their welfare was distinctly different from the responses of most of his contemporaries in colonial circles. And coming 'from Downside, in its lovely small English green countryside, to Australia and do the horseback travel that he did was amazing, absolutely amazing,' she said.[1]

Clare's interview was conducted at St Scholastica's Convent in Glebe, a quiet suburb of inner Sydney. The beautiful building housing the convent was originally Toxteth House, the elegant country home built for George Allen, a leading lawyer and one-time Mayor of Sydney. It is set within an estate of 90 acres, known as Toxteth Park. Purchased by the Sisters of the Good Samaritan in 1901 the house and remaining grounds became their premier school; for many decades it also housed their teachers' training college. Today, Toxteth House is the congregational headquarters of the sisters, and contains their archives, which include early correspondence with Archbishop Polding.

Clare first felt an affinity with Polding in the novitiate when she entered the Good Samaritans in 1969. The previous year, in 1968, the congregation's renewal chapter, required by Vatican II, had been guided by their strong and visionary congregational leader, Mother Mary de Lourdes Ronayne. In response to the call to return to their roots, the chapter produced a document entitled 'Declaration' urging the congregation to return to the Rule of St Benedict so that the sisters could reach a deeper understanding of Benedictine spirituality.

1 Downside Abbey, established in 1841, is situated near Bath in Somerset. The community of Benedictine monks traces its origins to Douai, France, in 1606. Their school is among the most prestigious in England.

'Our earlier sisters were very much formed in Benedictine spirituality,' explained Clare, but in 1917 Canon Law 'tried to make apostolic orders the same and to some degree we lost connection with out Benedictine roots'. While these roots remained, the emphasis on a 'structured lifestyle that Canon Law created' meant that 'the call of Vatican II to reclaim our founding charism was really taken very seriously'. The Good Samaritans thus reclaimed Polding as their founder and St Benedict as the source of their spirituality.

Clare remembered with gratitude the manner in which a previous novice mistress, Sister Philomena, introduced Benedictine spirituality into the novitiate 'in a strong kind of way'. To deepen the novices' knowledge and understanding of their Benedictine heritage, Sister Philomena invited monks from the Benedictine monastery in Arcadia in New South Wales to give lectures. This connection was maintained even more closely when Clare was a novice. Her superior, Helen Lombard, was also a key figure in her understanding of 'what the charism holds in terms of the seeking of God, the hospitality, the liturgy of the hours, stewardship, all those Benedictine values'.

During the years of renewal following Vatican II the Good Sams changed their vow formula from poverty, chastity and obedience to 'the Benedictine vows of stability, conversion of life and obedience, in which poverty and chastity are contained. Stability for the Good Sams means that we stay in community. We stay with the congregation. It's not stability of place; it's more stability of our relationships. Religious life is a total commitment to God, and there needs to be a communal dimension to that'. How this is achieved varies from one order to another. For the Good Sams, it lies in the 'commitment of one's life to this search for God'.

In the late 1960s another major shift for the congregation meant moving away from their emphasis on education. 'Pre-Vatican II most of our sisters were in teaching - primary, secondary, or tertiary,' said Clare, 'whereas our original purpose was to look after the women on the streets of Sydney'. She adds that while the Good Samaritans had never lost their connection with those on the margins, undoubtedly this had come second to their work in schools. In their re-examination of Polding's original intentions, the sisters saw other possibilities. 'One of our great strengths as a congregation has been the education of our sisters,' said Clare. 'Before Vatican II the focus was on teaching but post-Vatican II it was more in the fields of liturgy, theology and spirituality and a lot of our sisters went to the USA to study'.

Clare was educated by the Good Samaritans in Wollongong on the south coast of New South Wales, first at St Francis Xavier's primary school then at St Mary's College. She was born on a dairy farm in Jamberoo - not far from the place where the Benedictine Abbey would be established in 1988. Clare's parents moved to Wollongong when she was very young. After leaving school in 1964, she worked for four years with Wollongong Council while studying for a degree in accountancy. It was during those years that she had a 'sense of call' and decided 'I've got to get this out of my system'.

There were about 700 sisters in the Congregation of the Good Samaritan when Clare entered and the novitiate in the Sydney suburb of Pennant Hills was busy. 'About fifteen of us joined but only five of us were professed,' she recalled. Although she claimed her training was 'very balanced', nonetheless she found many aspects of life in the novitiate challenging, especially 'some of the nonsense' left over from the 'old ways'. At times she considered leaving but 'something kept me there'. But bearing in mind the women she admired, like Mary Ronayne and one of her successors as congregational leader, Helen Lombard, she thought, 'They've survived and they're great women…there's something in this'. As if to emphasise her point she adds, with undisguised joy, 'And I'm still here!' Clare is clearly deeply aware of the debt owed by the congregation to such women, who left a legacy of spiritually mature and professionally competent younger women well equipped to carry on the visions that grew out of Vatican II.

Attendance at lectures at Lavender Bay in North Sydney, where novices from several orders heard expert theologians and scholars expound on Vatican II and its thinking, had a profound effect upon Clare during her novitiate.[2] Among its advantages was the opportunity to meet novices from other institutes. Among them was Josephite sister Anne Derwin. Later in life, the two became good friends. The lecturers were brilliant. In particular, Chris Geraghty, recently returned from Europe and an expert on sacramental theology, 'blew our minds. He just opened up a whole lot of

2 The Xavier Institute of Sister Formation was established at St Francis Xavier's Jesuit church in Lavender Bay in 1967. Lectures were given in a range of subjects including dogmatic, ascetical and moral theology, scripture, history of religious life, liturgy, church history, catechetics and sociology. In 1974 the Institute moved to the Mercy Novitiate at Castle Hill.

different thinking'. Not surprisingly Clare spent as much time as she could in the novitiate reading; she also smuggled books into her bed at night.

As a young nun, and in spite of her degree in accountancy, Clare taught Grade four in the primary school at Balgowlah, a suburb of northern Sydney. She found it hard. 'I can remember saying to the students, "If I use words you don't understand, just put your hand up," and I'd said about three words and all their hands went up'. It came as a relief to be sent to teach the older primary students at the parish school in the rural town of Innisfail, North Queensland, before being asked at the age of 27 to be the principal at St Columba's, Charters Towers. It was widely accepted that even extraordinarily young women were capable of being principals of schools, often acting as project managers for maintenance and building works as well. When Clare was entrusted with the little school at Charters Towers, she observed that she 'grew through being stretched'. Throughout her religious life Clare has relished new challenges: 'I was constantly being stretched and I could respond to that'. While she was teaching at Charters Towers she was working on an arts degree part-time, with a major in sociology. Aware of the usefulness of this qualification, Mary Ronayne soon afterwards sent Clare to Lourdes Hill, the Good Sam school in Brisbane, with the task of remodelling the entire boarding structure.

The need to rethink boarding facilities was an issue for many religious institutes. By the 1970s and 80s the decline in numbers and the ageing of the sisters made a major impact on the viability of convent boarding schools. Many of the boarding facilities no longer met health and safety standards. Meantime, the Federal Labor government of 1972 to 1975 examined all aspects of the educational needs of isolated children, with particular reference to needs-based funding for non-government schools. More government schools were being built across the nation, and free transport was extended to students in both government and non-government schools. Gradually, the necessity and the desirability of boarding for country students waned.

Clare began her task at Lourdes Hill with a study on 'how we should separate the staff in the boarding component and introduce a welfare/ social science emphasis'. She and another sister, then director of boarding at Lourdes Hill, began to visit parents across Queensland, seeking their views about what was needed for their children. In itself this was revolutionary. Men in religious orders were accustomed to staying with the families of boarders, and while Good Samaritan sisters had made it a practice to visit the homes of students (some of the older sisters still do so) they had never stayed overnight with families:

> We went as far west as Windorah and as north as Cooktown. We drove, and we'd stay on stations and properties overnight with parents, and I think it really helped change the relationship between the girls and ourselves. They'd meet us at the gate, in the four-wheel drive and at the wheel, being just thirteen years of age. They were driving, and sort of saying, you won't let us go down the street to buy a coffee, or a Coke!

In 2000, Archbishop Leonard Faulkner invited her to be part of his pastoral team in Adelaide. She followed two Sisters of Mercy, Pat Fox and Meredith Evans. Archbishop Wilson took over the diocesan leadership in 2001, and Clare became his financial administrator, assuming the title of Chancellor of the Archdiocese of Adelaide, taking charge of some of the pastoral planning and financial management, and various other leadership responsibilities across the diocese. 'I think the role of Chancellor and the role of financial administrator are probably two roles that women can currently do, and are accepted into', Clare said, even though there were few dioceses where this is the case.

Whether ordination should be one of the criteria for taking up a role in decision-making, and when roles should be opened up for others, remains a question and a challenge for the church:

> My argument is that I don't want to be ordained into the current [clerical] structure, but I want my skills recognised as being able to contribute to the wellbeing of the church. Particularly when I worked in the dioceses, I used to get astounded that they thought ordination meant you were a competent counsellor, spiritual director, and financier, that you could do anything if you were ordained. That's where I think the church has failed itself at times, because it hasn't put the right expertise in place.

Clare was elected leader of her congregation in 2005 and will continue in the role until 2017. She has responsibility for the spiritual and temporal lives of the Good Samaritans in Australia, the Philippines, Japan, East Timor and Kiribati. Clare meets with representatives from the sisters across these countries in Plenary Council three times a year. She shares membership with Benedictine women around the world, meeting every year at the Communio International Benedictinarium, alternating between Rome and another of the nineteen regions across the globe. The international dimension and solidarity with women religious from all nations is a gift prized by many contemporary women religious, positioning their efforts for peace and justice at the local level in a global context as it does.

The work of the Good Sams within Australia has involved strongly supporting the Aboriginal people, a relationship that, in part, follows the example of Archbishop Polding. As Clare said, 'We've made a commitment to be there with Indigenous Australians, not to think what we can do for them, but to be with them'. The sisters are working in communities at Santa Teresa outside Alice Springs, on Palm Island and in Geraldton and the mid-west of Western Australia. At St Scholastica's College in Sydney there are nearly 50 Indigenous students, some from remote areas of the outback living as boarders, some from the inner Sydney suburb of Redfern.

Good Samaritans are also among the many institutes working with refugees, and they also continue their long tradition of working with vulnerable women. The Good Samaritan Inn in Melbourne was opened as a women's refuge in 1996 and three years later the order established the Good Sams Foundation in Brisbane to support women and children in crisis. Practical help includes transitional accommodation, providing safe houses and professional support workers, as well as offering educational and training opportunities to the women.

In 2008 Clare became the President of Catholic Religious Australia (CRA), the public name of the Australian Conference of Leaders of Religious Institutes (ACLRI). Membership comprises 180 sisters, brothers and priests all of whom are leaders of their congregations. Clare emphasises the importance religious leaders attach to connecting, communicating and acting with their peers. The CRA exists to represent religious life in the Australian church and the wider community, and aims to speak with a prophetic voice on social justice issues at both national and global levels. Its theme for its 2013 conference was 'Charism without borders', a clear sign, Clare said, that religious congregations 'will take initiatives together, rather than alone'.[3]

Religious women, Clare believes, have a responsibility to contribute to public policy-making, not only because of their religious lives but also because of their knowledge and direct experience of community needs, derived from their various ministries. Religious women have a responsibility to inform government of the reality of the lives of people with whom they work, and to advocate on their behalf when necessary. Bringing their Christian

3 In January 2014 Sister Annette Cunliffe rsc succeeded Clare Condon as President of CRA.

understanding of notions such as the common good into the public arena is of primary importance.

In her position as leader of CRA Clare wrote:

> The 'Common Good' is not only a Christian value, but it is a value that underlines any civil society...we need to cross boundaries and borders which previously were unthinkable...We need to open our horizons to include all who dwell on earth. In particular, we need to bring those who are most vulnerable to the table of discussion...Our current policies seem inadequate, even unjust, when tested against the principle of the 'Common Good'...As women and men religious we have a story of living for the 'Common Good' in our own communities and beyond...We have a creative voice that should be heard in these current debates and discussions. Let us exercise our voice at the local, national and global levels for a future of truly civil societies that can be built upon only on a deep understanding and practice of 'common good'.[4]

One of the issues Clare faces as congregational leader is 'looking at appropriate care for the future while at the same time holding the excitement of the mission and of the search for God. It is important to support those older women who are strong women and have been strong women all their lives and are now ageing'. It remains important to support the younger members of the congregation. 'I think that's the great challenge' she said, 'to keep the balance, to keep life going forward, but to care for the elderly as they move towards the end of life here'. The average age of the remaining 250 Good Samaritan sisters is 75. 'Benedict said that the young should love the elderly and the elderly should care for the young,' said Clare, 'so there's that respect both ways as it's not easy for different generations to live together'.

In 2011 Clare oversaw the creation of a new body, Good Samaritan Education, which has canonical status in the Church as a Public Juridical Person (PJP).[5] This body has taken over responsibility for the ten Good Samaritan schools in Australia, the nine secondary colleges and the special school for intellectually disabled children from preschool to Year 12. The schools are found in five separate dioceses. Clare and her council worked closely with the bishops to set up the PJP. The order founded in Australia is 'fundamentally Australian, so why wouldn't we do this together instead of heading off to Rome as some other religious orders are doing?' The bishops agreed, and Cardinal George Pell signed off on Good Samaritan Education in July 2011.

---

4 'The Common Good', www.catholicreligiousaustralia.org, 8 June 2012. accessed 17/7/2012

5 For an explanation of PJPs, see the profile on Sister Bernadette Keating.

In 2012 Clare received a new novice into the congregation, 35-year-old social worker, Sarah Puls. At her first profession, Clare welcomed Sarah to the community, saying, in part:

> In following the parable as an imperative in life, and not just as an optional extra, you are leaving your life and your future open to be neighbour in whatever circumstances you might find yourself. At times you will be the Samaritan to others, at times, Christ will be the Samaritan to you in your woundedness. This will be the shape of your journey of conversion, profound conversion into the very experience of the very life of God.

These words reflected Clare's own commitment in more than 40 years of religious life, in which she has followed a passion she described as 'living out of the combined Good Samaritan/Benedictine charism'. It has led her not only to reach out to strangers as the Good Samaritan did but, with her sisters and others, to offer traditional Benedictine hospitality and kindness in whatever form it is needed, whether that be a cup of tea with friends, housing for the homeless or speaking out for the dispossessed.

Clare Condon has moved far beyond what she described as being part of an outmoded idea of nuns as the 'public service of the Church', when women religious undertook what bishops asked of them, particularly in maintaining Catholic schools and hospitals, sometimes to the detriment of their founding visions. This is not to argue that women were victims of a system imposed upon them. They were frequently agents of change and exercised considerable control over their lives and apostolic work. But the paradigm shift following Vatican II enabled the next generation of leaders like Clare to confidently join in public debates about social justice and the common good, particularly as it applied to those on the margins in society.

In December 2013, Clare was awarded the Human Rights Medal by the Australian Human Rights Commission for her contribution over many years, and for the work of the Good Samaritans under her leadership. It was a public acknowledgement of her life's work. As she presented the medal, Professor Gillian Triggs, the Human Rights Commissioner, said of her that 'Sister Clare is a determined and compassionate woman…she is never afraid to stand up for what she believes in, nor is she afraid to take her message directly to Government, relentlessly lobbying politicians to help those in need'. What was said of John Bede Polding in 1839 in Sydney could be said of Clare Condon 175 years later: her labours are incessant, her zeal unbounded.

The Sisters of St Joseph of the Sacred Heart

Jointly founded in Penola, South Australia by Mary MacKillop and Julian Tenison Woods, the Sisters of St Joseph of the Sacred Heart are also known as the Josephites or Brown Joeys. Theirs was the first religious institute to be founded by an Australian. Born in Melbourne in 1842 of Scottish descent, Mary MacKillop was the eldest of eight children and started work as a stationery clerk at the age of fourteen to help provide for the family during her father's long absences. At eighteen she took a job as a governess in Penola where she met local parish priest Julian Tenison Woods.

Tenison Woods was born in England in 1832, and emigrated to Australia in 1855. After working in Adelaide, he entered the Jesuit college at Sevenhill in South Australia and was ordained a diocesan priest in 1857. He took charge of the large parish of Penola and concerned at the lack of education, especially Catholic education, in 1861 he invited Mary and her sisters Annie and Lexie to open a Catholic school. Mary was already thinking of entering religious life in Europe since no religious institutes for women in South Australia were then in existence. She was persuaded by Tenison Woods to found with him the Sisters of St Joseph of the Sacred Heart in Penola with the aim of living on alms and educating the poor. On 19 March 1866, the feast of St Joseph, Mary donned a simple black dress and took the name Mary, Sister of St Joseph. She always regarded this as the founding day of her institute.

The following year, in 1867, Tenison Woods left Penola for Adelaide to work with the newly appointed Bishop Laurence Sheil. That same year he wrote the Rule for the sisters of St Joseph, and Mary took her vows and the name Mary of the Cross. The institute slowly grew and in 1869 Mary went to Brisbane at the invitation of Bishop James Quinn. In 1871 she returned to a difficult situation in Adelaide where Tenison Woods had been in a serious disagreement with a member of the clergy who, upon becoming vicar general, influenced Bishop Sheil against him and the Sisters of St Joseph. Bishop Sheil decided he wanted the sisters' Rule changed so that it included lay sisters and placed convents under the authority of local priests. In 1871 he excommunicated Mary for insubordination, closed most of her schools and almost destroyed her institute. He lifted the excommunication five months later, nine days before he died.

In 1873 Mary went to Rome to seek approval for her institute from Pope Pius IX. This took almost two years and in the meantime she travelled widely, returning to Australia in 1875 accompanied by fifteen Irish postulants

Approval from Rome rested on her modifying the Rule allowing ownership of property among other changes. Julian Tenison Woods never forgave Mary for agreeing to this and the congregation split. Those sisters who remained with Tenison Woods changed their habits to black and were known as the Black Josephites, while Mary MacKillop's sisters in their brown habits were known as the Brown Josephites. The breach between Mary and Tenison Woods never healed though they reconciled on his deathbed.

During the 1870s the Brown Josephites spread in South Australia, Queensland and New South Wales, often being sent to remote settlements and townships in twos and threes. In the 1880s they were also established in Victoria and New Zealand. By 1890 there were 300 sisters in nine dioceses. They were unique among women religious in that they lived in the community rather than in convents. They were also unusual in that the sisters came under the authority of their superior general rather than the local bishop. Bishops in Bathurst (in 1876), Queensland (in 1880) and South Australia (in 1883) asked them to leave their dioceses on this account. In 1883 Mary transferred the mother house from Adelaide to Sydney where it remains.

Although Mary suffered a stroke at Rotorua in New Zealand in 1901, she continued to run the institute until her death in 1909, seriously incapacitated physically but fully alert mentally. When Archbishop Moran visited her before she died, he said, 'I consider this day to have assisted at the deathbed of a saint'. In 1925, Mother Laurence, Superior General of the Sisters of St Joseph, began the process for Mary MacKillop's recognition as a saint. It took 75 years before her canonisation was announced at St Peter's in Rome on 17 February 2010.

At the height of their numbers in the mid 1960s, there were about 2,000 Josephite sisters in Australia. They covered the full range of school education from kindergarten to the end of secondary day and boarding schools. Together with the Sisters of Mercy, they educated half of all children in Catholic schools. In addition to training their own teachers, they ran orphanages and other welfare agencies.

At the time of publication, there are 880 Josephites who continue to follow Mary MacKillop's maxim to 'never see a need without doing something about it'.

Maria Casey rsj

Maria was born in 1941 and entered the Sisters of St Joseph in 1958. She made her final vows in 1967. Her name in religion was Sister Maria Ignatius.

In the weeks before and during the canonisation of Mary MacKillop on the 17 October 2010, many Australians were introduced to their first saint, and indirectly, to the work of the Sisters of St Joseph, commonly referred to as the Josephites, who are even more affectionately known as the 'Brown Joeys', in recognition of their original brown habits. For generations of Australian Catholics, the Josephites have been part of their local communities, particularly those who relied on the sisters to staff their small country and regional schools. The sisters also ran orphanages, aged care facilities, boarding schools and St Margaret's Hospital in Sydney. They were spread throughout the country, and were second only to the Sisters of Mercy in terms of their numbers, which reached over 2,000 by the time of the Second Vatican Council.

The woman most frequently seen on Australian TV screens during the canonisation process was Sister Maria Casey, the canon lawyer who completed the 85-year-long process which culminated in the lavish ceremony at the Vatican, when the Pope pronounced to the world that Sister Mary of the Cross MacKillop was now a Saint for the universal Church. Maria's remarkable story is that of a young Irish girl who decided to become a sister at the age of twelve.[1] As a grown woman, she was to take centre-stage at the Vatican, shaking the hand of the Pope and leading the celebrations on behalf of hundreds of her sisters.

Maria Casey is a tall, dignified woman who gives no hint of being conscious of the magnitude of her work, much less of her status as one of the handful of women who have filled the daunting role as Postulator for the cause of canonisation.[2] She has an air of serenity combined with a sharp intellect, and a gentle sense of humour, all of which have obviously served her well during her long life as a sister, a teacher, community leader and Postulator.

1 During the hundred years following the establishment of the Josephites in 1866, over 700 Irish women migrated to join Mary MacKillop's sisters. Mary MacKillop visited Ireland three times and sailed back to Australia at the end of 1874 on the St Osyth accompanied by fifteen Irish women who would join her congregation.

2 A Postulator is a person who presents the case for canonisation or beatification.

We met Maria at Mary MacKillop Place in Mount Street, North Sydney, in the coffee shop which also sells books and souvenirs. The shop is obviously an important meeting place for local residents and the visitors who come to visit Mary MacKillop's burial site that is in the Memorial Chapel next door. Each day, a Josephite sister is available after morning mass and throughout the day for anyone who needs advice, or just to talk. Once the home of Mary MacKillop, and the convent of generations of Josephites, the complex includes accommodation, extensive conference facilities and the Mary MacKillop museum. It is a space to which innumerable pilgrims and local people flock, seeking Mary's intercession, or the company of the sisters who minister there.

Maria was born in 1941 in County Clare and attended the local National school. Quite by chance she met two Sisters of St Joseph. 'I was in sixth grade at a teacher school and used to help the teacher,' she explained. 'We were sitting in the sun on this particular day and these two nuns walked into the school playground. They were meant to go to another place but their taxi didn't turn up so they just walked in'. Maria listened to the sisters talking about Mary MacKillop and the Australian Josephites. 'Something just clicked,' she said.

Even before that fateful day, Maria had thoughts of religious life. She had been sick in bed and her mother had given her rosary beads belonging to Maria's grandmother. 'Mum said, "say those" and somehow along the way I got to thinking and I decided I wanted to be a nun…but I hadn't told anyone. I thought of Africa or China. Australia had never entered [my head]'. The two sisters told Maria they wanted to meet her parents and walked home with her that day, saying, 'you run ahead and tell your mother we're coming'. One of the women was Australian and had lived a long time in Ireland, and the other was Irish.

The conversation continued with Maria's parents and, said Maria, 'the long and short of it was I went to the Josephite Juniorate in County Cork'. The Juniorate was a boarding school for secondary students who were considering entering religious life. Maria estimates that three-quarters of her contemporaries did not go ahead with a decision to enter religious life 'but after three-and-a-half years I decided yes, I would still come'.

At the age of 16, Maria boarded a ship for Australia, accompanied by 12 other young women, all of them in the care of two Presentation sisters. She readily concedes that 'no-one in their right mind would come at 16 or 17 now', but in Ireland at that time most young people were in the work force at 14, and by 16 people were thought to be too old for school. Entering religious life at 16 was not uncommon.

Maria arrived in Sydney in February 1958, and went immediately to the Josephite's novitiate in Baulkham Hills, to eventually meet 73 other young women who entered that year from around Australia and New Zealand. When Maria entered the convent, Baulkham Hills was an outer suburb of Sydney, but still considered to be in the country. Her experience of the novitiate was a good one, even though, as she said, 'I was expecting things to be very difficult, but having been in boarding school, I didn't find it so difficult. The pattern of things was familiar, and we learned a lot of things that we didn't have at school, and of course the introduction to what religious life was all about, and it was a very monastic setting'.

Maria commented that some of her peers complained that they learned very little of Mary MacKillop in the novitiate, but that was not her experience. 'We did a project on her at the end of the first year,' she said, 'and then the more I'd read about her and heard [from the other sisters] the more extraordinary she was'. There were sisters still living who had known Mary MacKillop. 'We met one of them at Leichardt,' said Maria. 'She talked about the dancing. She was 96 or 97 and she played the piano for the young ones to dance and she knew Mother Mary, as she called her'. There were other sisters, too, who were able to relate personal stories of the foundress, and of the pioneer sisters who went in twos and threes to the most remote locations, living in appalling conditions. These were women who were, in Maria's opinion, 'extraordinary...I didn't realise how extraordinary really until many years later when I'd learnt a bit more about our Josephite history'.

At the time of Vatican II, some changes were already in place for the Josephites, the most notable being that English was gradually replacing Latin in the liturgy: 'that was the first whiff of change and it was great... though some people didn't like it, they'd got used to their prayer book with Latin down one side and English down the other'. At the time of the Council, Maria was already teaching. 'That's of course when the whiffs of change grew stronger...not that we knew a great deal about what was involved'. Information gradually began to filter through their superiors, 'rippling down through the ranks' as Maria said.

> There was a general air of excitement about the concept of *aggiornamento*, of a bringing up to date initiated by Pope John XXIII as he announced the Second Vatican Council. Then the document *Perfectae Caritatis*, came out on religious life, so we studied and pored over that and what it would mean for us. While many changes in significant aspects of life were made early it took longer to change our habits…the Josephites were slow, which wasn't a bad thing, when we look back. Some sisters felt we weren't moving fast enough and did rebel against it, and some left us. Our mother general who had been fabulous, an 'ahead-of-her-time' provincial, somehow got rather worried about the rapidity of change, and was very slow in some things, we thought, and the habit was one of them. But when you look back, change to an external (the habit) made us examine what were the real values and traditions we were trying to hold on to and espouse as far as ministry and mission were concerned.

Among the most obvious outward manifestations of change was the manner in which decisions were made within the congregation in the light of Vatican II directives. Decision-making 'that affected all of us without consultation' was no longer the mode. Now all members of the community were to be involved, through the processes of regular chapters, meetings and consultative processes in general day-to-day life. It was a 'breath of fresh air' for the women. Consultation, openness, and discussion on major issues and working on committees were 'great bonding times' as Maria said. 'Openness to the principle of subsidiarity was always being quoted, not only by the people from on high, but also by the people from below.' The openness engendered by Vatican II affected the special chapters held in the late 1960s and early 1970s. Structures that, in Maria's words, 'had been there forever', were adapted to meet the new circumstances in the opening up of new ministries and new ways of being in community.

Like most of her contemporaries in the Josephites, Maria trained as a primary school teacher, and again, not unusually, progressed to secondary teaching because of the need to staff secondary schools under their management, in her case at a new school at Milperra. It was at this stage that she began an arts degree through correspondence and, when the need arose after the introduction of the Wyndham Scheme,[3] switched to a science degree full-

3 The Wyndham Scheme was introduced by the New South Wales government in 1962 and extended secondary schooling to six years with a broad education in the lower years and increased specialisation for senior students. External examinations would be held at the end of Years 10 (School Certificate) and 12 (Higher School Certificate).

time, since all congregations involved in teaching had to ensure they had sufficient qualified science teachers to fulfill State requirements.

Interestingly, it was one of the conditions of the Wyndham Scheme that facilitated one of the great changes to community life. The Scheme required the nuns' attendance at conferences and meetings associated with their professional development, sometimes after hours. This outside contact with other teachers enabled women across different congregations to meet each other often for the first time. Combined with greater freedom to watch television, mix with seculars and read more widely, sisters were gradually moving away from their insulated and monastic style of convent life and joining the broader education community in a more apostolic and outgoing way.

At a still relatively young age, in her early thirties, Maria was put in charge of a school at Bellambi. With the principal of the nearby boys' college she shared the supervision of the amalgamation of the two schools, restructuring the curriculum, and melding two lots of staff – daunting educational administration work. Throughout her long teaching career, Maria took advantage of opportunities to do further study, gaining first a Bachelor of Science, Diplomas in Education and Media Studies, and later a Bachelor of Arts, a Master's in Religious Studies, and later still, her qualifications relating to canon law. While such achievements were not uncommon amongst the Josephites following Vatican II, they are remarkable in that in the 1950s no Josephite sister had specific secondary teaching qualifications.

In 1990 Maria moved to Western Australia to take up the role of leader of the Josephites, of whom there were 120 sisters then operating across the State, from Perth to Esperance and into the Kimberley. They moved into the most remote areas, sometimes at the request of parish priests or bishops, sometimes as a result of the sisters themselves perceiving a need and responding to it. Mary MacKillop had always wanted to work with Indigenous communities, prompted no doubt by her brother Donald, a Jesuit, who worked in the remote Kimberley. What Mary McKillop had not been able to do, her sisters were now able to undertake: for the first time, they could discern where their talents might be best used. This was a far cry from the days when the individual would sit patiently waiting for what were called 'destinations' or 'desties', instructions about where she was to go the next year. Before Vatican II, while the option to refuse to move to a new posting was available, in practice it was an option seldom exercised.

Towards the end of her time as leader in West Australia, Maria was asked if she would be interested in studying canon law. Considering herself a 'bit old to be working with teenagers' (even though she loved working with young people), and knowing 'that I needed to be reshaped or recycled', she talked to her friend, and Loreto sister, Mary Wright, one of only a handful of women religious who were canon lawyers. Before the Second Vatican Council, women religious relied heavily upon a few male canon lawyers specialising in the law as it applied to religious. Knowledge of canon law became essential for those leading and managing the changes required of all religious communities: Maria made the decision to specialise in religious law at Saint Paul University in Ottowa.

Three weeks into her course, Maria thought she would have to abandon the project, 'because, having been away from rigorous study for years, I read and nothing was going in'. But, following the advice of one of her lecturers, she stuck to it, and before long, began to enjoy the research and the reading time. The initial course was for two years, at the end of which she felt she was only beginning to 'scratch the surface', so she applied for and was accepted into a doctoral programme. Unlike all her previous experience, Maria found herself in a world of men, apart from a single woman lecturer and a part-time female tutor.

On returning to Australia, Maria worked in the Ballarat Diocese every second month, as Director of the Marriage Tribunal, a position previously occupied by a Brigidine sister, Rosemarie Joyce. It often involved listening to harrowing stories relating to the requests for annulments as she worked with people to prepare them for the final stages of the processes that took place in Melbourne. It was a lonely job, but she had colleagues she could call on, and would sometime sit in the car and to pray and reflect before going home to immerse herself in domestic life.

To hear Maria recount her experiences in the process of the canonisation of Mary MacKillop was an amazing privilege. The journey began with a phone call from the Jesuit priest, Paul Gardiner, asking if she would assist him in his position as the Postulator for Mary's cause. As she said: 'it started from there' in 2001. Her official title was Vice-Postulator.[4] She

4 See Paul Gardiner, SJ, *An Extraordinary Australian: Mary MacKillop*, E.J. Dwyer, Newtown, 1994.

held the post of Vice-Postulator until 2008 when Paul Gardiner resigned on the grounds of ill health. In July 2008, the Vatican appointed her Postulator. The first stage of Maria's work was to sift through the list of recorded cures, and identify any that 'could possibly be a miracle', with two doctors volunteering to scrutinise the cases. The process was extremely stringent in part, as Maria said, to avoid 'deception and bribery'. Very exact documentation was required, as well as scientific evidence. Maria's science background enabled her to make some sense of the medical terminology. As an aside, she thanked God for the Wyndham Scheme, which forced her into the study of science.

The question that the doctors had to answer was: could science explain this cure?

> The cure finally chosen for examination was that of a lady whose lung cancer was such that she was given only a few weeks to live. After prayer through the intercession of Mary MacKillop and no medical treatment whatsoever she was declared cured some months later when she returned to her doctors and had further tests. There was a rigorous inquiry in the diocese where the cure occurred with testimony, under oath, from the lady who was cured, her husband and family, friends and medical practitioners as well as receiving documentation from the hospitals and clinics.

The documentation was then taken to Rome, where Maria analysed it and presented it according to the specifications of the Congregation for the Causes of Saints. This analysis covered the life story of the cured woman, the medical documents, the testimonies given and the place of prayer in the cure.

Maria then had to write a concise history of Mary MacKillop, providing more documentation for analysis by the theologians, all of which culminated in another book, a 'slender little volume' which was delivered to the Pope, asking for the recognition of the miracle and, finally, a petition for the canonisation. In that process, documentation had to be produced. It gave details of 'who said what, when, where and how…a table, giving dates, and checking that none of them contradicted each other'.

> So it was very, very meticulous work. And then at each stage you'd get it translated, then check the translation, and set it out in a book where you'd have half a page of English, and half a page of Italian. Finally, check that it was exactly right, and that none of it ran over the page, or that the lady who put it together didn't have the headings in the wrong spot. When the third book

> was finished and presented to Pope Benedict XVI, he declared the cure was a miracle.[5] After the final two books he was ready to admit Mary MacKillop for canonisation. It was a time when learning curve was steep but very rewarding for all at the outcome.

Pope John Paul II had beatified Mary in January 1995 at a public rally and ceremony at Sydney's Randwick racecourse, since the Vatican had accepted evidence of the cure of a woman with leukemia in 1961. In July 2008, Pope Benedict XV1 visited Mary's shrine in North Sydney, informing the sisters that their foundress would be canonised as soon as a second miracle was proved. The Pope announced in February 2010 that the process was finally complete, and that the canonisation would take place in Rome on October 17.

Once the cure was accepted as the miracle, Maria began an exhaustive study of the life of Mary MacKillop, when she saw the extraordinary impact she was having on numerous people.

> I suppose what made Mary so holy was first of all, her profound acceptance of the will of God, and her dependence on the providence of God, no matter what happened. Then the fact that she had the courage to do what she did, whether it be in relationship to the clergy and the bishops in particular, or to the people she met, and her expansive acceptance of everyone, no matter who they were, whether they were rich, poor, Catholic, non-Catholic, or whoever. She had that enormous capacity to walk with all classes of people.

As a young girl, in a little known place in Ireland, Maria would have never imagined that she would meet the Pope, and complete the decades of work necessary for Mary to be named Australia's first saint. Talking of the difficulties of working in Rome, of dealing with the bureaucracies of both the state and of the Vatican, Maria also remembered the kindness and help she received in undertaking the work. People assisted with translation, with medical knowledge, and with practical advice as she found her way through the process. It was exacting, detailed work.

What she also hadn't been prepared for, and what presumably few people even imagined, was that she should also find herself in charge of coordinating the organisation of the event on the day. Back in Sydney, there were several hard-working committees planning for various aspects

5 For a detailed account of the process, see Sister Maria Casey Interview Transcript, *Australian Story*, ABC Television, Monday, 20 February 2012.

of the celebrations. Each committee held regular meetings and all were coordinated by an overall working party. Maria was an ex-officio member of each of the committees and regularly joined the meetings by phone, often during the Roman night.

In Rome, she helped design the pilgrim scarves (the design went back and forth six times), decide on the design and production of the official medal and of the banners that featured so prominently during the service. She liaised with the Vatican office for the liturgy, arranging who would be involved in the official ceremony, receiving and allocating tickets, and preparing texts. She decided what would be in the pilgrim packs for the nearly 8000 thousand Australians who flocked to Rome, booked space for the production on Mary MacKillop's life and the prayer vigil to be held on the night before the canonisation. She then organised the physical aspects of the celebratory mass to be held the day after the canonisation at the Basilica of Saint Paul outside the Walls, and the dinners given to thank those who had assisted. As she said,

> I got very good at pacing and knowing the area in square metres in order to estimate how many would fit in a particular church! (I think I paced most of the major churches in Rome on request). They told me that it was part of the postulator's job, so I said that no-one had told me that, but I didn't mind doing it, it was just that there was so much of it, and so slow. The whole canonisation event was one of amazing collaboration – between the sisters, the lay people and the government at all levels.

Throughout the whole process, friends and advisors supported Maria. In Rome, she worked closely with Tim Fischer who was then Australia's ambassador to the Vatican. The help of one of her Josephite sisters who spoke Italian was invaluable. She also valued the tireless work of committees of outstanding lay people and Josephites back home in Sydney, who were preparing for the 15,000 pilgrims who came to celebrate with them in North Sydney on the day. Most of all, she felt the presence of Mary MacKillop, to whom she used to say, 'Mary, no one else but you would I do this for'.

Maria was in constant demand from the media, including those back home who didn't necessarily take into account time differences, and were not averse to ringing at 2am.

> I spent hours and hours and hours with the media people when they'd come over, because they needed a story and hoped you would always be available. I remember saying to groups from varying TV channels, now, look, I'm meeting

> with such-and-such from a particular Channel, at this place at two o'clock. You're very welcome to come, and you work out between you who does what, and they did. There was wonderful co-operation and they were understanding, they really were very, very good, and some of them still keep in touch.

Of Mary MacKillop's contribution to Australia's life and spirituality, Maria said

> I think her acceptance of everyone, regardless of faith, or status, or anything else was an enormous contribution…that her respect for the dignity of people was foremost and is still needed today. I think that is something, especially now, in terms of the migrant and refugee input, that is a tremendous gift, if we can capitalise on it. She came from a broken home, and she suffered a lot of bereavements. A well-loved brother was killed, two of her sisters died fairly young, her other brother died of a heart condition, and her mother was drowned in a shipwreck near Eden on her way to Sydney to help Mary at a fund-raising bazaar. So there was a huge amount of sorrow in her own life; people can identify with that, and also with her own poor health, and her battle with authority figures, and the media in those days…and the hardships of travel. There were just so many things that people with problems can identify with today, and [feel] that she's there for them. The other thing that amazed me is how universal she is…[people] come to North Sydney from Egypt, France, from Germany, China and numerous other countries. You just wonder how the message gets out.

After a short break in 2011, Maria continued to work for the Sydney Archdiocese on a part-time basis as Vicar for Religious. In the meantime, she was involved with Catholic Communications in the production of a DVD of the canonisation ('A huge task for them'), winding up the company set up by the Congregation for the canonisation process, and then 'sending a lot of thank you messages to numerous people'. Another set of letters of thanks had to be sent when she was awarded the Medal of the Order of Australia in 2012 for her work on the canonisation.

Maria still does consultancy work in canon law, and is working on archiving all the material relating to the canonisation. She belongs to the Canon Law Society, writing papers and opinions when requested; time consuming work. On the one hand, she acknowledges how far women have advanced, not least in areas such as her own work in canon law, and the fact that women are now accepted as Postulators. The acceptance of women in the Canon Law Society has also been slow, but is now established, allowing much easier acceptance of women amongst the bishops and other canon lawyers. Maria was elected the first woman President of the Canon Law Society of Australia and New Zealand in September 2012.

> So things are changing. I think women are really extremely powerful in the church. You look at who runs the parishes, and it's not always the parish priest. If you look at the power that women have in running schools, and always have had it in religious orders, and in running of hospitals, women run budgets far above anything that may be run in a diocese…I've never regretted the power that women have in the church. What I think is lacking very much is the acceptance in the hierarchical circles, but I'm not sure that we're losing too much…I'd love to see women priests, but not in the mould that has developed over centuries for our clergy. I look forward to a day when there is much more genuine collaboration.

Our final question to Maria was asking her to describe the essence of the religious life of the almost 800 Josephites: what sustains a Josephite woman?

> I think we have a great care for one another, we sustain each other, and we mightn't be lovey-dovey, but when the chips are down, we do care, and we do support each other. We have a lot of sisters now in individual ministries who are right out at the edges, and sometimes, we don't know, or understand precisely what they're doing, but we know that they're with the people who are marginalised, who are suffering, and that is truly Mary MacKillop territory. We have moved beyond the need that was expressed in the earlier days, which was education, as have many other religious, because now the state is able to look after that. Good Catholic Education Offices and Catholic Health Care are now able to manage those. So going out in to the back of beyond with many of the Aboriginal groups, refugees, supporting the women being trafficked, and helping those who are prostitutes, the prison ministries…there is still that urge to go out to the edges, or the margins, to where the need is. I think it is that sense, and that sense of commitment to the religious vocation, and the spirituality of Mary MacKillop that sustains us. Pope Francis brings a new vision and new hope for a Church being transformed – a church of which we are part.

Anne Derwin rsj

Anne Derwin was born in 1949 and entered the Sisters of St Joseph in 1969. She made her final vows in 1978.

Speaking at a dinner at Sydney Town Hall in August 2010 held to celebrate their founder Mary MacKillop's life and work, and to raise funds for her canonisation, Josephite congregational leader Sister Anne Derwin quoted the American Benedictine, Joan Chittister, saying that 'saints are models of people who fire the soul of their own culture or who swim against the current and offer resistance where needed'. Anne continued: 'Perhaps that's why Australians generally admire Mary MacKillop – she does fire the soul of our culture and she does show us a dignified way of swimming against the current and offering resistance when needed'.

Anne has been a Josephite for more than 40 years but her connection with the sisters began two decades before that. As a small child she went to the Josephite kindergarten in the north western Sydney suburb of Beverly Hills an spent the remainder of her school days at Regina Coeli, the Josephite school there. 'We were pretty ordinary poor kids', she recalled. She was impressed by the sisters and the lengths they went to ensure their charges did as well as they could in exams by devoting extra time to them after school and on Saturday mornings. 'They were quite amazing,' she said, 'so I guess their witness was what drew me to the Josephites'.

It was at high school that Anne first heard about Vatican II and she has never forgotten the day her Josephite principal, who also happened to be her religion teacher, bounced into the classroom and wrote, 'The church is the People of God' on the blackboard. 'She kept saying it with great delight and satisfaction in every religion lesson for the rest of the year,' Anne recalled, adding, 'At 15 I felt the same excitement and freedom Sister Raymond did .'

On leaving school, even though she already knew she had a call to religious life, Anne took up a Commonwealth scholarship to do an arts degree at the University of Sydney. 'When you're a young teenage girl you don't really want to say yes to that,' she said. 'You think about other things you should do with your life.' University was something of a shock. 'It was the late 60s after all with its flower power, free love, and students demonstrations through the streets. ' The call, however, 'was still nagging at me' and Anne felt she wouldn't be happy until she responded to it. Her parents urged her to finish her degree but she was adamant she didn't want to wait that long, knowing she could finish it later. It took a while for this to happen, she admitted, but she was happy.

In 1969, the same year that the Sisters of St Joseph held their renewal chapter after Vatican II, Anne entered the novitiate in Baulkham Hills. Her novice mistress she said would not have had a lot of background to the documents of Vatican II 'but she was reading them and teaching us what the Council was saying about religious life'. Looking back she remembered being given a good grounding in theology, scripture and prayer with an emphasis on a new approach to the vows of poverty, chastity and obedience.

Obedience was no longer taught as unquestioning acceptance of the rule of superiors, of 'saying "yes Sister" when you were told to do something'; it was about 'listening to the voice of God, where God is leading us in our personal lives and community life'. Chastity was no longer to be thought of as a negative virtue, but a choice to love more broadly and generously. Poverty was more than the frugality common to all religious in the earlier days of their apostolic work, it was about sharing and about the generosity of God.

There was little talk of Mary MacKillop. That came later when Anne was a young nun. In the second year of her novitiate, however, she enjoyed trips to the Jesuit church in Lavender Bay to hear a wide-ranging group of scholars lecturing on the documents of Vatican II. These trips were in themselves a contrast to the pre-Vatican II days when novices rarely left the novitiate. At Lavender Bay the young Josephites enjoyed meeting novices from other congregations, found the lectures 'brilliant and stimulating' and shared 'an excitement about religious life'.

After the novitiate everyone in Anne's year was trained to teach in primary schools, including Anne, even though she had partially completed her degree. 'They had a real need because in the 1960s the schools were huge,' she said. Her superiors also considered that starting at the primary level gave a 'more solid teacher training'. The newly professed young nuns had moved from Baulkham Hills into the convent at Mary MacKillop Place where the Josephites had their teacher training college. 'It was pretty hard work,' Anne said. 'There were a lot of older sisters living here then and we looked after them at the same time as studying hard. We used to go to the infirmary after college and look after the sick ones, and cook for everybody, and it was a big community…there would easily have been 100 here then or close to that. So we were very busy young sisters.'

Once trained, the young nuns were sent off to different schools, 'usually back to our home places in Australia or New Zealand,' said Anne, 'and we got on with life and teaching and studying and all those things you do'. Anne was sent as a secondary teacher to Mount Saint Joseph, a Josephite-owned school in Milperra in western Sydney. During her first few months living in this smaller community of between 12 and 14 sisters, she realised how very different her formation was from those who had gone before her. 'I can remember vividly in the dining room one day the superior saying, "We don't understand what you've been taught about obedience"'. Anne remembered thinking, 'My goodness, we have had a very different sort of formation and preparation for religious life'. She could see that it was a 'time of struggle' for many of the older sisters.

For a young woman formed according to the more liberal ideas of Vatican II, and immersed in the excitement of the new teaching of theology and scripture, Anne was shocked by the resistance of some of her companions in community to losing past and cherished ways of being a religious. At about this time, in order to ease the transition, the congregational leadership team began to bring in speakers from overseas to talk to the sisters about Vatican II, 'opening the doors of our understanding of what our life was about'. As a result of these sessions, said Anne, 'we all began to understand what the Council was saying'.

It is curious that one of the side effects of the sameness imposed on apostolic religious congregations by the 1917 Code of Canon Law was to understate or even lose sight of the stories and visions of their founders. Anne acknowledged that even though she had spent the whole of her schooldays with the Sisters of St Joseph, she heard little about Mary MacKillop; this was true of the novitiate too. 'We had her life read at meal times when we were sitting there in silence, but that was it…it's funny when you think of it now.'

One of the most powerful edicts arising from Vatican II was to 'go back to the spirit of the founder' which, for the Josephites, meant 'go back and see what Mary MacKillop was really about'. Anne described their rediscovery of Mary MacKillop as truly liberating for the Sisters of St Joseph. 'Mary MacKillop wasn't bound by a lot of the canon law stuff – she was before all that, as that came in later to religious life,' she explained, 'so to go back and feel the freedom of those days [in which the founding sisters were able] to respond to the poor and live a life they could shape themselves was extraordinary'.

The Josephites discovered that their founder was a remarkable woman whose story continued to resonate with men and women in the twenty-first century. What was especially significant for the Sisters of St Joseph was that Mary MacKillop's life was not just a great story, but that it was a great Australian story. One aspect of this was Mary's flexibility as founder. 'She used to call the nuns who came from Europe the real nuns,' said Anne. 'She didn't want that form of religious life, she said it did not suit this country. To learn this was very enlightening for us and going back to the spirit of the founder became a real catch cry.'

As in all orders in the years after Vatican II, a number of sisters left the Josephites, among them women who had been in the novitiate with Anne. She believed that if change had come more quickly, perhaps more would have stayed. For younger sisters sent out to remote rural places, often living with an older sister, it was a matter of loneliness and life was hard. Many of those who left stayed in touch, said Anne. 'We meet up every now and again.' She herself did not consider leaving. 'I've always been happy and was enjoying my life. You know you belong if you're happy.'

After a year at Milperra, Anne went to St Joseph's High School in Kogarah, a southern suburb of Sydney where she taught maths and religion. She loved being with teenage girls, 'they really kept you young.' Her congregational leader at the time, Sister Elizabeth Murphy, told her she had to wait until she had taken her final vows before she could go back to university and finish her degree, and that she had to switch from arts to science. Anne, concerned that her scholarship time was running out, and also determined to do arts, decided she was justified in being 'a little bit disobedient...I did try to explain to her that that was silly, that I would miss out if I didn't finish my degree, so I did pick it up before my final vows'. Like so many of her contemporaries, she taught all day and studied at night. She was grateful she wasn't teaching in a boarding school.

The Josephites have always seen themselves as very ordinary. Their history is marked by service to the very poorest, to communities on the goldfields, along railway tracks, in tents and humble houses in small rural towns. In

Anne's words, 'we haven't had a history of being behind closed walls in convents, we've been out there in twos and threes all over the country… we've always lived among people…we're very much at home being with whoever we are with'. Elizabeth Murphy's time as congregational leader from 1977 to 1989 was transformational in that she encouraged the Sisters of St Joseph to look beyond Australia and New Zealand when considering Vatican II's emphasis on the 'option for the poor' as well as Mary MacKillop's admonition to 'seek the poorest and most neglected'. 'She was the first leader who opened our eyes to the world and got us out of this Australian mindset,' said Anne.

Under Elizabeth's guidance, the Josephites considered a number of invitations to make foundations overseas and decided on Peru. Initially a number of Josephite volunteers went to support the work of the Australian Columban Fathers, mainly in parish and pastoral work and catechetics, but also in visiting psychiatric prisons. They were particularly active in supporting women to establish small businesses in local craft work, undertaking fund-raising in Australia and assisting with marketing their finished products. 'The women are off and running with this and doing it themselves now,' said Anne, explaining that the Josephites currently work in small communities supporting local projects with funds raised in Australia.

In 1991 Josephite Irene McCormack from Western Australia, was shot dead in Peru by Shining Path terrorists after a kangaroo court in the tiny hill top village of Huasahuasi. It was a tragedy for the congregation and a trauma for villagers who tried to stop the killing by calling out that Irene was Australian and 'not a Yankee'. Anne described Irene as 'a vivacious and wonderful woman'. Anne paid a visit to Peru before Mary MacKillop was declared as a saint, and Irene's local bishop asked if the Josephites had considered Irene's case for canonisation. 'I said no – this one has taken us 125 years so far and we're not there yet.'

Another enterprise that began under Elizabeth Murphy, and one that Anne said would have delighted Mary MacKillop, was to establish a presence in the Kimberley to support the Gija people. 'Mary MacKillop wanted to go to central Australia from the beginning.' Among a number of other ministries, the sisters opened Ngalangangpum (Mother and Child) School combining formal education with Gija language, songs and dances. 'We've had a very strong group of sisters committed to the Aboriginal ministry over the years, being with people and fighting for their rights,' Anne explained. 'It's been educative and transforming for the rest of us.'

After three years at Kogarah in 1980, at the age of 33, Anne was finally given time to finish her arts degree full time at Macquarie University. She spent the rest of the decade back at Milperra, first as teacher and religious education coordinator and, from 1983, as principal. She also continued her own professional education, gaining a Graduate Diploma in Religious Studies in 1984 and a Masters in Education in 1990. 'It was an exciting time, that period of nine years,' she recalled. It was also a challenge when the decision was made that any enterprises the sisters owned would be incorporated as companies. 'Some of us had to quickly learn about governance,' she said, 'and the difference between governance and management. I did get a bit of basic education, particularly through our solicitor…we'd go to courses, and lectures [by people] like John Carver, the Canadian expert on governance… we went and learnt everything, I can tell you'.

She was so happy at Milperra that when a number of sisters asked Anne if they could nominate her for the leadership of the New South Wales Province in 1990 she said, 'No, no, I love school and I'm staying in school'. There were more than 400 sisters in the province at the time and Anne knew that being a member of the leadership team of six women was a full-time job. Two months later, one of the sisters on her staff came to talk to her. 'She was an older sister so she could get away with it – she sat down in front of me and said, "you know you're being very selfish about this. You're just doing what you want to do, not what the congregation might want you to do." So in the end I said yes to the nomination and then I was put on the team.'

This was the end of teaching for Anne and the start of finding herself in a series of leadership roles that were to occupy her for almost 25 years . It was not what she expected when she entered the Josephites, but, she said, 'It's a privilege to be asked to do leadership of any group, isn't it? It's not what you pray for but it's a privilege when you're asked to do it '.

Anne spent six years on the provincial leadership team (1990-1995), and another six (1996-2002) immediately afterwards as provincial leader of the Sisters of St Joseph in New South Wales. This was followed by a sabbatical year which included studying theology at the Irish College in Leuven and four years as Director of St Joseph's Spirituality and Education Centre in Kincumber on the central coast of New South Wales before, in 2008, being elected congregational leader of the Josephites. In her words, 'I had to be prime minister now, not just the premier'.

The first rung of the ladder for Anne had involved assisting the provincial leader oversee all the many ministries of the sisters in the state, including education, health care, welfare works, justice works and pastoral works in urban and rural New South Wales. The second was assuming final responsibility for all these elements. The third was taking on the care of 800 Sisters of St Joseph across Australia, New Zealand, Peru, Brazil, Ireland, Scotland and East Timor. In addition, from July 2010 until July 2012, Anne was president of Catholic Religious Australia.

It is impossible to imagine any job description that would encompass such far-reaching responsibilities at so many levels. Among the many facets of the work Anne undertook during these years was monitoring the activities of the MacKillop foundation which sits at the heart of the work of the congregation in Australia; the stewardship of properties, institutions and places of residence; financial oversight of the congregation; ensuring the proper governance of companies associated with the congregation; support of several hundred volunteers; and advocating to government on behalf of the most marginalised in the community with particular emphasis on refugees and trafficked women.

Part of Anne's training in management came from her experience at Milperra. Becoming a Board member of the St John of God Health Care in Perth, one of the largest health care organizations in Australia, added to her experience. When she was first invited, she declined, but just as she was urged onto the NSW leadership team, once again, she responded to one of her sisters. This time it was her provincial leader who said, ' You're always saying we should share around, we shouldn't just be doing our own thing, so practice what you preach'. Her membership spanned 2004-2009. Once on the Board, it was recommended that each member undertake a company director's course, which she did, ' Glad of the opportunity seeing we were so heavily into it'. Her Diploma from the Australian Institute of Company Directors in 2005 added to her expertise in her role as Chair of St Anthony's Family Care (2003-2007).[1]

1 A not-for-profit organisation, St Anthony's Family Care carries on the work of Mary MacKillop in caring for children and families in need. www.safc.org.au.

When she was elected congregational leader Anne was thrown onto the world stage because of the canonisation of Mary MacKillop. Along with her sisters, she was challenged, not only by the enormity of the process itself, but also by the stewardship of the legacy of Australia's first saint and the women who followed her. When asked how she got through it all, Anne replied:

> I don't know. It must be the grace of God, I think, which gets you through, because I didn't enter the convent to do this…I entered the convent to teach kids. Who'd have thought we'd entered a convent to do media training? But together we did it; you've got your team and all the other people who are so great at helping us, and you just take it in your stride.

No doubt Anne's sense of humor made the process a little easier. Perhaps the Australian characteristic of taking badly to structured authority also helped. The hundreds of Australian pilgrims, including the nuns who were in Rome for the canonisation, demonstrated this. Even though they were told by the 'Roman men up there', as Anne put it, that they were not allowed to clap at the moment of canonisation, the millions watching on TV delighted at the sisters' obvious joy when spontaneous cheering and clapping broke out in St Peter's Basilica. Anne was unperturbed when the Australian Prime Minister of the day, Kevin Rudd, remarked on their 'disobedience'.

Overwhelmed that the canonisation meant so much to all Australians, Anne said: 'everybody seemed to find a place and could identify with what was being celebrated. It was very inclusive'. The great gift of the canonisation for the Josephite sisters, she added, 'was that people have articulated [back to us] our identity, even if we thought we weren't articulating it very well…a lot of people wanted to affirm that the sisters have kept doing [Mary's work] all these years…it was wonderful to keep hearing it; it was very humbling'.

From the public's perspective, another significant Josephite activity during Anne's leadership has been their commitment, alongside other Australian religious congregations, to the people of East Timor. The Josephites responded to an invitation from Bishop Belo in 1993 during the Indonesian occupation to help 'the building up of a new society in peace, reconciliation and forgiveness'. He specifically asked them to help preserve the Tetum language which was under threat and this has been a major focus for them ever since. Working with university linguists, they have produced their own curriculum materials and trained new teachers in literacy and maths.

The work the sisters have done over two decades in the fledgling nation has moved far beyond their involvement in teaching and community development. They were leaders in advocating for the civil and human rights of the East Timorese. Former deputy leader of the Labor Party, Tom Uren once remarked that 'the Josephites had such an influence that the cause became respectable'.[2] A later Federal Labor Minister, Peter Garrett, maintained that it was the Josephites who kept the plight of the East Timorese front and centre before government officials. As Anne said, 'One of our sisters, Josephine Mitchell, just kept driving to Canberra every three weeks…she just kept at them…[the Josephites] probably drive the government mad at times, but that's good.'

In 2012 Anne visited East Timor as congregational leader to celebrate the opening of the Institutu Mary MacKillop, the first permanent residence for the sisters. A small three-bedroomed convent, it also has an office attached and facilities for training staff as well as a music room. The sisters have both a carpentry and sewing team whose work helps to raise funds. Resources are so basic, added Anne, that the sisters are required to make their own teaching materials.

In the spirit of Mary MacKillop, whose travels within Australia and internationally have become the stuff of legend, Anne has been on many journeys during her years in leadership. Highlights have been times of sharing the Eucharist sitting on the red earth with an Aboriginal community in East Kimberley; being in crowded churches full of people in East Timor; climbing stony paths to gather in hill-top chapels in Peru, and being with thousands of refugees from Berundi in a camp in Tanzania.

The role of women religious as advocates for social justice is not often recognised in the mainstream media. Yet women like Anne see this as central to their mission. In her case, this aspect of her work increased when she became President of Australian Catholic Religious (ACR), one of whose functions is to lobby governments, based on the research arising from their work with the most marginalised in society. In her last message as President in June 2012, Anne wrote:

> In the seventies, Johann Baptist Metz defined religious life as the 'Holy Spirit's shock therapy for the Church', as 'the institutionalised form of a dangerous reminder in the heart of the Church.' Religious life must be the thorn, the

2 *The Age 'Good Weekend'* 30 August 2003.20.

> restlessness, the constant impetus, forbidding the Church to make its peace with the powers of the world. In the bourgeois Church it should clamour urgently and persistently for adhering to the roots of the gospel and for radicality of discipleship…Religious life can be defined as exactly that impetus in the life of the Church which keeps that dynamism alive. Its most appropriate place is on the edge, in company with the outsiders. Its greatest temptation is to belong to the centre, or to transform itself to become the centre.[3]

The radical nature of leadership as Anne has described it is arguably well suited to women's leadership style, which often includes a more consultative approach, less aggression and more respect for the inclusion of others. She nominates the art of truly listening as essential for any leader:

> I don't think women are frightened to make decisions, but we might go about it differently to men. We spend time discussing together, listening to everyone in the group, finding ways to listen to them…we weigh out what needs more time and deliberation. I [also] think women are collaborative leaders, I think we like to work together. I think women leaders have got a lot of courage, they're risk-takers.

Mary MacKillop urged her sisters to seek the poorest and most neglected and Anne found this confronting 'where many of us are living in an affluent country and are quite comfortably off'. Poverty for the Josephites, she explained, is about sharing their resources with those in need. 'It's about this sharing and the generosity of God and being part of that because it's not as if we don't have a house to live in. We are secure, we've got a house, and we've got whatever we need so we're not poor in that sense but hopefully we are poor in the sense of not being attached to anything and receiving graciously what we're given but moving on or giving away… I guess our shared life is really very much part of that. And reverence for the earth and good stewardship of the earth these days is all part of our poverty.'

She asked herself as religious leader, 'How do we as a group keep seeking the poorest and most vulnerable, and make sure we're there with them in whatever capacity we can be?' The sisters talk about such issues a great deal, they keep themselves informed. 'Immersion is the best thing,' said Anne. 'We send women out to go and see what's happening in other parts, in other places and usually our hearts are grabbed.'

---

3 Sister Anne Derwin, *Message to the CRA*, 17 June 2012, www.catholicreligiousaustralia.org, accessed 19/7/12.

While she was provincial and congregational leader, Anne lived at Mary MacKillop Place in north Sydney, where Mary once lived herself. It's a big place, she admits, and greatly valued not only by the sisters but also by its thousands of visitors. It is a place of pilgrimage for Australians and also for people from around the world. The sisters trust that the people who go there 'are drawn to the same things as Mary MacKillop in her life – to care about the poor and to put God first and rely on God as she did, and hope to find God'.

The Sisters of Mercy

The Sisters of Mercy were founded by Catherine McAuley in Ireland. Born in 1778, Catherine inherited a considerable fortune and in 1827 at the age of 49 built a house in the centre of Dublin in which she and a small group of like-minded women established a community to shelter and educate women and girls. Under pressure from the Archbishop of Dublin to take on the status of women religious, Catherine and two companions entered the novitiate of the Presentation Sisters in 1831 and at the end of the year, on 12 December, took their vows as the first Sisters of Mercy. Catherine's vision was that works of mercy be the distinctive feature of her institute.

In the following ten years, Catherine established 14 independent foundations in Ireland and England. Determined to avoid the centralised form of government common to many women's institutes at the time, her model, based on that of the Presentation Sisters, meant that each independent house was able in turn to establish further foundations that also became autonomous. One of the advantages of this system of governance was that local young women following religious vocations could stay within their own communities. It followed that many parishioners knew the women either through family ties or shared life experiences in the tightly knit Catholic life that prevailed until the years following Vatican II.

The first Sisters of Mercy to arrive in Australia came to Perth in 1846 under the leadership of Ursula Frayne. They were the second group of religious women to come to Australia after the arrival of the Sisters of Charity in Sydney in 1838. The Sisters of Mercy made 17 separate foundations in Australia, principally from Ireland, and a further 34 independent houses stemmed from these. They have long been the dominant religious institute in Australia, with a membership of 3,500 women at the height of their numbers in the mid-1960s, responsible for kindergartens, schools, hospitals, teacher training facilities, orphanages, aged care facilities and welfare agencies in both the major cities and in regional areas in every state.

Bathurst Sisters of Mercy

Seven pioneer Sisters of Mercy arrived in Bathurst from Charleville in Ireland at the invitation of Bishop Mathew Quinn. At that time, the Bathurst diocese covered the whole of New South Wales west of the Blue Mountains. The Bathurst Sisters of Mercy educated children, boys and girls, in the region from kindergarten to the last years of secondary schooling. They trained their own teachers at St Joseph's Mount, their convent and novitiate in Bathurst, cared for orphans in both Bathurst and Orange, managed aged care facilities in Forbes and Bathurst, and a hostel for young women in Bathurst.

Of the 17 congregations of the Sisters of Mercy, Bathurst fell into the mid-range in terms of numbers, with a few less than 200 women in the mid-1960s. This number was comparable to that of other regional Mercy congregations such as Ballarat, and about one-third the size of the congregations in Melbourne and Brisbane. The overwhelming apostolic commitment of the sisters has traditionally been to education, with relatively few engaged in welfare and health care before Vatican II.

At the time of reconfiguration in 2011 there were 60 women remaining in the congregation, many of whom were still actively engaged in a diverse range of works, including the traditional works of Mercy that involve pastoral care, visitation and advocacy on behalf of the marginalised in society. Over the past 25 years, they have become heavily involved in justice issues through the Mercy and Justice Centre they established at St Joseph's Mount. The property has evolved into a centre for environmental education.

The Ballarat East Sisters of Mercy

The Ballarat East Congregation of the Sisters of Mercy was established in 1881. They founded the Sacred Heart Convent, and staffed the local parish primary school, setting about their long history of teaching across the Ballarat Diocese. Like the other 16 Mercy congregations spread across Australia, the Ballarat East Sisters of Mercy soon attracted young women as entrants to religious life, most of whom had been educated in their schools. A high proportion of the women had sisters, cousins, aunts or nieces already in the congregation, and many of their families were well known as local Catholics in Ballarat, and in small communities and medium sized towns in the district.[1] *Until the 1970s, their corporate work was within the Ballarat Diocese, which stretched from the Murray River to the sea, covering the western half of the State of Victoria.*

The Mercy novitiate and their teachers' college, Aquin Training College, was located in Ballarat East until the 1970s. It was the home and training institution for nearly 200 women by the mid-1960s when this, a mid-sized Mercy congregation, was at its most numerous. [2] *Their leaders were*

1 A statistic that illustrates the local character of the nuns profiled in 1960, shows that of the 20 sisters teaching at Sacred Heart Convent, 19 had themselves been students at the school.

2 During this period, the largest of the Mercy congregations were located in Melbourne

tenacious in their support for their novitiate and their teachers' college, established in 1909. Aquinas College, as it became known, was one of only a handful of teacher training colleges operating outside the capital cities prior to the late 1970s, and its continuous operation is one of the community's proudest achievements.[3]

In the early years of the twenty-first century, fourteen congregations of the Sisters of Mercy, including the Ballarat East Sisters of Mercy and the Bathurst Sisters of Mercy, went through a process of reconfiguration resulting in the establishment of the Sisters of Mercy of Australia and Papua New Guinea in 2011.

---

and Brisbane, with numbers exceeding 500 in each. By comparison, those in the regional areas similar to Ballarat East, numbered between 100 and 200. Unlike many other Mercy congregations, the Ballarat East sisters did not have responsibility for vulnerable children, aged persons or for a hospital, these functions being the responsibility of the Sisters of Nazareth and the Sisters of St John of God respectively who managed these institutions of care in the city of Ballarat.

3 The College was responsible for training Sisters of Mercy and lay women (and later, men) who would teach in Catholic schools, first within the Ballarat diocese, later extending to the rest of the State and into New South Wales. Early pioneers and congregational leaders of the Ballarat East Congregation, particularly Mother Xavier Flood, and following her, Mother Bonaventure Healy, ensured that from the earliest days of the community women were allowed to attend Melbourne University, maintaining the highest educational standards in teacher training and in secondary education for students of Sacred Heart College in Ballarat East.

Veronica Lawson rsm

Veronica Lawson was born in 1941, and entered the Sisters of Mercy in 1960. She took her final vows in 1968.

Biblical scholar Veronica Lawson was asked recently how she developed such a love of learning, growing up as she did on a dairy farm in Central Victoria. Her answer conjured up the picture of a lively, intellectually stimulating and happy home. 'My dad loved poetry and reading and mum was just wise. We had this wonderful extended family. Some of my earliest memories are of my maternal grandparents who lived with us. Grandpa Manassa was Lebanese, originally from a place in Syria called Joudaidah Marjayoun. He told stories of walking from southern Lebanon to Jerusalem and sitting on the Mount of Olives. Granny Manassa was the fount of all practical wisdom and love. I can hardly ever remember our house without lots of people in it and open doors and eating carefully during the week to be able to entertain relatives from the city on the weekend. Grandpa Lawson and his border collie dog came to live with us when I was about seven and that was another blessing in our lives.'

The Lawsons were strong Catholics and involved in a vibrant local parish but Veronica insisted 'we weren't a rosary sort of family'. Her father was secretary of the local Labor Party so conversations round the kitchen table frequently centered on religion and politics. Looking back, Veronica acknowledged that she 'inherited my mum's appreciation of art, my dad's love of poetry, and both parents' commitment to public life'.

Born in February 1941, Veronica was the middle child of five, two boys and three girls. Her primary education was at the Macedon State School, which both her father and his father before him had attended. The Ursulines came to Macedon when she was in Grade 5 and she and her sisters transferred to their school. Veronica loved and admired the Ursulines but the range of subjects they taught was limited and numbers never rose above 50. The school closed at the end of 1954. After two weeks at Sacred Heart College in Kyneton, which offered neither art nor Latin, Veronica's favourite subjects, she was told by her parents to find a school that suited her. On the advice of her parish priest, she chose Sacred Heart College run by the Sisters of Mercy in Ballarat East, and went there as a boarder in 1955 at the age of 14.

Veronica and her contemporaries at Sacred Heart College had the advantage that the sisters who taught in the Sisters of Mercy teachers' training college, Aquinas, also taught at their school. Many of these women were highly proficient in music, science, languages and the arts, and were committed to providing the best education they could for the girls in their care, whether they were trainee teachers or secondary students. Outstanding amongst the teachers who influenced her, Veronica said, were Sisters Genevieve MacDonald and Anne Forbes, the latter unintentionally responsible for introducing Veronica to the works of Karl Marx. Anne was studying political science at night, Veronica recalled, and kept her books in a cupboard in the back of the classroom. 'When she went off to prayers, I would borrow a book, take it to bed and read it by torchlight under the blankets.' Anne caught her returning a book one morning and was horrified. 'You'll have me excommunicated,' she said.

Anne's sister, Clare Forbes, was senior school religion teacher and, well before Vatican II, was introducing students to the liturgical renewal movement, the works of Johannes Hofinger, and the teachings on the church as the mystical body of Christ, 'and I was fired with it', said Veronica. Even though Clare had no formal studies in theology or religious education at that time, she was 'simply attuned, through her reading and acute attentiveness, to the groundswell of renewal in the Church. She educated herself and us in its movements.'[4] Not many secondary school students at that time were being introduced to Pope Pius XII's encyclical, *Divino Afflante Spiritu* (1943) and to the study of Genesis: 'It was 1958 and we found ourselves doing critical biblical studies,' Veronica said.

On finishing Year 12 Veronica was awarded a Commonwealth scholarship and enrolled in an arts degree at the University of Melbourne. It was during her first year that she decided to enter the Ballarat East Sisters of Mercy. 'Don't ask me why,' she said many years later in an interview with the Ballarat Courier. 'I come up with a different answer every time I am asked that question. It surely had something to do with that never ending God-quest that leads us all on different paths.' As a student in Melbourne, Veronica shared a house with her brother who was cross with her about her decision to become a nun, but she was clear about it. 'I just knew I wanted

4 Veronica Lawson, 'Gospel imperatives for a changing church (Mark 1:15 and 16:15)', *The Swag: Quarterly Magazine of the National Council of Priests of Australia*, Vol. 20, No. 3, Spring 2012, 23-26.

to join the Mercies and I thought, if I don't do it now I won't do it…I had to give it a go.'

Veronica entered the novitiate in Ballarat in 1960, at the age of 19. 'There were five in my year,' she said, 'and seven in the year ahead of me and seven in the year ahead of them'. The hardest part, she found, was saying goodbye to her family and friends; having her younger sister boarding in the school at the same time helped to some degree. Much about life in the novitiate Veronica considered 'lunacy…but we got through and in the grand scheme of things…I didn't find it an enormous hardship. I was really healthy and that included a healthy skepticism, I think'. Her respect for the Mercy women who had taught her, she said, kept her going. 'When I was at school I saw these women as people with a mind of their own,' she said. 'I didn't realise the extent to which they were expected to conform until after I was professed, but they were great role models because they took the best of it.'

Veronica liked the novice mistress, Mother Columba, who had come to Australia from Ireland when she was 12, lived with a priest uncle, and was educated at the Mercy's school in Ballarat. 'She'd had a tough life and I think I understood her somehow,' said Veronica. 'I didn't take too seriously some of the stuff that she thought was important and I just knew that I had to put up with it…if I wanted to be a Sister of Mercy, which I did.'

Veronica found being cut off from newspapers and magazines in the novitiate difficult, especially during an election campaign. She was old enough to vote but Mother Columba, a Democratic Labor Party supporter, was not sympathetic to requests for information on other political parties. Veronica's brother, horrified at her ignorance of local issues, organised a subscription to *The Age* and friends sent her copies of *Time* magazine, but Mother Columba chose not to pass them on when they arrived.[5] 'I knew she put the copies of *Time* in the cupboard in the priest's flat,' laughed Veronica, 'and three of us would come down very late at night and read them…so we kept ourselves informed as far as we could'.

As a postulant Veronica was allowed to continue her university studies and later completed her degree as a second year novice. She travelled to

5 In the 1960s Australia had four major political parties, the Australian Labor Party (ALP), the Liberal Party and the National Party. The Democratic Labor Party (DLP) was formed out of a split in the ALP in 1955 and was strongly Catholic and anti-Communist. It lost all its representatives in 1974 until 2010 when one candidate was elected to Federal Parliament.

Melbourne University one day a week and relied on notes from friends for the sessions she missed. She also attended geology classes at the local School of Mines and sat for both Melbourne University and School of Mines examinations.

At the end of her novitiate, Veronica, now a junior professed, moved into the main community of about 100 women. Clare Forbes, she said, who was responsible for the continuing formation of the junior professed, insisted that their faith would be strengthened through study of the whole Bible, not just the New Testament. 'She taught us to pray in a way that engaged both the pain of the world and the sacred stories of our tradition.'

Vatican II had begun and, said Veronica, 'we were surrounded by people who were keeping us informed and engaging us in discussion. Clare Forbes was keeping tabs on absolutely everything that was happening in the Council'. Veronica and any of the sisters interested would avail themselves of the lectures delivered by the local Redemptorist priests, including scholars of the calibre of Leo Branagan, Kevin O'Shea, Peter Callachor and Tony Kelly. They introduced the sisters to the Pontifical Biblical Commission's 1964 'Historical Truth of the Gospels', and to '*Dei Verbum*, the Dogmatic Constitution on Divine Revelation'. 'We were taping their lectures, going back over them and discussing everything,' recalled Veronica.

Veronica's degree was in Latin and English, and although it would have qualified her to teach secondary students, had she completed the required diploma of education, her superiors decided that she was to undertake primary teacher training first. In 1965, when biblical studies was introduced into the curriculum, she taught the senior classes at Sacred Heart, at the same time expanding her own knowledge of the subject. She was also teaching French and later took up biblical Greek and Hebrew, learning her verbs while supervising meal times for the boarders. She wrote:

> In those heady days of the Vietnam moratorium and student demonstrations, I was being introduced to critical biblical scholarship by the professors from the Redemptorist studentate in Wendouree, just out of Ballarat. There were no formal qualifications for such students, simply the satisfaction of a thirst to move more deeply into the mysteries of the word of God. I learned my Greek and Hebrew verbs and vocabulary while the boarders at St Martin's in the Pines at Mount Clear ate their breakfast. The 150 Year 11 and 12 boarders had less need of meal supervision than I had of those languages, though I was not to know where that informal study would lead me over the subsequent decades.

> None of the formal studies in theology and scripture and the ministry of the word that followed would have been possible for me as a woman in the church without the impetus that Vatican II gave to the study of the bible…and to the opening up of religious life.[6]

Towards the end of the 1960s, the Redemptorists decided to move their studentate to Melbourne as part of the proposed Yarra Theological Union in Box Hill. This meant the loss of all the Redemptorist lecturers at Aquinas College. Bishop Mulkearns suggested to Mother Carmel, then leader of the Ballarat East Sisters of Mercy, that Veronica be sent overseas to study theology and scripture 'so that I would be able to lecture at the College'. Clearly her potential as a fine teacher and scholar was already evident.

Mother Carmel consulted Peter Callachor, the Redemptorist Professor of Hebrew and Greek, whose classes Veronica had been attending.

> He said he thought the best thing for me to do was to go to the École Biblique in Jerusalem, which is where he went after he did his licentiate in Rome, because it was not possible then for a Catholic woman to get a theology degree in Australia. The only place Catholics could study theology in Australia then was the seminary, and they didn't do degrees anyway, and it was unthinkable for a Catholic woman or lay man to go to a place like the Melbourne College of Divinity.

Veronica passed the requisite language examinations and Professor Callachor contacted the great Dominican scholar, Jerome Murphy-O'Connor, on her behalf. Based at the École Biblique in Jerusalem, he also taught in two or three American universities in the summer months and agreed to arrange for Veronica to enroll at one of these universities and write her thesis at the École. 'The plan was that I would do my masters, then come back and teach at the teachers' college…the Bishop offered to pay for me but the Congregation refused because they wanted to be able to decide whether I went to the teachers' college or not.'

Flying for the first time in her life, Veronica set off in June 1973, initially to a summer school in San Francisco, then on to Jerusalem, via New York, Brussels, Paris and Rome. She arrived in Jerusalem in August and before

---

6 Veronica Lawson, 'Vatican II in Hope and Memory: The Power of Vatican II and the Structures of Power', *Compass*, Vol 38, No 1, Autumn 2004, 21. Paul Collins reports that by the beginning of the 21st century, 74% of those undertaking undergraduate studies in theology were women. They also made up 64% of postgraduate students. Collins, *Believers: Does Australian Catholicism Have a Future*? Sydney, UNSW Press, 2008, 68.

beginning her studies enrolled in a course in modern Hebrew. 'Six weeks into the course, the Yom Kippur War broke out and my teacher's 17-year-old son was killed on the first day of the war. The course was disbanded and the building requisitioned by the army.'

The École Biblique Archéologique Francaise had been established in East Jerusalem by the Dominicans at the time of the modernist crisis and became a world-renowned centre for biblical scholarship.[7] The Jerusalem Bible was produced at the École, originally in French, and later translated into other languages. The 25 research students present when Veronica arrived were 'of all different nationalities…the only other woman was an Anglican Cambridge University graduate who lived at the British School of Archaeology'.

The men lived at the Dominican Convent, a magnificent building set in extensive gardens located near the Damascus Gate outside the walls of the Old City, but finding accommodation for Veronica was difficult under the conditions of the curfew then operating in the city. She and a young French woman archaeologist boarded at the Chaldean Patriarchate until arrangements were made for them to live on site at the École. The local superior decided to take advantage of a visit to the École by the superior general of the Dominicans so that the community could formally consider what was a radical proposal. 'The Dominicans operate by consensus,' said Veronica, 'and they had to get the vote of the community to say yes to allowing women to live in'. The vote in favour was unanimous, overturning a long-standing tradition and making it possible for future generations of women students to enjoy the same access to accommodation and the same library borrowing rights as the men.

Veronica spent two academic years in Jerusalem at the École Biblique during which time she immersed herself in studying the lands of the Bible as well as of the biblical texts, a preparation for what would later be study tours of the Bible lands for groups of Australian Catholic University students. During her time in Jerusalem, she received unwavering support from her community in Ballarat. Barely a day passed, she said, without an aerogramme from one of the sisters. Jerome Murphy-O'Connor supervised her masters thesis and 'gave me confidence in my own judgement'. They

7 The École Biblique was founded in 1890 when the Modernist movement sought to modify traditional beliefs with modern ideas, especially in the Catholic Church.

became firm friends. 'Jerry was interested in the gospel being real for people and I resonated with that,' said Veronica. 'He was as interested in what was happening in the world, in what was going on in people's lives, as he was in the text'.

Veronica loved Jerusalem and found her time at the École to be 'life-changing'. An unexpected part of this was a visit from her mother. 'I began to understand myself and to understand her in a new way. The people of East Jerusalem embraced her because she was at home there, even though she only had the few words of Arabic her father had taught her. For me, it was somehow part of discovering more about what it means to belong to the global community…some of my best friends there were Protestants and I made really good Jewish and Muslim friends, so that another world opened up for me'.

On her return home at the end of 1975, Veronica went back to secondary school teaching at St Martin's in the Pines and was appointed principal at the beginning of 1977. In January of that year, the Ballarat East Sisters of Mercy had a general chapter. 'I walked into that chapter as one of the sisters in the community and walked out as the vicar-general', she said. 'I came out of the chapel in shock and remember Mother Marie Therese saying, "I have no objection to your being vicar but we can't have a vicar with a ponytail"'. She was, in effect, deputy to the congregational leader, Valda Ward. As well as her new responsibilities, Veronica continued as principal of the boarding school. 'It was crazy really,' she said. 'I was too young for one thing and once more I found myself on a very fast learning track.'

This was the first of several occasions when Veronica was to be elected to positions of leadership within her congregation, including that of congregational leader. Reflecting on the reality of religious life, she said that taking up a leadership role in relation to women who had been her teachers, and who had been in authority over her was 'not really an issue, because one day you're a rooster and the next day you're a feather duster… you don't think of it in hierarchical terms or in terms of a career'.

Valda Ward, then leader, was involved at a national level in the establishment of the Institute of Sisters of Mercy of Australia (ISMA), and Veronica often found herself attending to the business of the congregation. One of the difficult aspects of her position was handling with sensitivity the concerns of those who were discerning whether or not they would remain in the congregation.[8]

At the same time that she was given increasing responsibilities in the congregation, Veronica was becoming known outside it as a biblical scholar, and was in demand as a public speaker and writer. A measure of her national standing is her election as President of the Australian Catholic Biblical Association in 1987/88; she was the first woman to hold this position.[9] Her commitment to professional development and networking among scholars has become a feature of Veronica's scholarly life. She was an inaugural member of the Women Scholars of Religion and Theology Association, formed in 1992 as a professional association of women scholars of religion and theology in the Pacific, Oceania and South-East Asian regions.[10] She was also a major contributor to a groundbreaking collection of essays published in 1994 exploring the issues of women and theology and their growing importance as participants in academic debates.[11]

In January 1991, Aquinas College was incorporated into the newly formed Australian Catholic University, and became the university's only non-metropolitan campus. Veronica, who had been teaching at Aquinas for some years, never ceased to deepen and expand her own knowledge and in 1992 took the opportunity to study with another eminent scholar, Sean Freyne, at Trinity College in Dublin.[12] Her doctoral thesis, completed in 1996, is entitled, 'Gender and Genre: The Construction of Female Gender in the Acts of the Apostles'. It took Veronica to another level in her understanding of the representation of women in the Christian Scriptures.

Veronica defines herself above all as a teacher and describes teaching as 'essentially an act of respect and generosity', something she also attributes to biblical scholars, as theologians. One of her own acts of generosity to thousands of people every week is her reflection on the Sunday gospel. It is printed in innumerable parish newsletters and is available on

8 Of the 60 women who joined the Ballarat East congregation between 1961 and 1970, 45 eventually left religious life; of the nine who joined between 1971 and 1988, five left.

9 The Association was formed in 1964, at which time women were not admitted as active members.

10 See Elaine Wainwright, 'Sea changes land living and loving: Women scholars of religion and theology over ten years', http://wsrt.asn.au/index.php?p=1-15, accessed 17.12.2013.

11 Maryanne Confoy, Dorothy Lee and Joan Nowotny (eds), *Freedom, Entrapment and Women Thinking Theology*. North Blackburn, Dove, 1995.

12 Both Sean Freyne and Jerome Murphy-O'Connor died in 2013.

various websites. It is written out of Veronica's deep knowledge and lived experience.[13] Ironically, Veronica and religious and lay women like her around Australia, well qualified to bring the gospel to life, are not officially authorised to give the homily in Catholic churches. The people of Ballarat, for example, cannot hear Veronica give a homily in church even though they can read her commentary on the gospel in the newsletter.

Veronica has written about her frustration at the limits imposed on women's participation in church life: 'As a woman committed to the proclamation of the gospel, I yearn for the day when women as well as men might, at the very least, break open the word in our liturgical celebrations'. On another occasion she has said that

> The story of women in the post-Vatican church is a story of one step forward and one step back. There is no denying the power of the data that emerged from the enquiry into the participation of women in the Australian Catholic Church…The constraints imposed by papal teaching on the place of women in the Church can only function as a powerful deterrent to any substantive change.[14]

Veronica and others like her have chosen to concentrate their efforts in supporting those who want to shape a renewed Church, one which incorporates new ecological and feminist approaches to the scriptures. As a member of the Sisters of Mercy, she feels 'part of something that is making a difference, something that's worthwhile', a movement that was founded by a woman, Catherine McAuley, who was practical and down-to-earth in her view of ministry. A grounding in the reality of people's lives and the life of the planet is just as important to Veronica as is her dedication to study of the scriptures. For her, there is no disjunction between life and engagement with the gospel since 'our sacred texts came out of reflection on life experience and provide a mirror for our own experience'. She uses as an example of this engagement the close association of the Sisters of Mercy with the struggles of the people of Timor Leste. Since the 1970s, the community has provided hospitality and housing for refugees, as well as educational opportunities for them in Ballarat, at their schools and through ACU. It is not possible to walk into their administration building without learning something about the plight of those they support, nor

---

13 Veronica's reflections can be accessed on line at http://catholicreligiousaustralia.org

14 Veronica Lawson, 'Vatican II in Hope and Memory', 21.

leave without being given the opportunity to assist in some way, financially or through some show of solidarity.[15]

Alongside this on-going involvement in the social justice and social mercy issues of the day, Veronica is now part of a resource group of Sisters of Mercy who are offering whatever expertise and service they can provide for the newly created, reconfigured Institute of Sisters of Mercy of Australia and Papua New Guinea. This 'Circle of Mercy Theologians' consists of ten sisters who identify themselves as theologians and/or biblical scholars. The process of offering their expertise where and when needed builds on the work Veronica and others did to assist the reconfiguring process. As Veronica said, these women see themselves not as the experts, but as resource people for others in their ministries of environmental justice, of mercy and justice for refugees and asylum seekers, indigenous communities and the people of Papua New Guinea. The process relies on what Veronica calls 'deep listening', hearing the experiences of others, helping them to analyse their situations, and bringing all of this into dialogue with 'our sacred stories' for the sake of transformative action.

In her room Veronica has a copy of the Claretian Bible Diary lying open at a page that captures her understanding of the potency of the scriptures.[16] She explained that it tells a story about one of the Rabbis. 'He is asked why the scripture said of God, "I will put my words on your heart" instead of "in your heart"? And the Rabbi said, "Even God can't put them in your heart. God puts them on your heart so that when it breaks, they'll slip in"'.

'The heart in Jewish thinking,' Veronica explained, 'and in the whole Jewish biblical tradition, is not just the locus of the emotions, but also the seat of cognitive awareness and understanding. With students, there's always the question of readiness. They may not be ready when you are teaching them, but if the words are on their hearts something might slip in when their hearts break. God's word might then become part of their thinking, part of their whole being'.

15 The Ballarat East sisters provided a home for Isabel Guterres during her studies at ACU. Isabel was a Commissioner on the Reception, Truth and Reconciliation Commission for seven years, then Secretary General of Timor Leste Red Cross, and most recently Minister for Social Solidarity. The Sisters also provided a home for seven Timorese students, supported schools in Timor Leste and missioned sisters to teach and minister there.

16 The Claretian Communications Foundation in the Philippines publishes a Bible Diary each year.

Now in her early seventies, Veronica's appearance belies her age. She has a smile that lights up a room and a joy for life and an energy fitting a person half her age. Her endless curiosity is infectious, and it is easy to imagine her engaging students of all ages. She has a confidence that stems from her education, but also, one suspects, from a strong community of independent and educated women. She is extremely comfortable with the latest technology and rarely seen without her iPad. She is an inveterate traveller for the sake of the mission, a great reader, and wonderful company. A true Vatican II woman, Veronica epitomises the best of teaching and learning, combined with a determination to use her own resources and those of her community to confront ignorance and injustice and, above all, to place words on the hearts of those whose lives she touches.

Patricia Powell rsm

Patricia Powell was born in 1942 and entered the Bathurst Sisters of Mercy in 1960. She took her final vows in 1966. Her name in religion was Sister Mary Emmanuel.

In many ways, Patricia Powell's life in religion is the quintessential example of the thousands of Sisters of Mercy, the largest women's religious institute in Australia. In telling the story of her individual contribution, some of the features of the lives of her fellow religious and the experiences shared by women in apostolic institutes across the country can also be seen. To put it another way, it is easy to imagine walking into any of the 17 congregations of Sisters of Mercy in Australia and come across someone whose story is very like that of Patricia Powell's.

The Bathurst congregation of the Sisters of Mercy 'has always been rural based', Patricia said:

> These rural roots provide the congregation with some of its personality and flavour. As a group, I believe we are practical, down-to-earth, resilient and resourceful. We place importance on respect for human rights, mutuality in relationships and direct responses to need, in partnerships with others who share our vision…Achievements of the congregation include maintaining a sense of faith and humour and zest for life in the face of diminishment and decline.

Patricia's local experience is a characteristic she shares with many of her Mercy companions. She was born in the Bathurst diocese, attended the Mercy-run Santa Maria College in Orange, and entered the novitiate at St Joseph's Mount, the Mercy Convent in Bathurst, with other young women from the school. She has remained attached to the region most of her religious life. Many of her companions come from families she has known since she was a girl, families generally of Celtic, often farming, backgrounds.

In a pattern familiar to women of Patricia's era, the gap between leaving school and entering the convent was small, only six months. Like all the women with whom she entered in 1960, she presumed that her life would be spent in teaching, 'which I would have been happy doing as I related well to children and was a good teacher', she said. The majority of the sisters attended the training college attached to the novitiate, and were taught by their own sisters, with practical training supervised at St Philomena's primary school in Bathurst, also staffed by the Sisters of Mercy. Patricia's was the first generation to leave the convent to study and she completed a Bachelor of Arts degree at the University of Sydney and a Diploma of Education at Sydney Teachers' College in 1966.[1]

From 1967 until 1972, she was deputy principal and acting principal of the same high school in Orange that she had earlier attended as a schoolgirl. The Sisters of Mercy, like many other teaching orders, frequently appointed women in leadership positions who were young compared to their counterparts in secular schools. In 1974, at the age of 32, Patricia became superior of the community at St Joseph's Mount and novice mistress and also principal at St Philomena's, the primary school. It was a heavy workload. Of her experience as novice mistress, Patricia said that the 'six years were years of failure and disappointment for me':

> My contribution to the community in this role was to assist most of the junior professed sisters leave without guilt or grudge. And those who remained soon taught me that they were on a spiritual journey for which I was ill-equipped to accompany them.

Reflecting further on this time, Patricia commented:

> My efforts to assist women not much younger than myself grapple with the discernment of vocation, quickly demonstrated to me the inadequacy of my own pre-Vatican II theological and spiritual formation. I had been instructed in the vows and religious life, introduced to scripture and basic theology and the rules and rubrics of the church. But much of my prayer life was devotional or prescribed, whereas educational methodology in the wider community was already embracing process and enquiry and the emphasis in prayer was more personal. I had received all I was told by people I accepted as experts in the field. These young women accepted nothing I said without question.

The awareness of her inadequate formation led Patricia to embark on a deeper spiritual journey. She had already completed a Diploma of Theology in 1973 at the Mater Dei Institute in Sydney, and, in the same year, a counselling course at the Archdiocese of Sydney Institute of Counselling. During the 1980s she undertook a number of renewal programmes in Ignatian spirituality, as well as counselling, psychology and facilitation. In 1988, she travelled overseas for further study and renewal, completing a

1 With the exception of St Mary's Convent in Bathurst, the Bathurst Sisters of Mercy did not own schools (or orphanages) in either Bathurst or Wilcania-Forbes diocese; all were owned by the diocesan authorities.

spiritual director's programme at Regis College, Toronto, Canada, and a six weeks course in the Global Agenda of Feminist Theology at the Maryknoll School of Theology, New York. She graduated from the University of Toronto *magna cum lauda* in 1991, with a Bachelor of Sacred Theology and a Masters in Divinity, which included a thesis on feminism and the Church. Patricia is not alone in extending her intellectual life of study well beyond her first degree; it is an experience that many post-Vatican ll women religious share.

When she looks back on her early years of study and leadership, Wordsworth's words on the French Revolution come to mind: 'Bliss was it in that dawn to be alive but to be young was very heaven'. She said:

> It was a bit like that in the heady days of religious life after Vatican II, when everything seemed possible. The practice of electing and appointing senior religious to positions of leadership in communities and apostolates gave way to electing and appointing younger women to these positions. Indeed, I often felt that my youth and tertiary education were significant factors in decisions about my suitability for positions of responsibility and leadership – a fact that was not always welcomed by women who were senior to me in the community.

When Patricia was elected as a general councillor of the Union of the Sisters of Mercy between 1978 and 1981, she lived at the generalate in Canberra. She played an important role in winding down the generalate structure of the Union and the reconfiguration of the Mercy Sisters into the Institute of the Sisters of Mercy (ISMA) in 1981.[2] It was during this time that she attended the first international meeting of Sisters of Mercy in Ireland, an experience that enabled her to experience the strengths of the worldwide Mercy community.

On returning to Bathurst from her years in Canberra, Patricia was asked to go to Dubbo, a town about 200 kilometres north, to join Sister Miriam Gibbons, another sister from the Bathurst Congregation. The two women established a ministry of support and advocacy for the local Indigenous community, which Miriam continued for many years. The ministry gave Patricia daily experience of the issues the Indigenous communities faced, one that would profoundly affect her later ministries and enrich her spirituality.

---

2 The move towards unity saw the Union Provinces such as Bathurst revert to independent congregational status and the 17 autonomous congregations form one structure with a common constitution in 1981.

In 1992 Patricia was elected community leader of the Bathurst congregation. This marked the beginning of a period in which she carried local, national and international responsibilities. She fulfilled her role as leader with astonishing energy: an executive member of the NSW Congregation of Leaders of Religious Institutes between 1993 and 1997, she was also a delegate to the International Union of Leaders of Women Religious in Rome between 1995 and 1998. She was Vice-President of the Australian Conference of Leaders of Religious Institutes in 2002, and represented that body at meetings of the Australian Catholic Bishops' Conference.

Within the diocese, Patricia was a founding member of the Bathurst Pastoral Council, a founding member of Catholic Health Care, and in her capacity as an adult educator, undertook consultancies on behalf of the Bishop of Bathurst to ascertain the needs of local Indigenous communities and of adult faith educators. The Bathurst community received a Papal Award, *Croce pro Ecclesia et Pontifice,* for distinguished service to the Church conferred by Pope Benedict XV1 in January 2007. The Bishop of Bathurst, Patrick Dougherty, sought it for Patricia, and for the Sisters of St Joseph in recognition of the work of women religious in the diocese.

Patricia became community leader at a time when religious orders were facing difficult decisions about the use of the convent buildings that once housed large numbers of novices and professed sisters. The Sisters of Mercy in Bathurst had expanded the convent and novitiate in the late 1950s when the number of young women entering religious life was increasing, but the situation had changed dramatically by the late 1990s.

St Joseph's Mount, the Mercy convent in Busby Street, Bathurst, was just a few doors down from the home of Ben Chifley, Prime Minister of Australia from 1945-1949. In contrast to the modest Chifley home, St Joseph's Mount had originally been a mansion built by Dr John Busby in 1884 for his wife and eleven children. Known as *Logan Brae,* it was set amongst 4.7 hectares of beautiful land and gardens and given to the sisters by local philanthropist, John Meagher, in 1909. The fine property had heritage and sentimental value, not only for the sisters, but also to the local community. Alternative uses for the house and site were not easily identifiable, nor was its outright sale acceptable to the sisters whose congregation had lived there for more than a hundred years. It was their convent, novitiate and teacher training centre.

Years of discernment and consideration of the needs of the people around them led the Bathurst Sisters of Mercy to reimagine the use of their land and buildings to include new ministries focussed on mercy and justice. The entire Mercy community was involved in decision making and in 1994 space was set aside at St Joseph's Mount for a Mercy and Justice Centre under the direction of Sister Pat Linnane. At the centre, the sisters not only continue their work as educators, spiritual directors and justice advocates but have greatly expanded it.

Room was made available to a variety of community groups, 'people of all faiths or none'. The Catherine McAuley cottage in the grounds, named for their founder, was earmarked for retreatants. A small house, once used by the live-in gardener and his eleven children, became a house of hospitality for refugees or survivors of torture in need of rest and recovery. It was named the Kath Knowles House of Welcome to honour a former Mayor of Bathurst who was responsible for the city's nomination as a place of welcome for refugees.

Building on her experience from the Dubbo days with Sister Miriam Gibbons, Patricia encouraged the public advocacy and practical support given by the Mercy and Justice Centre to the local Indigenous community; the Centre provided a home for those supporting local land-rights and reconciliation in the region. Close ties in the cause of reconciliation were forged with local Indigenous leaders, and local service clubs such as Rotary, as well as the local Art Gallery.

Inter-faith partnerships were formed with local communities to support refugees and to sponsor lecture series on environment issues, supported by staff from the Charles Sturt University. In partnership with the local Area Health Service, the sisters formed a support group for people suffering depression. Partnerships were also formed with government departments such as the Department of Correctional Services, through which men on periodic detention were able to work on the property, as were people on the Work-for-the-Dole scheme.

In 2001 the sisters redesigned their grounds in tribute to the original owners of the land, the Wiradjuri people. Patricia welcomed the then Governor of New South Wales, Professor Marie Bashir, who opened the gardens officially.

During her years as community leader, reflecting the down-to-earth and practical commonsense which is a feature of her congregation, Patricia was outspoken on issues that directly affect the regional area within which she was born, bred, and has worked most of her adult life. Speaking against the injurious effects of economic rationalism which dominated the political and economic debates, and representing the ACLRI, she and Sister Janice Ryder addressed a Senate Select Committee, highlighting the effects in regional areas of the withdrawal of services and the resulting high levels of unemployment.

Factors such as these motivated Patricia and her team to work assiduously in maintaining their Mater Hospital in Forbes and the St Catherine's Aged Care Facility in Bathurst. Both express the Mercy charism and commitment to service, and also have the practical effect of supplying much-needed employment for professional staff and local suppliers of goods and services. The economic benefit that women religious have provided through services such as hospitals and schools is seldom referred to as part of their contribution to the health of the communities in which they live, but it has been and remains vital in smaller cities and regional areas of Australia.

The history of large institutions of care has come under intense scrutiny during the past twenty years with information emerging on the mistreatment of and criminal assault upon children.[3] During Patricia's time as congregational leader, the Bathurst Sisters of Mercy, began a process to deal with complaints lodged by ex-students in the orphanages by the mid-1990s. The sisters educated themselves about the issues and about the processes for dealing with them, ensuring that all sisters understood and observed the conduct required of religious outlined in *Integrity in Ministry, a Document of Principles and Standards for Catholic Clergy & Religious in Australia* first published in 2004.

Patricia, with the help of the local media, encouraged victims of abuse to contact her, resulting in two people requesting further action in relation to their complaints. A local Resource Group of Professionals was established, 'to keep us honest and assist us with our process', she said. 'It was a time of feeling disbelief and denial and even depression that this was happening.'

3 A series of government enquiries into the issue of abuse of children, culminated in the establishment of the Royal Commission into Institutional Responses to Child Sexual Abuse in 2013.

The complaints received have been settled through mediation, and counselling for the victims has been made available.

In 2000 seventeen of the sisters most closely associated with the Sisters of Mercy's children's homes met at St Joseph's Mount to exchange stories of their experiences and to consider a proposal which had been put to them to organise a 'get together' of girls who had been resident at St Joseph's orphanage. Preceded by meetings and rituals that enabled the sisters who had worked in the homes to reflect upon their lives as religious while they were working in the homes, and organised by a committee comprising five of the sisters and a number of ex-residents, the 'get-together' was held on 27 and 28 October 2001.

By 2002, at the end of ten years as congregational leader, Patricia was happy to pass the baton to a new leader with a fresh approach. 'I knew I would miss the contact with the wider national and international worlds that leadership of a congregation afforded,' she said, 'but not the responsibility and or the authority of the position.'

Speaking of the low points of her leadership period, she added:

> It was hard to be a religious and a religious leader at the time when revelations of abuse of power and trust by priests and religious were first made. By association, if not by actual fact, all religious felt under scrutiny and suspicion. And the revelations in the media were shocking and tragic. Morale among priests and religious was low and the challenge to respond justly and compassionately to the allegations of complainants was a complex and difficult process for the Bishops and religious leaders of Australia at the time...It takes a lot of faith and courage to be a religious today.
>
> One of my superiors with whom I often found myself at odds, used to say, 'Anyone can have hindsight. But at the time, you make the best choices and decisions you can, based on the knowledge and understanding you have then.' We agreed on this point and I think it applies to the issue of sexual abuse. Sadly, in society generally in the 1970s, there was no outrage about this issue. It existed. But in families it was hidden. And parents and people in authority were frequently in denial about its occurrence. The victim was blamed or not believed because this behaviour from people in privileged positions such as clergy or religious was inconceivable. I suspect the sexual revolution of the 1960s did much to enable such behaviour, if not encourage or excuse it. And certainly, a more open and educated attitude to sex since then, has allowed the issue to be brought into the spotlight and addressed appropriately.

Following her time as congregational leader, Patricia and a number of other Mercy sisters began a process of reflecting about the qualities of mercy and justice in the context of compassion for the planet. Patricia had been particularly affected by the world-wide movement culminating in the Earth Charter launched in 2000, and in the call from Pope John Paul II a year later for 'ecological conversion', a concept supported by the Australian Catholic Bishops in 2005.[4]

Given that the sisters based their concept of caring for the planetary community on the acceptance of the common origins of all species and the inter-relatedness and interdependence of everything in the universe, they began to see eco-justice as an extension of their traditional care for the poor and the sick. Incorporating care for the earth seemed a natural fit for an institute whose foundress had stressed service to the most vulnerable in the community. 'With the call of the Church to ecological conversion, the mercy, justice and charity we have poured out on the human species is now expanded to comprehensive compassion – a compassion that embraces the whole of creation,' Patricia said.

Inspired by their new understanding of the theology of eco-justice, Patricia and her sisters decided to do something to transform their ideas into reality. Following their first proposals for change to the Bathurst congregational leadership ten sisters, including Patricia, formed a working party followed by a committee of five, Patricia among them, who worked on developing details of the new ministry. They drew up extensive plans including mission statements, objectives, strategies, expected outcomes, evaluation tools, financial projections and fund-raising options, all of which they shared with the congregational leadership with input from any sisters interested in participating in the project. They set out clearly for the rest of the congregation the underlying spiritual and theological basis for their vision as they called on the congregation to respond to the call for 'ecological conversion'.

In the tradition of Sisters of Mercy as educators, members of the committee attended local, inter-state and national conferences and workshops, educating themselves in the science of water management, alternative energy sources, soil regeneration, the effects of climate change and how to

4 'Climate change: Our responsibility to sustain God's earth', Position Paper from Catholic Earthcare Australia, Canberra, Bishop's Committee for Justice, Development, Ecology and Peace, 2005.

mitigate them locally. They consulted widely with experts, as well as with local groups involved in conservation and environmental protection. 'We were exploring new ways of doing the works of mercy in the context of comprehensive compassion for the whole earth community,' said Patricia. 'Our desire was to nurture an ecological learning community where we could share that exploration with experts and novices alike.'

This extensive process of discernment, fact-finding and decision-making led, in 2007, to the Mercy and Justice Centre being re-named *Rahamim,* the Hebrew word for mercy, as the sisters dedicated the property to earth-care awareness. With Patricia as its first director, the centre offered a series of programmes entitled People, Planet and Spirit which, taken together, demonstrated the connection which the sisters saw as necessary for a healthy community committed to ecological conversion. Looking back, Patricia recalled:

> We were all on a steep learning curve to understand what it means to relate differently to the natural environment. The big insight for our time is the realisation that everything in nature is in relationship with everything else. And the balance is very delicate.

True to the spirit of Catherine McAuley, who instructed her sisters to 'make sure they have a comfortable cup of tea', hospitality and welcome have always been important at *Rahamim*, and are offered in equal measure to volunteers, retreatants, professional experts, students, people looking for support for personal problems, trades people and general visitors. Hundreds of school children have also visited the site since *Rahamim* was established to experience environmental education programme.

At the time of establishing *Rahimim,* Patricia, together with Bathurst Mercy Sisters Margie Abbott and Mary Dennett, formed the eco-justice sub-committee of the Institute of the Sisters of Mercy Justice Network in 2007. Reporting to their sisters across Australia via their internal journal, *Listen*, they defined eco-justice as:

> A perspective on what it means to be human, not in isolation, but as part of God's creation, living lovingly and justly within the interconnected web of life, within the cosmos, within society, within churches and communities, and within families and friendships.

In 2010 *Rahamim* was registered as an incorporated association managed by an elected Board and legally distinct from the congregation.

Nevertheless it is very fully integrated into Mercy ministry both locally and nationally. Mercy sisters have supported the initiative in a range of ways from contributing their prayers, their time and even money from their own patrimony while a range of scholars, including Mercy sisters Veronica Lawson and Elaine Wainwright, run regular workshops and programmes.

When she was congregational leader Patricia said she found that the most rewarding aspect of her role was 'nurturing partnerships with clergy and lay people to further the mission of mercy and justice'. The same, she explained, applies to her time as director of *Rahamim*. 'I think the day of the 'one-man-band' is over,' she said. 'The way forward seems to be to work together in mutual relationships, building up the Body of Christ, recognizing designated leadership, but that we are also interconnected.'

Patricia stepped down as director of *Rahamim* in 2013 and was succeeded by Josephite Sister, Mary Ann Casanova. She remains closely involved, however, presenting workshops and contributing in a number of ways such as talking to visitors or supporting those in need, who may be refugees, Indigenous people or men in detention. She is often to be found in gumboots and work clothes clearing out the hen house built by men from the Bathurst Correctional Outreach Team. Aptly named the 'Chook Chapel' or the 'Poultry Detention Centre', it was built in 2008 to mark the occasion of a visit from a group of Karen refugees to the Survivors of Torture programme.

Patricia celebrated her golden jubilee as a Bathurst Sister of Mercy in 2013 and reflected that she 'never really lived religious life in the pre-Vatican II form in which I was introduced to it. Questioning of its basic elements began almost as soon as I was professed, and continued throughout my years at university and as a young teacher. This questioning took on a very radical dimension when many of my contemporaries began leaving religious life.'

While all the women who appear in this collection would acknowledge the need for the support of their sisters as they developed their professional lives, Patricia's work, more than most, embodies the collective contribution of her community, and of the laity, both of whom sustain her apostolic work in pursuing eco-justice. Her continuing hunger to further her understanding of ecological conversation led her, to enroll in the Doctor of Ministry programme at Sydney College of Divinity in the year she turned 70.

Patricia's life-long commitment to her own education and the education of those with whom she has shared mission covers both formal study and community development in the best tradition of adult education. Her role as a public advocate in the pursuit of social justice has been constant, and has met with the same successes and frustrations experienced by most who pursue that path. Her experience of what it means to live in community stretches from near-monastic enclosure to individual housing. She has been a member of a congregation that has made significant contributions to the educational and economic welfare, and to the social capital of the region where they live and work. Patricia's individual contribution is significant on any criteria by which it might be judged. As a member of a religious congregation, it has been multiplied in manifold ways.

The Institute of the Blessed Virgin Mary (Loreto Sisters)

The Institute of the Blessed Mary (IBVM) was founded in 1609 by a woman from Yorkshire, Mary Ward (1585-1635) in St Omer, then part of the Spanish Netherlands, and now in France. Modelled on the Society of Jesus, it was self-governing and its members were active in the community meeting the needs of the time, one of the most pressing of which was education for women. However, a monastic, enclosed life under the authority of a local bishop was then mandatory for nuns, and the freedom and independence of Mary Ward's women was unacceptable to the Vatican. Mary Ward was condemned and briefly imprisoned for heresy, her schools closed and her followers dispersed. Nevertheless, her institute survived and slowly grew. With the decree Quamvis iusto *of 1749 it became the first female religious order to win concessions from the Vatican over enclosure and self-governance, but Mary Ward was not formally recognised as its founder by the Church until 1909.*

By this stage her institute was scattered across the world either in independent houses or separate branches. These gradually came together and after the union of the North American and Irish branches in 2003, only two IBVM branches remained: the Irish branch and the Roman. The latter changed its name in 2004 to the Congregation of Jesus. Both branches continue Mary Ward's work, not only in the field of education but also meeting needs wherever they find them. In 1951 at the World Congress of Catholic Action Pope Pius XII told his largely lay audience that the two great role models for apostolic work in the history of the Church were St Vincent de Paul and Mary Ward. He called her 'that incomparable woman given by Catholic England in her darkest hour'.

Mother Frances Teresa Ball founded the Irish branch of the IBVM in Dublin in 1821. Frances Ball came from a wealthy Dublin family and was educated by the sisters of the Institute of the Blessed Virgin Mary at the Bar Convent in York. At 18, she told her parents that she felt called to religious life, and was urged by Daniel Murray, coadjutor Archbishop of Dublin and family friend, to establish the IBVM in Ireland with the aim of educating upper-class Catholic girls. She agreed, returned to the Bar Convent, and was given the religious name of the great Spanish founder Teresa, spending the next seven years preparing for her future undertaking.

When Teresa Ball returned to Dublin, Archbishop Murray bought a magnificent property at Rathfarnham outside Dublin for her first foundation. She named it Loreto Abbey after the shrine in Italy, a small house that, according to tradition, was the home of the Holy Family in Nazareth, miraculously transported to Europe by angels when threatened by destruction in the thirteenth century. Thereafter the IBVM sisters in the Irish branch of the institute became commonly known as the Loreto Sisters. Teresa Ball opened a number of schools in Ireland and sent sisters to North America, Gibraltar and India. Her successor, Mother Scholastica Somers, asked Mother Gonzaga Barry to lead the first group of Loreto Sisters to Australia in 1875 at the invitation of Michael O'Connor, Bishop of Ballarat and previously parish priest at Rathfarnham.

In the following 40 years, Mother Gonzaga opened boarding schools in every state other than Queensland and Tasmania. Her Loreto sisters also ran six parish schools, opened two day schools, two teacher training colleges and one free kindergarten. The Loretos currently own seven schools in Australia and for 96 years, until 2014, ran St Mary's College at the University of Melbourne. Few sisters now teach in the schools but work instead in such areas as social justice, parish ministry, pastoral care, the arts, spiritual guidance, canon law and theology. Two sisters teach in Timor-Leste and until 2013 one represented the IBVM in New York at the UN. The Australian Province is also part of Mary Ward International, supporting social justice projects round the world. In 2009 Mary Ward women round the world celebrated Pope John Paul II's declaration which afforded their founder the title of Venerable.

Deirdre Browne ibvm

Deirdre Browne was born in 1936 and entered the Institute of the Blessed Virgin Mary in 1954. She took her final vows in 1964. Her name in religion was Sister Mary Cecilia.

Music was in the air for Deirdre Browne from the beginning. It was her first language. Celtic influence came to her through her mother Winifred Davies's Welsh and English background, and also from her father Frederick (Fred) Coleman Browne's Irish and English heritage. Winifred died of heart failure when Deirdre was nine; music sustained father and daughter.

Celebrated political and industrial journalist with the *Sydney Morning Herald*, Fred started work at three in the afternoon, went home for a meal and a break in the early evening, and then returned to the office to file his story. During these breaks he and Deirdre would sit together by the soft light of a standard lamp and Fred, an accomplished pianist, would play the piano, often Chopin or Beethoven, or put on a record, Beethoven's Ninth or a Tchaikovsky Symphony. 'I think it sensitised my ear and my spirit, it fed my soul,' recalled Deirdre, 'and it was relational to somebody I loved and relational to the music. At the same time I was learning what it was to ponder and to be deeply quiet and to listen, as well as to be lifted out of the here and now. Faith and music share this ingredient, if such you can call it. Looking back it was a very significant time.'

An unusually sensitive child, Deirdre watched her mother suffer ill health for years, yet maintain the highest standards at home. She remembered her kneeling in prayer, Deirdre quietly beside her. She also remembered her devoutly Catholic Lancastrian grandmother repeating 'Man proposes, God disposes'. She had no idea what that meant, but 'the rhythm of the words stayed with me for the day when meaning did unfold,' she said.

Deirdre started learning the piano at four or five, her father often sitting beside her as she practised. Later, when her older brother Winston was at boarding school and only the two of them remained at home, Fred would sometimes take her to a concert at the Sydney Town Hall with his great friend, *Sydney Morning Herald* critic Lindsay Brown, 'I remember Handel's *Messiah* and things like that and thinking; it's as if the heavens are opening. This is beautiful. This is very beautiful. When I started to write about aesthetic and religious experience much later on and either taught or studied courses on that area, I went back to that experience because it's quite deep in me. I don't know whether that was a religious or an aesthetic experience - and does it matter?'

In her secondary school life, first as a day pupil at Loreto Kiribilli and then as a boarder at Loreto Normanhurst, Deirdre's musical gifts developed not only with piano, but also violin, singing, choir and orchestra. She emerged in Year 12 as dux of the school with the accolades of a NSW Exhibition to the Conservatorium of Music and a Commonwealth Scholarship to the University of Sydney. Her success presented Deirdre with something of a conundrum. Keen to go to university and further her musical studies, she felt called to religious life at the same time. 'I think sometimes that deep calling is particularly strong in children who have lost a parent,' she said. 'It makes you very reflective. In boarding school I lay in bed at night and gazed at the galaxy. I tend to contextualise everything, to make connections. Even as a child I recognised something infinite beyond the every day.'

Deirdre thought she could spend a year at the Conservatorium before entering religious life but her father felt it wrong to deprive somebody of a full scholarship by only doing part of it, and so she gave it up. She worked in a bank, keeping up her music by taking lessons with Haydn Beck, one of the most eminent violin teachers in Australia at the time. A fellow student of the violin, Joan McKerras, suggested to Deirdre that they both go to the Royal College of Music in London but Deirdre was determined to follow her religious vocation.

In early February 1954, at the age of 17, she left Sydney for the Loreto novitiate in Ballarat. Among the 13 women in her 'set' was 'a hugely strong spirit' in spite of religious practices she found 'archaic'.

> There was a message in the novitiate scrolled across an arch that said *Agere Contra:* go against yourself. It was Ignatian, but I saw it going way back beyond Ignatius in terms of asceticism. What we had in the convent was more like monastic asceticism. That austerity seemed to be part and parcel of religious life no matter what order you were in.

Looking back, Deirdre said the message was clear: 'if you were a religious you were expected to carry out ascetic practices. You weren't regarded as an equal with lay people. You were a cut above, a bit special, therefore you needed to do more, to take on more suffering, to identify with Jesus.'

She was, she said, young and idealistic and happy 'There was great energy in the communality of vision and faith that we shared. You felt encouraged, supported, befriended in this enterprise, and it was a damn good enterprise.' Appropriately she was given the religious name 'Cecilia' after the patron saint of musicians.

Her first few years were spent teaching kindergarten and primary school children. In spite of her lack of training, she found this creative and immensely enjoyable, using the piano whenever she could to sing about everything from times tables to Bible stories. She expected that this would be her life when, to her surprise, the provincial, Mother Dympna McNamara, sent her to live at St Mary's Hall in Parkville while she studied for her Bachelors Degree in Music at the Conservatorium of Music at the University of Melbourne. Clearly aware of Deirdre's talent, Mother Dympna was looking ahead. It was 1960 and the Wyndham Scheme was soon to be implemented in New South Wales, requiring formal qualifications in the teaching of arts and sciences, and more structured music teaching in classrooms. Even though she had done very little serious music since entering, Deirdre performed so well at her audition that she was encouraged to undertake a double major in piano and violin with additional singing.

There was inevitable tension in the contrast between Deirdre's two selves at St Mary's Hall. On the one hand was the gifted young musician studying with some of the finest teachers in Australia, on the other was the enclosed nun in full habit abiding by the timetable of her religious life and forbidden to leave the convent unaccompanied, or to eat in public.[1] It was particularly difficult for Deirdre because, as a music student, her hours were different to everyone else's. She had orchestra rehearsals at 5.30pm, for example, and if one of the sisters wasn't available she had to ask a student to accompany her on the 20-minute walk to the Conservatorium. Understandably the students were often reluctant and Deirdre felt 'a bit of a pain'.

The musical opportunities, however, were exciting. Staff at the Conservatorium included pianist and harpsichordist Roger Heagney, the great flautist Margaret Crawford, composer Noel Nixon and organist, choral master and Associate Director of the Conservatorium, Percy Jones. Deirdre was taught keyboard by the legendary Nancy Weir, violin by John

1 Enclosure (and wearing habits) was imposed on women religious by Pope Boniface VIII in 1298 and re-emphasised by the Council of Trent in the 16th century.

Glickman and singing by Elsa Haas. The dashing young Irish musician Basil Deane lived next door to St Mary's Hall and occasionally, strictly against the rules, Deirdre accepted a lift home in his Volkswagen.

For the first time in her life Deirdre was fully immersed in music and loved it. It was a heady time, and she remembers being at a crossroads when she came to take her final vows in 1964. Her results at the Conservatorium had been impressive and she could well have gone on to pursue a professional career in music outside the convent. It was a moment that was not so much one of deep hesitation, she said, but rather of a pause.

> I had to make a decision and I remember it being a real decision, as I'd come to the stage where I could see that you could be following the spirit either way. Whether I was a nun or not I would still have this deep love of music and religious sense. I decided single heartedly that my commitment was to religious life and I would take the risk, whatever it offered. I took as my motto, 'Into your hands, Lord, I commend my spirit'. It was like a consecration of myself to God through my hands. They were the best part of me, the way my music streamed through, and the way I communicated.

Deirdre left the Conservatorium with her Bachelor of Music and Diploma in Education and was promptly made head of music at Loreto Normanhurst, taking over from her old piano teacher, Mother Lua Byrne. Significantly, the choral director resigned the week she started so as well as managing the music staff, teaching general and elective classroom music, piano and violin, and conducting the orchestra, she taught singing at every level.

At Normanhurst the possibilities offered by Vatican II were seized on with enthusiasm by a group of forward-thinking Loreto nuns. They included future province leaders Noni Mitchell, Chris Burke and Deirdre Rofe, as well as Deirdre Browne herself.[2] The nuns would meet together during Profound Silence when the borders and the rest of the community were in bed and pore over Council documents and the writings of avant-garde theologians such as Karl Rahner and Yves Congar. Out of these gatherings came a radical new approach to teaching religion to older students. The nuns enlisted young Jesuits from nearby Canisius College to teach the senior girls in tandem with them. They used the liberal Dutch catechism

2 Sister Noni Mitchell was province leader of the Loreto Institute from 1974-1983 and general leader from 1986-1999; Sister Deirdre Rofe was province leader from 1990-1995, Sister Deirdre Browne was province leader from 1999-2005 and Sister Chris Burke from 2005-2011.

and discussed such issues as primacy of conscience and *Humanae Vitae*, the document forbidding the use of artificial contraception. For the first time in a Loreto boarding school, morning mass for borders became voluntary.

The creative significance in Vatican II for Deirdre lay in *Sacrosanctum concilium* – the document on the Sacred Liturgy that sought a balance between the push of the progressives to support and expand the work of the liturgical movement and the pull of the conservatives to hold it in check. The liturgical movement had began in the early twentieth century and slowly gained momentum, especially in the 1940s and 1950s, winning such concessions as evening mass and active congregational participation in the mass. The emphasis on collegiality in *Sacrosanctum concilium* gave local bishops a degree of flexibility in implementing what the document termed 'legitimate variations and adaptation to different groups, regions, and peoples'. This opened windows for teachers of religion such as Deirdre, keen to devise liturgies that would be meaningful to young people.

It was evident to Deirdre that the hymns the students were singing meant little to them and did not carry contemporary conciliar theology.[3] She wrote numerous hymns for both primary and secondary levels of the school with Chris Burke, Noni Mitchell and Jo Little helping with the words. Weekly class masses were an opportunity for working with students on music and ritual. There was so much creative energy around, 'the whole place was abuzz', said Deirdre. She recalled that running down the stairs one day a new idea for a song was in her head by the time she reached the bottom. She and Noni Mitchell wrote 'A Man Forsaken', a hymn that appealed strongly to young people who were rebelling against church-going and were concerned about racism, religious prejudice, financial greed and the threat of nuclear war. 'The sorts of kids we were teaching were changing dramatically,' she said. 'There were the Beatles and rock and roll and protest songs. They wanted to sing protest songs in the liturgy so Noni and I wrote Man Forsaken. It was based on incarnational theology. It was something quite new to use the word 'man' to emphasise the humanness of God. The kids loved the song.'

One of Deirdre's most intense periods of creativity at Normanhurst occurred during the writing of *Mass for Young Christians* – a striking model of aural

3 Theology emanating from the Vatican Council documents.

composition and possibly the first time such music was composed in a school. 'Different classes would gather in the lecture theatre,' said Deirdre.

> It took about 120. We would built up concepts first, talk about the meaning of the words and look for the rhythm in them, then see if we could find a tune. Someone would sing out, 'Lord have mercy', for example, and I would sing back, 'Christ have mercy', and we'd build it up and build it up with Bernadette Allen, our accompanist, putting the piano underneath it. It was amazing. It worked. It was a new way of talking about God and a new way of singing music. It was a period of wonderful fertility across the school.

Allans Music, Australia, published Deirdre's *Mass for Young Christians* in 1967. The following year a collection of her hymns, *Throw Open Your Hearts,* appeared under the same imprint.

The quality of the choirs at Normanhurst was important for Deirdre. Within four years they began to take the top prizes at local eisteddfods, and attracted the attention of the Australian Broadcasting Corporation. Deirdre and the Normanhurst students made a number of appearances on radio and television including a recording in 1969 of Christmas carols which leading up to Christmas, featured nightly on national television before the 7pm news. The Normanhurst choir also represented Australia in the international choral competition, 'Let the Peoples Sing' and reached the semi-finals in the British Broadcasting Corporation Silver Rose Bowl section.

Deidre's time at Normanhurst was followed by five busy years as superior of the Loreto Convent and school at Coorparoo in Brisbane, beginning in 1974. She settled the religious community into a new home, closed the boarding school, demolished and rebuilt the school chapel and opened the parish primary school. She kept her music alive by forming a parish choir, and developing strong links with the local Anglican choir. 'We came together and swapped choirs in each other's churches and combined for Easter and Christmas, so the creativity was there.'

When she left Brisbane in 1979, Deirdre had been in the Institute for more than 20 years, and Noni Mitchell, now province leader, suggested she would benefit from time studying music overseas. Noni was not particularly concerned about what Deirdre chose to study, 'she just wanted us to be opened up'. Deirdre consulted her past teachers at the Conservatorium and at Basil Deane's suggestion enrolled in a Masters course at the Institute of Education at London University, combining education and music.

In 1980 Percy Jones sponsored her for a grant of $20,000 from the Moodie Heddle Trust to be paid in instalments from 1981-83.[4] The money enabled her to subscribe to the English National Opera and concerts at the Festival Hall, to attend summer schools at Dartington Hall and Canford and go to music festivals in Cheltenham and Winchester. In London she also arranged private singing and conducting lessons and did a six-week programme of study with the BBC Symphony Chorus and the London Philharmonic Chorus.

When Deirdre left Australia for London in 1981 she had no idea that she would be away for four years, or that her time would be filled with experiences beyond anything she could imagine, and that, as Noni had hoped, she would be transformed. The key for her was not only the broadening of her musical horizons in England but an introduction from Nancy Weir to Malcolm Williamson, Australian composer and Master of the Queen's Music, who was living in London. He took Deirdre under his wing, and introduced her to people in the musical world including Dame Eva Turner and Eileen Joyce. His faith in Deirdre helped her recognise her own outstanding gifts.

Although there were exciting aspects of her course, such as observing the teaching of gifted students at the Yehudi Menuhin School, spending time at Pimlico Comprehensive, and teaching in the East End of London, Williamson declared it 'too dull for Deirdre' and asked her, as a church person, whether she knew what was happening with church music in Spain and France and Germany? With his encouragement, Noni's agreement, and Deirdre's own concern that she should not go back to Australia before truly experiencing the impact of *Sacrosanctum concilium* on religious music and liturgy in Europe, she left the Institute of Education after 18 months and took the ferry for France.

In Europe Deirdre created her own study programme exploring liturgical centres in France, Italy, Spain and Germany with a high reputation for church music. Wherever she went she sought the answers to three questions: What is being sung? Who is composing for the new rites? What might this repertoire say to people in Australia? Immersing herself in the experience, Deirdre enjoyed a new found independence and trust in her own judgement, 'In the way that our founder Mary Ward said I ought'. She said:

4 Set up by Enid Moodie Heddle, with money left by her friend Muriel Horlock, the Trust enabled adults who had never left Australia to broaden their musical horizons overseas. Deirdre was the last benefactor of the Trust before it was wound up.

> In Paris the experience of liturgy at St Ignace, St Severin, St Sulpice, La Trinité and Notre Dame Cathedral was seminal in my development. I also visited Solesmes to learn more of Gregorian chant. In Spain I visited pastoral centres in Madrid, Barcelona, Monserrat, and in Germany those in Munich, Regensburg, Augsburg [and] Cologne put me in touch with the history of the liturgical movement that led to Vatican II. And key abbeys in all these countries opened me to the riches of our musical tradition.

Her expectation was to return to Australia at the end of 1982, but Malcolm Williamson suggested Deirdre take her studies in sacred choral music further, working with the great choral teacher Michael Cordovana in Washington. In a letter to Noni and the council in July 1982, he wrote, 'I believe it possible that you are still not fully aware of Sister Deirdre's gifts as a musician in three aspects: one; director/conductor; two, musicologist/mentor/tutor; and three; creative artist'. He pointed out that no one else in the Australian Church had this same combination of gifts and that 'the IBVM has something musically spectacular in Deirdre'. After pleading for her to be given time to further her studies at the Music School at the Catholic University in Washington, he concluded that 'the harvest will be richer than we can at the moment see'.

Noni and the Council decided that rather than concentrating on sacred choral music, Deirdre needed to know more theology, since in Australia she would be working with liturgy in music. So Deirdre enrolled in a two-year Masters in Liturgical Studies at the Catholic University in Washington.

On her return to Melbourne, Loreto sister Joan Nowotny, then Dean of Yarra Theological Union, asked Deirdre to take on the teaching of liturgy from one of her staff, who resigned because of illness. 'I was ready for it,' said Deirdre, even though she had never taught liturgy nor taught at tertiary level. Coincidentally at about the same time a chance meeting with Roger Heagney, founder of the Bachelor of Church Music course at Mercy Teachers' College, Ascot Vale, (later to become part of the Australian Catholic University) was significant. He asked Deirdre if she would consider creating and teaching a course on the philosophy of music as part of the Bachelor of Music degree.

This was the start of another ten-year cycle for Deirdre, one of immense energy, creativity, activity and musical output interspersed with great personal satisfaction in what she was doing. At the same time she extended herself well beyond the institutions where she taught. She established *Musica*

Camara, a monthly choir named after the great Latin American Bishop and music lover, Helda Camara, who said, 'You must never deprive the poor of their music'. Originally intended for young musicians between the ages of 18 and 28, *Musica Camara* met at St Francis Church in Melbourne and people stayed on and matured with the choir. Organist Beverley Phillips usually accompanied the choir but on special occasions other instruments were introduced including strings, woodwind and brass, forming something of a chamber orchestra.[5]

Fiona Dyball, Director of Music (Choral) at the Catholic Regional High School in Wodonga, a student of Deirdre's at Ascot Vale, and a member of *Musica Camara,* described singing in the choir as an expression of joy and deep faith:

> Deirdre had a way of crafting liturgy to make it meaningful and richly layered. We all loved the masses and enjoyed the camaraderie of creating something alive, contemporary and timeless with her. 'God Beyond all Names' and 'Restless is the Heart', both by Bernadette Farrell, were just two of the wonderful little musical jewels Deirdre introduced to the choir. After singing, we would all go and eat! Hospitality, laughter and fun were all part of the experience with DB and that rounded, life-giving relationship has continued over the years with so many people.

Fiona emphasises that she and her fellow students and choir members always felt that Deirdre cared for them as individuals as well as encouraging them to create 'music and liturgy that would make God's presence real and immediate'. Fiona and countless other young musicians were inspired by Deirdre to continue to share the gifts they received from her in their own work. Past students are 'all over the place', said Deirdre, and include Paul Taylor, Director of Liturgy in the Melbourne archdiocese and lecturer in liturgical music at the Catholic Theological College in Melbourne.

Deirdre's close friend, Good Samaritan sister Margaret Smith, whom she had met in 1983 while working on her MA in liturgical studies in Washington, was on the staff of the Archdiocesan Office for Worship during these years working under its Director, Frank O'Loughlin. Deirdre joined in 1988 on a part-time basis in the capacity of Liturgical Music Education Officer and she and Margaret ran workshops, seminars and events in parishes. 'We did what we could to ensure people had good liturgy,' recalled Margaret. Re-

5 When Deirdre left for Sydney, *Musica Camara* merged with the Julian Singers, another long established group, under the baton of Beverley Phillips.

reading past copies of *The Summit*, the Diocesan Liturgical Centre journal, Margaret is astounded to recall how active she and Deirdre were. She and Deirdre bring different gifts, she said. She sees herself as the support person while Deirdre's is the creative side – the music, language, poetry, and facility with words. In particular she admires Deirdre's capacity to bring music out in people.

Yet another layer in Deirdre's life in the 1990s was her involvement with the Royal School of Church Music, an interdenominational educational organisation for church musicians. Deirdre was national liturgical advisor on music for the Catholic Church and contributed to a number of summer schools convened by leading Catholic laywoman and civil celebrant, Mary Williams. Under the auspices of the National Council of Churches in Australia, Mary co-chaired an international conference in 1996 called 'Household of God – Living under the Southern Cross'. It was a five-day event held at Newman College and Deirdre was part of the team planning the ritual and liturgy each day. Mary Williams recalled the conference as the high point of her association with Deirdre:

> Deirdre's contribution was outstanding. She brought the best of the Roman Catholic tradition using music from plainsong, to medieval, traditional and contemporary while also incorporating music from other traditions. Symbols, water, light and movement were used with great artistry and skill, with generosity of heart and spirit. People still talk about those liturgies. Deirdre stretches our imaginations to see how we can experience liturgy authentically. She is one of *the* outstanding liturgical musicians in Australia. While others are writing music, she is *doing* it.

One of the highlights in this decade for Deirdre was co-conducting the papal Mass in Sydney with Brother Colin Smith to celebrate the beatification of Mary MacKillop. Another was her invitation to give the keynote speech for Australia at the National Music Liturgical Convention at the World Congress Centre. It was the first to be held in this country and to find the peace she needed, Deirdre took her computer to Tarrawarra Abbey for two weeks to write a paper on 'where we'd come from liturgy and music-wise, our history and our response to Vatican II'. It was a seminal address combining music and words in a way that people present later told her was breathtaking.

While it is possible to be creative living in community Deirdre acknowledged the tension that arises between the need for solitude and the distractions of what she calls 'common life'. In 2010 and 2011 she lived in a flat in the

Melbourne suburb of East Malvern, alone for the first time in her life as a Loreto sister, and found it a remarkably productive time. She was working on a major presentation inspired by the words of the poet Heinrich Heine, 'Where words leave off, music begins'. Drawing on her years as a performer, composer, public speaker and conductor, she presented words and music with images and once again drew high praise from her audience.

Between the years 1999 and 2005, Deirdre was leader of the IBVM Australian Province and stepped back from active involvement in music but it was always there, not far below the surface. The many talks she gave as province leader were full of musical imagery and symbols. She saw herself not as a solo instrumentalist but as a certain kind of conductor, one who also plays the violin in the orchestra. In her musical life she enjoyed collaboration, and it was collaboration that sustained her as province leader. 'I always really loved playing chamber music and being in an orchestra or bringing a choir together,' she said. 'I learned from the group and that helped me with the decisions I had to make as province leader.'

At the end of her six-year term, Deirdre was very surprised to be asked to write a modern version of the IBVM constitutions by Mary Wright, the institute leader in Rome. It was a sensitive and daunting task. Members of every religious order live according to their constitutions and for Deirdre it meant encapsulating the original charism of Mary Ward and the spirituality of St Ignatius, so as to present the result in a way that was meaningful to the Loreto sisters in the new millennium. Mary Wright, who had preceded Deirdre as the leader of the Australian province, knew that Deirdre could do it. 'When the Irish branch of the IBVM joined with the North American branch one of the things we noted that the style of their constitutions was feminine and poetic,' said Mary Wright. 'Ours in comparison seemed pedestrian and uneven in quality and not suited to reflection. We made a commitment that we would write new constitutions that would be reflective, poetic and feminine. Deirdre has a flair for poetic writing and is theologically well educated. I knew she would get it done and get it done properly. And she did.'

The work was a collaborative process, drawing on all Deirdre's creativity. Her words had to speak to more than 1000 sisters in 25 countries and incorporate their combined contributions. It took four years of working closely with a steering committee and suffering the agony at times of seeing cherished passages discarded. When her work was considered at the general chapter in 2009 there was an especially anxious moment when Deirdre felt she needed time out with music.[6] 'I remember going off at morning tea, pounding around the garden of the retreat house where we were meeting, the Mormon Tabernacle Choir on my iPod in full bore playing Masagni's 'O rejoice that the Lord has arisen, he has burst through the gates of the prison,' she recalled. 'I came back into the chapter room with a degree of equilibrium again'. The revised constitutions were accepted by her peers and the Vatican and published in 2010.

That same year another unexpected project came to Deirdre's door, this time through her Good Samaritan friend, Margaret Smith. Margaret was explaining to a class at Yarra Theological Union how the new liturgy had been developed in Europe after Vatican II, when one of her students suggested visiting places that had played a significant role in that work. Margaret took the idea to Deirdre, to Blessed Sacrament priest Tom Knowles and Paul Taylor. They decided to plan together a month-long tour of places of historic significance for the liturgical movement. They drew on Deirdre's own liturgical exploration of Europe in the 1980s and the extensive research she had done for her paper at the 1993 liturgical convention.

Twenty-five people went on the tour, led by Deirdre and Margaret, and the group included a number of students whose participation earned them two units towards their Bachelor of Theology degrees or post-graduate work in theological studies. Highlights included a visit to St Theodore's in a poor area outside Cologne, a church that had been burned and rebuilt on three levels to include an area for liturgy and an area for practical outreach. Another memorable place was Bose, an ecumenical monastery of lay people in the foothills of the Italian Alps. As part of her contribution, Deirdre had put together a CD that filled the bus with music wherever it went. Each time it crossed a border, the local national anthem played and the bus was flooded with both folk and classical music from the region through which they were travelling. It was a Deirdre touch that added to the joy and beauty of the liturgical journey, said Margaret Smith.

It could be argued that by making the decision to take her final vows in 1964, Deirdre gave up the possibility of a brilliant musical career. Clearly

6 In the Institute of the Blessed Virgin Mary delegates from every country assemble in Rome in a general chapter every six years. The chapter's main task is to elect a new general leader and her council.

Malcolm Williamson, a musician who reached the peak of his profession, did not believe Deirdre was living up to her musical potential. Their friendship suffered when Deirdre went to study liturgical theology rather than choral work with Michael Cardovan and, in Deirdre's words, 'become the next Percy Jones', although, she added, 'I doubt the church would ever have allowed me to take that role'. Deirdre herself acknowledged times of self-doubt, especially in her early years in religious life when young nuns were being told to walk straight and not slam doors and she yearned for music. She remembered feeling that no one understood her, nor did she understand them. 'I've always come alive 200 per cent when I'm anywhere near music in my life,' she said, 'and if that balance isn't there my world shrinks'. The words of a hymn she wrote in the 1960s reflects this ache in her heart:

> Don't clip my wings, please let me fly
> Don't stifle my song, please let me try
> To open my heart and share with you
> The best that's in me, self that's true
> Please let me fly.

Before taking final vows she could have flown. She chose to stay. Collaboration, not solo performance, she maintains, has given her the greatest satisfaction in her life both as a religious and as a musician. 'I love being part of a group,' she claimed, 'and have always learned most from groups'. Admittedly she is most herself when in the music and she has used her musicality, her creativity and her artistry in a way that is unique in religious life. It fills her prayer life, her public presentations, her sharing – whether with fellow sisters or musicians – with unexpected beauty. Her impact both spiritually and musically is incalculable. Her music has touched thousands through her teaching, concerts, public presentations, rituals and hymns. Deirdre's 'Come as you are' is one of the most popular hymns worldwide. Her students are scattered inter-state and around the world. In some ways Deirdre's is a story of compromise but also fulfilment. As a Loreto sister, she has opened her heart and sung her own song.

Libby Rogerson ibvm

Libby Rogerson was born in 1943 and entered the Institute of the Blessed Virgin Mary in 1968. She made her final vows in 1976.

To call Libby Rogerson a Mary Ward woman is to offer the greatest compliment a Loreto Sister can receive. It suggests that she is a woman of integrity, authenticity, warmth, strength and lively intelligence, a woman, in Mary Ward's words, who has the maturity to do God's work in 'freedom and love or not at all'.

Libby entered the Loretos on the eve of the Institute's renewal chapter held in Rome three years after the Vatican Council's document *Perfectae Caritatis* was to bring about immense changes for religious orders.[1] For the Loretos in Australia, the return to the 'spirit and aims' of their founder proved to be particularly poignant. Not only had Mary Ward been erased from the history of her own foundation, but when she was formally recognised by the Church in 1909, many of the members of the Irish branch preferred to acknowledge Dublin-born Frances Teresa Ball as their founder rather than an Englishwoman. The Mother House in Ireland had rigorously imposed this view on its Australian sisters from the early 1920s and it took considerable courage for those Australian sisters loyal to Mary Ward to stand firm.[2] The story of this struggle was shrouded in secrecy until recently, and is perhaps one of the reasons why Australian Loretos, as noted by members of the Institute around the world, strongly identify with Mary Ward and have such an independent spirit.

Thus Libby Rogerson entered the Loretos when they were wrestling with immense changes, many of which amounted to a return to the vision of Mary Ward. Ward had originally imagined a company of women who would live simply together, wear the dress of the day, and work actively in the world to meet the needs of their time. Like the Jesuits, they would

---

1 A general chapter is an assembly of representatives from all provinces within a religious order, the term originally being derived from the reading of a chapter from the order's rules at such meetings. Vatican II required that all aspects of the renewal programme introduced for religious orders be considered at a general chapter held within three years of the close of the Council in 1965.

2 See Chapter 9, 'The Terrible Years', in Mary Ryllis Clark, *Loreto in Australia*. Sydney, UNSW Press, 2009.

govern themselves and be answerable to the Pope in Rome rather than local bishops. Their greatest strength, May Ward claimed, was their free and open access to God.

To ensure the Institute's survival, Ward's version of religious life had been modified after her death to include enclosure and a monastic structure. The demands of *Perfectae Caritatis*, therefore, were not only liberating for most religious orders, but in the Institute of the Blessed Virgin Mary in particular they were closely linked with the resurgence of Mary Ward's vision.

Inevitably there were tensions in every Loreto community. For many, Vatican II was a breath of fresh air but there were those, including Libby's novice mistress, who loved the old monastic practices and found the changes distressing. For a modern young woman like Libby entering at this shifting time, the effectiveness of certain older practices was questionable.

One centuries-old practice was the chapter of faults in which members of the convent confessed their failures in observing the Rule to the gathered community. It was an important exercise in collective humility. In the twentieth-century Loreto novitiate the novices sat in a semi-circle and admitted their failings in breaking crockery, being unpunctual or speaking during Profound Silence.[3] When Libby and the other novices learned that speaking at the chapter of faults was to be optional, they decided not to speak: the chapter did not seem an effective means of inner renewal. 'There was this incredibly long silence,' she recalled, 'and the novice mistress became more and more agitated. After that the practice in the novitiate was dropped'.

Significantly this change highlights one of the major aspects of the Vatican II renewal, which involved religious men and women (and indeed secular people as well) in taking personal responsibility for their inner lives. For the Loretos, this was very much in tune with Mary Ward's Ignatian-based spirituality. A daily individual examination of conscience became one of the foundations of the Loreto Sisters post-Vatican II spirituality.

For many religious, their habit was their identity and represented their commitment to religious life. It is not surprising that the habit came to symbolise change, nor that the first indications to the outside world of the

3 During the ancient monastic practice of Profound Silence members of a community refrain from speech in order to deepen their spiritual focus. In the Loreto Institute Profound Silence began at 9pm and continued until after breakfast at 8am.

major shift happening within convents was the nuns' appearance. Libby and her five fellow novices were in the process of making their long religious habits at the same time that the Loreto leadership team was debating new styles of dress at the general chapter. The novices were eventually instructed to abandon the habit in favour of a simple dress and veil. 'I entered, thinking I was going to wear all that long gear and then it was changed', Libby said, 'a lot of things changed'. The novice mistress and many of the sisters, she added, continued to wear their full habits and 'the move to change took place over a number of years'.

The young novices, however, and open-minded Mary Ward women, were impatient to erase those customs that were not lifegiving for them. 'The only thing that kept me sane in the novitiate,' recalled Libby, 'was Veronica Brady who taught us literature. She told us that when she joined she thought you had to be mad to be a nun and so she decided to just be mad'. For Libby, however, the only madness she was interested in was making a difference. She had come to Loreto with a political and social conscience ignited by travel.

She had left Australia for Europe by ship in 1966 at the age of 21 and was away for two years. She taught at a school in Edinburgh where the children were separated in the classroom into two groups, those who had head lice and those who didn't. Growing up in slums, they had been moved out of 'those sixteenth century closes into new public housing estates. Both were just terrible,' Libby recalled.[4] After Edinburgh, she worked in schools in London's East End before going on to weed sugar beet in a kibbutz in Israel. There she took note of the treatment of Arabs by the otherwise delightful Israelis. Even later she crouched in a youth hostel in Damascus while a military coup took place in the street outside. The starkness of the poverty she saw in her travels moved Libby profoundly. 'There was nothing romantic about it, nothing theoretical when you saw it first hand,' she said. Her decision to enter Loreto was not, however, only a result of her experiences overseas, but was something she had been considering for some time. 'It doesn't leave you alone, this feeling that it's something you have to do,' she explained. 'I already had a well-developed sense of social justice, and an understanding that there were a lot of things wrong in the

4 A close is a Scottish term for a narrow lane or alleyway on private property. These were gated, therefore 'closed'.

world. My decision was something to do with service, to do with making the world a better place.'

A country girl from Binalong in New South Wales, Libby had boarded at Loreto Normanhurst, as had her mother and greataunts. But she learned little of Mary Ward there. She only came to know her upon entering and believes it was extraordinarily important for the Institute after Vatican II to examine the founding precepts thoroughly. 'I think I saw Mary Ward's education of girls in the seventeenth century as a way of freeing up a totally dominated group in society and helping them out of an inequitable structure. It gave me a new way of looking at the Church,' she said.

Throughout the seventies Libby was involved in intense discussions in Loreto communities about the meaning of religious life and the implications of concepts such as the priesthood of all believers, the equality of all vocations, the introduction of community discernment and consultation, and new ways of interpreting vows of poverty, chastity and obedience. She was also developing her understanding of social justice issues, inspired by Liberation Theology and its teaching on the 'preferential option for the poor'.[5] She said:

> It was a turbulent social justice time. There was the Vietnam war with thousands of boat people arriving here in Australia, the land rights movement for Indigenous people and equal rights for women. What had helped me a lot in my thinking was going to university in 1975 when Gough Whitlam made it possible for mature-aged people to study. I majored in politics, and one evening tutorial included a union leader from the Swallow and Ariell biscuit factory, a French horn player from the Melbourne Symphony Orchestra, the wife of an Anglican minister and two women who argued about politics over the back fence. The brilliant young academic who ran the tutorial didn't actually have to teach us anything, she just gave us guidelines and let the discussion go. Melbourne was a really active university then.

While living as a student at St Mary's College, Libby became involved with Action for World Development, an initiative of the National Council of Churches and the Catholic Bishops and inspired by Vatican II. She also

5 Liberation Theology was a radical movement developed largely in South America in the 1950s and '60s in response to widespread poverty, social injustice and inequality. Noted proponents were Gustavo Gutiérrez of Peru, Leonardo Boff of Brazil, Óscar Romero of El Salvador and Juan Luis Segundo of Uruguay. It was influential though controversial in the Church throughout the 1970s and 1980s, increasingly attracting criticism from conservative forces that saw it as aligned with Marxist ideas.

worked with the Jesuits' Asian Bureau Australia. Such agencies were at the forefront in shaking off the traditional approach to charity, welfare and good works. 'It was a huge and formative thing making the political theory and structures actually applicable,' said Libby, who was appalled by blistering attacks on the Jesuit Director of the Asian Bureau, Mark Raper, and several of his colleagues, published in the conservative Catholic press *News Weekly* in Victoria and *The Record* in Perth which accused Raper and his colleagues of being communists.

Libby had an unexpected and invaluable opportunity to present her ideas to her Loreto sisters when an Australian chapter was organised for 1980 in preparation for the next general chapter of the Irish Branch in Rome. The mother general, Agnes Walsh, highlighted social justice in her guidelines for provincial chapter discussion papers. 'Charity and justice must be clearly distinguished,' she wrote. 'Charity – what can I give you to eat; Justice: why are you hungry?' Libby's passion for this subject was clearly well known to the Loreto leadership team and the Australian provincial, Noni Mitchell, asked her to write a paper discussing how effective the institute in Australia had been in meeting the challenge of 'building a more just and humane society'.

Libby believed that at the heart of the debate facing the Loretos and other religious congregations, was the need to find new ways of supporting, and if possible, working with, rather than for, the poor and marginalised, and making the shift from the traditional notion of 'charity' to one of seeking genuine justice through confronting structural economic and political inequality.

In her discussion paper she suggested that, apart from a few Loreto sisters who had left the schools to find new roles working in welfare, most members of the institute did not understand the issues well. 'How alert are we as a province?' she asked.

> Not much at all. We come from behind scratch (because of wealthy schools and our own upper-middle-class backgrounds). Insofar as grappling with the real issues means being critical of our present social scene – not at all for most people. On the issue of women and justice – minimal awareness. Justice in the Church – non-existent awareness.

In her paper Libby went so far as to question the Australian Province's subscription to *News Weekly*, the mouthpiece for Bob Santamaria's National

Civic Council.[6] (Earlier she had tried to cancel *News Weekly* when she was at St Mary's College but did not succeed.) To her surprise, a letter objecting to her paper was circulated among the nuns before the chapter. She had underestimated the conservative convictions of some of the sisters, some of whom, particularly in Victoria, had voted DLP for years, equating it with loyalty to Bob Santamaria and the Church.[7]

It is not surprising that Libby ruffled feathers. Loreto sisters had faced considerable change in the structure of their lives in the years after Vatican II: Libby was relatively newly professed and, with other younger nuns, was challenging the way the community thought. The nuns were also experiencing a different style of government with Noni Mitchell. A physician, Noni had worked extensively in education and had been principal of the Catholic teacher training college in Melbourne. She also served on a number of important state and federal boards. A true Mary Ward woman in her strong leadership, her openness to Vatican II, her freedom and readiness to take risks, Noni encouraged communal and individual discernment, personal initiative and balance. She understood that Libby and the other fine young nuns in their 30s were the emerging Loreto leaders.

Libby claims that living in a lively community in West Australia cushioned her. 'You get a bit disconnected,' she laughed,

> We were a little secessionist state so far from head office in Melbourne. We had great leadership with Mary O'Brien, who always believed the best of everybody and would sit up half the night so that she could chat with Veronica Brady when she wheeled her bike in at midnight or whatever.[8] Friday nights people like the Jesuit John Hart came to dinner, red wine would be flowing and there'd be arguments for hours of the most stimulating variety.

---

6 The political activist B.A. Santamaria founded the right-wing National Civic Council in 1957. He edited its newspaper, *News Weekly*, for many years. Subscriptions to *News Weekly* were made through direct bank debits, which made cancellations complicated.

7 After their split from the Labor Party in 1955, Bob Santamaria's followers formed the Democratic Labor Party. The party's main platform was fighting communism in the Labor Party and Trade Union Movement.

8 Veronica Brady was one of the first nuns in Australia to teach in a university. In 1972 she was appointed to the University of Western Australia and became a household name through her work on radio, her publications and her outspoken comments, which were often at odds with the Church hierarchy on social and political matters.

Libby may well have felt she was under the radar in the West but this proved an illusion. In July 1994, within days of Noni Mitchell's election as the new mother general in Rome, Libby received a call from the Australian Provincial, Sister Deirdre Rofe, telling her she had been elected to the general council. 'Jesus,' she said in shock, and heard Sister Deirdre saying to whoever was with her, 'She's saying, "Oh Jesus" but I don't think it's like Mary Ward'.

For someone as outspoken and independently minded as Libby, her new appointment held a number of personal challenges as well as offering an invaluable opportunity to expand her understanding of the world. The Loreto generalate was located in a house in the centre of Rome where Libby lived with Noni and five other Loretos from different parts of the world. She said that 'living in an international community is very, very difficult because you come from totally different views about what religious life is, what theology is, what culture is, what everything is. Mary Ward was about the only common factor. Australians are not by nature obsequious. I couldn't believe all the kowtowing to authority'.

One of the most fascinating aspects of being on the general council, Libby found, was the profound difference between the provinces in the institute. Doubtless Australia's geographic isolation meant that the Loreto province there had to be largely independent and self-sustaining. Australia at that time had more members with post-graduate degrees than other provinces and had sisters of the calibre of Veronica Brady, Margaret Manion and Joan Nowotny teaching at tertiary level.[9] It also had the greatest number of women who had moved out of schools to work in the community.

In Rome Libby saw the best of the Church and the worst of it. 'What it did,' she said,

> Was cement my view that there are two churches – the one that existed with cardinals wearing red socks and the one represented by a Spanish priest I met in Peru. We drove up in to the Andes to a church that only had mass twice a year. He gave the simplest and clearest catechesis I have ever heard before baptising the illegitimate baby of a profoundly deaf girl and the terminally ill child of a

9 Veronica Brady is Professor Emeritus of Australian Literature of the University of Western Australia; Margaret Manion is Professor Emeritus of Fine Arts at the University of Melbourne and was the first woman Chair of the Academic Board at Melbourne; and Joan Nowotny, who died in 2008, was Dean of Yarra Theological Union, the first woman dean of a theological institution in Australia.

> young couple. He and his heroic band of fellow priests, mainly Spanish, were ebullient and fun and did amazing work. Meanwhile in downtown Lima, Opus Dei was taking over the key positions in the Church and making their lives unendurable.

Again travel was a vital component in opening Libby's eyes and heart. One of the biggest things she learned about herself was her lack of awareness that 'there is a certain cultural arrogance that comes out of a country that runs very efficiently'. She experienced the frustrations of dealing with impenetrable and corrupt bureaucracies in countries such as Italy and India 'where so much energy goes into dealing with the barriers that are put in your way'. She had to train herself not to talk about Australia 'because I made it sound as if it was the best place in the world'.

During Libby's time in Rome, Pope John Paul II gave a talk at Castel Gondolfo stating that women should hold positions at the highest levels. She was impressed until a colleague gave her an article from *L'Osservatore Romano*, the Vatican newspaper, containing a list of all the Vatican curias and departments, even down to the Vatican Radio and including the newspaper itself. 'The list contained the names of heads and deputy-heads,' she said, 'There were cardinals, archbishops, bishops, fathers and even a few secular men, but not one woman. I wrote a very polite letter to the Pope implying he had a credibility problem. He never answered. I used to walk across St Peter's Square and think to myself, this is the last trumpeting of the dinosaurs!'

Libby also learned not to be so quick to judge others, and to understand that things were not always what they seemed.

> I thought anyone who wore a religious habit was a right-wing reactionary locked in a past dimension. In Rome I found that people wore the habit because it gave them protection in the slums. Women from Eastern Europe wore the habit because they had been forbidden to during the Communist regime and so it was a sign of their identity. Other people wore the habit because it wasn't worth fighting about when there were bigger battles to be won.

In 1998, towards the end of her time on the general council, Libby attended an important international human rights conference in Rome. Bishop Manning from New South Wales was there from Australia, as was Sandy Cornish, head of the Australian Council for Social Justice. About half of those attending were women, but men chaired all the discussion groups. Groups were organised on the basis of language and an archbishop from

Turkey was asked to chair one of the English speaking groups. He refused saying his English was not good enough and as no one else was willing to take it on, Libby stepped in, to great encouragement from a group of Scotsmen. When reporting back to the full conference, she said that, given the fact that loss of human rights had a greater impact on women and children, it was somewhat problematic that the Swiss guards in the Vatican gave a full salute to archbishops, a half-salute to other clerics and no salute at all to lay people and women. At the next tea break, a Good Shepherd nun ran over to her laughing, and told her there was an American bishop outside asking a stony-faced Swiss guard why he didn't salute women!

Such occasions in Rome were important in raising awareness of the injustice inherent in the way women were regarded. More than 30 years had passed since Cardinal Suenens, in the second session of Vatican II, had asked why there were no women in the Council, since they made up half of humanity.

For Libby personally, the conference bore fruit. Back in Australia from Rome, and looking for work, she was approached by Bishop Manning who asked her to set up a social justice commission in his diocese of Parramatta, an outer suburb of Sydney. She worked with him for ten demanding, fulfilling and fruitful years as Coordinator of Social Justice and Director of Caritas. A strong advocate for social justice, especially workers' rights, Bishop Manning gave Libby carte blanche.

> There were lots of positives, lots of negatives, lots of things that didn't work well and things that did and a couple of things that stood out. One of these was doing something for the African refugees who were coming, especially the Sudanese. We worked with the Catholic Education Office and some fantastic local youth officers and actually employed a young Sudanese man ourselves. It all went really well. Another big thing was our involvement with Your Rights at Work. Bishop Manning and I were on the hustings morning, noon and night. I spoke on a box down at Circular Quay on behalf of the cleaners, he spoke at the Police Union and I marched with the then leader of the opposition here, John Robertson, and spoke at the big rally in Blacktown. I'd say we were extremely influential. We spoke at heaps of gatherings, went to numerous meetings, were invited to everything and really got to know all those union men and women.

Libby and Bishop Manning were surprised when they were asked to support the bikies in their fight against what they considered to be unjust legislation. They listened to their arguments against the State's attempts to bring in legislation to prevent them assembling and wearing insignia and concluded they were right, and it was unjust. 'We supported them and the legislation was not passed', said Libby.

Perhaps the hardest thing Libby did in Parramatta was reviewing Centacare. It was not meeting the needs of the people of the western suburbs and Libby argued for a review. In the face of considerable opposition, changes were introduced and the welfare-related work expanded. It continues to develop.

Some of Libby's most moving experiences during her years in Parramatta occurred while she was travelling. In 1999 she was one of the people Caritas sent to East Timor to be in solidarity with the people working in Caritas projects. 'I was working at the Caritas office in Dili,' she said, 'which was absolutely shocking because no one was doing anything as they were all anxious and on edge. After a month I was evacuated when it all fell apart. However, I went back for another couple of months helping Caritas with food distribution and things like that'. Evacuated again from Dili, Libby became the spokesperson on the situation in East Timor since she had witnessed it. She resisted the Australian media's pressure to issue a blanket condemnation of the Indonesians, stating that justice demanded supporting the people of East Timor against the military, and stressing that not all Indonesians knew what was happening and should not, therefore, be condemned.

In December 2000 Libby, together with 13 other Caritas Australia volunteers, was awarded the Humanitarian Overseas Service Medal by Bishop Francis Carroll, President of the Australian Catholic Bishops Conference. He thanked them all 'for the witness they gave to the struggle of the people'.

Church organisations, Libby believes, provide among the best structures and support for action on issues of social justice because so many Catholics have worked in organisations with experience in this area and have some idea about structural injustice. 'For example,' she said, 'I've been on the Congregational Leaders' Justice Group in New South Wales for a long time and the work done by the small sub-committee on prisons is so effective, committee members are invited to contribute every time there's anything to do with prisons. When I first went to Parramatta, for example, we had a picket outside the women's prison for days because they wanted to build a new one and we said no, that we wanted the women out of there, as prison was hopeless and stupid for most of the offences they committed'.

Libby's standing is such that she was invited to support the motion that 'the Catholic Church is a force for good in the world' in a public debate at the Melbourne Town Hall in November 2011. She began by attacking the portrayal of the Church in the media as defined solely by its hierarchy of Pope, bishops and clergy, and argued that just as Tony Abbott in his bathing trunks is no more the measure of Australian manhood, so cardinals in their silk robes are not the measure of Catholicism.[10] She pointed out that the Catholic Church is the sum of all its parts - the 1.2 billion people who call themselves Catholics. It is 'a flawed human institution with a 2000 year old history of triumphs, tragedies, betrayals, closed minds, extraordinary heroism and, at times, lamentable behaviour,' she said, 'but its goodness outweighs the many negatives'.

Confining herself to the nine minutes allotted to her, Libby could not possibly do justice to the thousands of Catholic agencies meeting needs in every corner of the globe. Instead she spoke of those of which she had direct knowledge. As a member of the Board of Caritas Australia, for example, she had seen transformational programmes in place in East Timor, Bougainville, Botswana and South Africa. As the Coordinator of Social Justice in the Diocese of Parramatta she had been involved with a network of social welfare agencies – Centacare, Jesuit Social Services, Marist Youth Services, MacKillop Family Services - working with Indigenous communities, alienated, homeless youth and children at risk. As a Board member of CentaCare (Wilcannia-Forbes) she had seen the effectiveness of programs such as Strong Young Mums and free financial counselling. She also praised the effectiveness of Jesuit Refugee Services, the largest non-government refugee agency in the world, which offers education, health, counselling and support programmes to over 500,000 refugees in 51 countries.

Libby's fellow speakers in favour of the motion were barrister Julian McMahon and former Liberal Senator Helen Coonan. Those against were author and journalist Anne Summers, former Catholic priest Peter Kennedy and author and journalist David Marr. At one point speakers on both sides of the debate were caught up in an altercation about the Church's condemnation of the use of condoms in countries where AIDS is a major problem. To the surprise and delight of the audience, Libby steered the argument back on course by stating

10 Tony Abbott is a Liberal Party politician who became leader in 2009 and Prime Minister in 2013. He has been frequently photographed in sporting apparel.

firmly, 'I don't agree with the Church's stand on this issue. I think it's wrong.' It was a comment based on the fact that she had seen for herself the ravages of the disease and the nonsense of not doing everything possible to combat it. In the event the motion was lost, but Libby's faith, feminism, clear thinking, sincerity, articulate understanding of social justice and humour were well received by the audience.

Libby had three main focuses in her life when we interviewed her in 2013. First was working with the Sudanese community in Blacktown in Sydney helping to set up an after-school homework centre. The Sudanese parents are very excited about this, she said, as they want to boost their children's education. The project comes under the CentaCare umbrella. Second is her active involvement in a number of not-for-profit boards including Jesuit Social Services, St Francis Social Services and the Loreto Normanhurst School Council. Third, she is leader of the Normanhurst community. In addition she is a member of the Conference of Leaders of Religious Institutes (NSW) Social Justice Committee.

Libby had a wide range of choices when she returned from her trip overseas in the late 1960s. Her two years away had given her invaluable practical and personal skills, and job opportunities for women, though still limited in comparison with those for men, were nonetheless opening up. She believed that joining the Loreto Sisters was not only what God was asking of her but would offer her the means of making a difference in the field of social justice. At 70, the passion that drew Libby to Loreto has not faded.

Sisters of St Brigid

The Brigidine Sisters were established in Ireland in 1807 by Daniel Delaney, Bishop of Kildare and Leighlin, to serve the needs of the Catholic population denied an education under the Penal Laws of the eighteenth century. Daniel Delaney had been educated in Paris at the Sorbonne and ordained in 1770. After working as a curate in Tullow, County Callow, in the diocese of Kildare and Leighlin, he was appointed Bishop in 1783. He opened Sunday schools for both adults and children through which he hoped to improve the faith and the morals of his parishioners, but his strong desire was always to establish schools for both the rich and the poor. To this end, he enlisted six women he had trained as catechists in his Sunday schools to form the first community of Sisters of St Brigid.

Rather than seeing this initiative as the founding of a new order, he believed he was refounding the fifth century Order of St Brigid. Delaney had great devotion to Brigid, prophet, peacemaker and patroness of Ireland, and placed his small band of sisters under her protection. Their first convent was in Tullow. Because the pioneers were not well educated, Bishop Delaney brought in a laywoman, Judith Wogan Browne, who had been educated by Benedictine nuns in Europe, to oversee their spiritual and secular studies. Daniel Delanay died in 1814, seven years after the establishment of the first convent. The community by then had grown to 21, a figure which increased to 250 by 1886, with the sisters spread across six convents.

It was not until the 1880s that the Australian bishops discovered the Brigidines as a potential source of teachers for their dioceses. Six Irish sisters from Mountrath responded to a request from Bishop Murray of the Maitland diocese in NSW. In 1883 they established themselves in Coonamble, a remote town of 800 people 500 kilometres northwest of Sydney, where they opened a parish school, day school and boarding school. A second group of four sisters came from Tullow in 1886 to the Victorian diocese of Sandhurst to staff the parish school in Echuca, situated on the River Murray. Six Irish sisters, two from Cooma (where sisters had gone from Coonamble in 1887) and four from Coonamble established a foundation in New Zealand in 1898.

The Brigidine Sisters initially served communities in small regional centres, where they often provided boarding facilities and were known for the high standard of their education. In the early decades of the twentieth century, they expanded their commitment to education to the larger cities, and became a vital component of the Catholic education system, meeting the needs of both primary and secondary students. As they attracted local girls to join them in religious life, their reliance on Ireland for recruits diminished. In fact by the end of the nineteenth century, there were more Brigidines in Australia than in Ireland, living in six individual foundations. These amalgamated as an Australian province in 1893. Victoria became a separate province in 1896.

The Brigidines continue their involvement in education through their ongoing ownership of schools in Queensland, New South Wales, Adelaide and Victoria; a number of schools for which they were responsible have either closed or been handed over to the relevant Catholic Education Offices.

The Brigidines are one of eight congregations that formed Earthsong, an inter-congregational group focused on environmental education, and they continue to advocate for peace and justice through the United Nations and other international and national organisations. In Australia, there are three Brigidine sponsored spirituality centres, two in Melbourne and one in Canberra.

Brigid Arthur csb

Brigid Arthur was born in 1934 and entered the Brigidine Sisters in 1953. She made her final vows in 1959.

Brigid Arthur is one of the leading advocates for both the needs and the rights of refugees. Supported by the Brigidine community to which she has belonged for over 60 years, and a number of volunteers and friends, Brigid and Sister Catherine Kelly run the Brigidine Asylum Seekers Project based at Kilbride, their convent in Albert Park, Melbourne.[1] The Project offers not only practical support for asylum seekers, but a strong base for advocacy on their behalf, which has led Brigid to appear in the High Court, to tackle Members of Parliament face to face and to speak regularly in public to raise awareness and stir consciences.

In 2013, Australia became a nation in which asylum seekers are used as political pawns. Brigid said; 'the country descended to new depths. What we're doing is awful. I feel a great sense of sadness at the way we punish people who try to come here. Pregnant women are sent to Nauru, children are born in detention centres with little prospect of leaving, men are put on Manus Island even though we know how depressing it is.' She thinks the death of Reza Berati in February 2014 brought about a slight shift in public opinion in Australia.[2] 'More people are saying enough is enough.'

Brigid's work is demanding and challenging but she was born into a family with a strong work ethic and sense of justice, especially on the female side. She grew up near Kaniva, a small town in the Wimmera-Mallee region of western Victoria, an area so tough for farmers that some of the original selectors walked away.[3] Her grandfather on her father's side stayed the course and her father, inheriting the farm, lived there all his life. On her

1 Kilbride closed down as a Brigidine school in 1978. In 1990, a community of Brigidine sisters took up residence with hospitality named as their corporate mission. The buildings currently house the Asylum Seeker Project, as well as providing accommodation for visiting nuns and holiday groups. It is also a centre for renewal courses and a base for women working in individual ministries.

2 Reza Barati was an Iranian asylum seeker who was being held in Australia's detention centre on Manus Island in Papua New Guinea when he was killed during riots.

3 To encourage settlement, Land Acts legislation in some Australian colonies offered 'free selection before survey' of crown land.

mother's side she is descended from Scottish and Irish settlers. Brigid's maternal grandmother, Jessie, was one of fifteen children; seven of her sons fought in the First World War. Brigid's mother, Winnie, was ten when Jessie died of cancer and she was sent to the Sisters of Nazareth's Ballarat orphanage to be educated. She was obviously bright, so the sisters entered her for a scholarship to the Sacred Heart Convent run by the Ballarat East Sisters of Mercy. However, the sisters got the time wrong and sent Winnie in the afternoon instead of the morning. 'Even though the Nazareth nuns argued with the Ballarat East nuns that they should give her a chance,' said Brigid, 'they wouldn't change it.' Winnie stayed at the orphanage in Ballarat as a monitor until she was 17, and then worked for several years as a domestic servant before marrying. She raised eight children, of whom Brigid was the eldest, and Winnie was determined they would get the education she had been denied.

The children loved the freedom of the farm, but since there were no high schools near, they were sent away for secondary schooling, the girls to the Brigidines at Horsham, the boys to Mount Gambier or Ballarat. 'To send eight of us away to boarding school, one after the other, and often several of us at the same time because there was only ten years between us, was incredible,' said Brigid. 'We hated it and I remember mum saying one day, "It's costing us a fair bit to send you, so if you are going to moan and groan, well maybe you just stay at home." So we stopped a bit of the moaning.'

Brigid's mother was a powerful influence on the family and her word was paramount. Brigid recalled her 'taking on' a man in the district about his neglect of his wife and family, and of standing up to the convention of always being ready with food for the men coming in from shearing: 'Bugger the men, I'm not ready yet.' It is not surprising that at school Brigid was frequently in trouble for speaking her mind or asking questions. 'Mum was very gutsy and I just grew up thinking women could say their piece,' said Brigid. She was the bane of Mother Bernadine who taught religion. 'It was just dreadful,' Brigid remembered.

> We had a number of books, including one on apologetics. They were all awful. One big row I got into was when was Bernadine was talking about the resurrection and asking could it have been anything else other than Jesus – God – being raised from the dead. Being silly I said he could have been in a state of suspended animation. Well, I was disgracing the family, the faith, the Irish nation! I got sent out to Mother Bernard next door.

Brigid described Mother Bernard, who taught every Year 12 subject, as 'a very tough woman' who 'impressed me more than anyone else' at school. 'She would put a brown paper bag around the outside of her books so that no-one would know what she was reading. She often gave me books to read...we didn't talk much, but we had this really good relationship.' Brigid acknowledged that she differentiated a bit 'between those whom I thought were people in their own right, independent thinkers and human and so on, and those whom I think were warped by the system'.

Brigid's memories of her school days are reflected in those of one of her best friends, Pauline Toner, who became the first woman Minister in the Cain Labor government in Victoria, elected in 1982. Pauline wrote:

> The 12 years or thereabouts I spent surrounded by the gentle, poor and unsophisticated women in the Brigidine convent [in Horsham] meant that we were exposed to a narrow view of theology and apologetics for a significant period of our lives. [But] my last three years at school were quite happy. Mother Bernard, an Irish nun, took us for all subjects. She was a warm and witty woman and gave me some leeway to express my radical views in my essays and in debates.[4]

Undoubtedly the biggest influence on Brigid during her years at school was the Young Christian Students (YCS).[5]

> The nuns gave it over to us to run, which in retrospect was the best thing they could have done. So we actually read all the stuff, found out how you did it, went to conferences...it was extraordinarily good, because we took social issues and actually explored them...you brought something that you had seen, then tried to [contextualise and ask] 'What does that reveal...we were talking about power, about who controlled what, and who shouldn't. We were like little Marxists really... It had the same underlying philosophy as the YCW (Young Catholic Workers) – see, judge, act...We started with a gospel discussion...it

4 Pauline Toner, 'Martha, Martha, Thou art too worldly', in Kate Nelson and Dominca Nelson (eds), *Sweet Mothers, Sweet Maids: Journeys from Catholic Childhoods*. Ringwood, Penguin, 1986, 43. A second woman Minister in the Cain/Kirner governments who is a past student of the Brigidines in Melbourne is Maureen Lyster, Minister for Local Government and later, for Health. A third is Senator Rosemary Crowley, representing South Australia, Minister assisting the Prime Minister for the Status of Women in the Keating Labor government.

5 The Young Christian Students started in Australia in 1942 as an official arm of Catholic Action. YCS was modelled on the groups of Young Christian Workers and Young Christian Students in Europe inspired by Belgian Cardinal Joseph Cardijn. They had their origin in the Young Trade Unionists which Cardijn founded in Brussels in 1919.

> certainly began my interest in looking at the gospel, not just literally. What's this all about? What's this saying?

It wasn't until her final year at school that Brigid considered entering. 'I had this nagging thought,' she said. 'It certainly wasn't what I wanted to do, this was what God wanted me to do. My fallback position was, OK – go and prove it's wrong. And here I am still! There's probably some psychological interpretation of this whole thing that might be less than flattering!'

Like the majority of the women's apostolic orders, the Brigidines were involved in education alone, so joining them meant becoming a teacher and Brigid was happy with this:

> [I was] fairly naïve. I was imbued by the whole See, Judge and Act stuff and what I'd understood the gospel to mean. I think I was intent on doing something to change the world. I thought, well, there are not too many things that I, or women can do. I had been keen on being a doctor. But then I realised I didn't have the right subjects and I didn't know how I'd get to university and that sort of stuff. I thought, well, teaching's pretty good. You can have a fair bit of influence on people. That was my main motivation.

Brigid entered the novitiate in Malvern with thirty other young women in 1953. Their two and a half years of formation was combined with the Brigidines own teacher training college and in Brigid's opinion, both the spiritual and the intellectual training 'were a little bit suspect but I don't think I took things too seriously. Some people talk about the long-term effects of the novitiate, but I couldn't claim any of that. I sort of put up with it. It wasn't a lifetime sentence'. Most of her companions were afraid of the novice mistress, Imelda O'Collins, but Brigid liked her even though she was 'a bit cracked and frequently in bed sick'. She admits they did clash now and again:

> I remember once saying to Imelda, well, you can make me do all sorts of things, but you can't stop me thinking what I'm thinking. She wanted me to go to the priest in confession and tell him that I had been insubordinate! I said you've got to be joking! You can tell me to do anything you like. You can even make me go into the confessional – which I didn't -- but you simply can't tell me what I can think! I thought it was a self-evident truth that no one can make you think what he or she wants you to think. She gave up in the end.

At one stage during her novitiate Brigid had the thought that she should be a lay sister and devote her life to cooking for the other sisters and boarders. 'That was one of my few pious moments', she said. 'By this stage, Bernard

O'Mahoney had become provincial, and I told her I was going to change over and become a lay sister. She was so incensed, she said, "You will not! You're a clever girl! You're going to be a teacher!" And there I was thinking it was up to me!'

Mother Bernard, of course, was right. Brigid began her teaching career at Kilmaire, the Brigidine school in Hawthorn, and proved to be a natural. 'From day one I loved teaching,' she said. 'I loved the kids. I have, over the years, taught everything. I'd done the primary training when I was in the novitiate but I virtually didn't teach primary much, probably three years or so…I was also in charge of the boarders, but I loved all that. The work I've always loved. That's what kept me going, I loved the kids, loved the families. I really enjoyed teaching.'

Brigid's obvious passion for teaching was combined with an apparently inexhaustible energy for study. This was very much her initiative. 'We weren't pushed to study,' she said, 'but if you wanted to you could and it was always on top of a full working life which some people refused to do'.

> I started studying straight away at Melbourne University part time. I did humanities - an arts degree. I've studied a lot, mainly part time, mainly in my own time. I did science eventually, I did maths because there was no one else around teaching that…I've always been pretty energetic and although it was mad I didn't mind. I'd be reading a novel on which I had to write an essay at 3 o'clock in the morning, and then trying to work out the maths problems for the kids for the next day. But I was very fit and it didn't unduly perturb me.

Behind the scenes in the post-Vatican II years, changes were taking place in religious life. Brigid pointed out that the thinking behind them started well before the Council:

> It certainly wasn't that we were all waiting round and then Vatican II happened - yippee, now we can do things we couldn't do before. It wasn't like that. Things were already moving in a particular direction. Many of us like-minded people were having discussions in the 1950s saying this has got to change or it's not for us. We were reading good stuff that was around before Vatican II, arguing it and debating it. In my mind it was a time of a lot of good intellectual tussling and Vatican II just made sense of it in that context.

Meetings, endless meetings, became a feature of religious life in the post-Vatican II years in response to the call for greater consultation. This in itself was revolutionary. Brigid recalled one particularly Brigidine gathering at Harrietville in 1971:

> A fair few of us went and we had two priests giving us this renewal stuff, and it was very intense. It was all the Vatican II stuff, but put into our context, and a lot of it was around authority and obedience. So for the first time we were being told things that we wanted to hear, like your primary obedience is to God, your primary obedience is to your own conscience. There are constraints on authority. Authority means authorship and therefore it's got something to do with your own authoring, what you're going to do inside. I suppose I can remember the bits I wanted to hear! But we found it really, really fascinating. It had all these ramifications, however, round the province.

Brigid remembered some of the sisters 'falling apart' at what they were hearing. 'People cried during some of the sessions about things that were really dumb because they were peripheral to what we were talking about which was philosophical and theological,' she said. 'One woman was convinced the changes would inevitably lead to other things such as drinking.' Brigid was one of those who spoke out in favour of the changes and clearly her voice carried weight since after the Harrietville meeting the provincial leader, Mother Carmela, accused her of 'tearing the Province apart'. Looking back, Brigid knows she was seen as one of the young troublemakers and adds ruefully that even the two priests were implicated:

> The talk was that they had whipped us up as though we were automatons just sitting there and taking in whatever anybody would tell us, whereas by this stage we were ready to think for ourselves. We had been debating stuff. We had been getting these lectures and they were an interpretation of the documents coming out of Vatican II...it was hugely exciting.

Mother Carmela, however, must have been struggling to steer a path on which all the sisters could progress together. 'She became increasingly worried about the divisions in the province,' admitted Brigid, 'She was absolutely traumatised. That would be the only word for all that'. Looking back 'with a little more compassion', Brigid acknowledges that there were casualties and realises some members of the congregation really suffered such as the sister concerned about 'our possible drinking splurges'. She also thought 'we might all go to hell because we were all getting into cottontail pants'. But nearly 50 years later, Brigid's memory of those tumultuous years is less of the casualties and more of the excitement of following this new path, even if some 'went at different paces'. She laughed when thinking about the sister's concerns about alcohol, 'Her worst dreams have come true. I usually have a glass of wine at night! She'd say, "I told you it would come to this!"'

In another visible sign of turmoil numbers of women were leaving religious life. Before the Vatican Council it was rare for sisters to leave subsequent to taking their final vows. She recalled the shock when a nun who had been in the order 15 years left when Brigid was in the novitiate. This would have taken courage, she pointed out. In the years after the Council, as the rigidity of the system loosened, it became easier to leave. Brigid could see no pattern to those who left her congregation, commenting that a number of the 'holiest ones' were among the first to go. Some of the women to whom Brigid was closest left and she, too, thought seriously about it, and admits she would not have found it hard. After Vatican II her family, who placed no expectations on her, asked 'Are you sure you want to be there?' She decided that she did: 'My sense was that this was what I was meant to be doing'.

Brigid, like her friends in the community, found the new ideas coming from Vatican II intellectually stimulating and so were the things happening in education. Brigid became principal of the Brigidine school in Horsham in Victoria in her late twenties and welcomed the opportunity to work with new lay teachers, especially the younger ones, to implement new ideas in educational thinking.

As the dust of renewal gradually settled, Brigid was given more leadership responsibilities within the congregation, eventually being elected to the province leadership team. In the early 1970s, the Brigidines, like all the other congregations, foresaw the need to rationalise and plan for a future that would not include nuns in the day-to-day teaching and management of their schools. By 1974, Brigid was one of seven members of the Brigidine's Education Committee responsible for planning future educational programmes. Subsequently, she became a member of the resource team that planned and carried out a development programme for eleven Brigidine schools in country and metropolitan Victoria.

> I've had very satisfying opportunities to do things, like to initiate what we call the Brigidines Secondary Schools Council. I was given that job to do…so I had to stop being a principal – I loved that, so I wasn't real keen. But [we needed] to set up a network so that the schools could operate together, and that meant starting common policies, eventually a common policy structure, so that's been hugely challenging but also immensely satisfying.

Brigid retired from active involvement in schools in 1991 although she remains a member of many education groups. Throughout her working life, social justice has been a passion and on the day of our interview, she was leaving to mediate in a school between students and a member of staff:

> I think it's so important to break down the stereotypes. Truth is not to be found in stereotypes. The kids went through a democratic process about what charity they want to support. They chose a group in South Africa that builds houses for the poor and a staff member decided that they should support Catholic groups because she thinks that is what the local bishop wants. I am going up there to put her straight. One: The kids' process is to be honored and two: who said the Church or the gospel is about Catholics? The gospel is primarily about outsiders and how we can bring them not into the Catholic Church but into humanity and treated like everyone else. Now that's stereotype stuff.

Brigid and Cathy Kelly established the Brigidine Asylum Seeker Project under the auspices of the Brigidine Justice Community in 2001. Brigid insisted that was not a cause suddenly discovered upon retiring.[6] 'I have a long history of involvement with justice groups, so setting up the BASP did not come out of nowhere,' she said. During her 20 years as principal of Marian College, the Brigidine school in Sunshine West, for example, she came to know asylum seekers well as 'wave after wave were coming into the country'.

BASP encompasses all aspects of a support and advocacy service, from information dissemination through its regular newsletter to appearances before the High Court. The practical support it provides for asylum seekers includes accommodation in one of the three houses the Brigidines manage, assistance with finding, furnishing and equipping rental accommodation, visiting asylum seekers in detention centres, supporting family reunions, organising English language programmes, partnering with the Edmund Rice Centre in Richmond to running a drop-in centre, and distributing donated goods to individuals and families.

The regular newsletter reports on their information nights, book launches and public meetings and speaking engagements in schools, as well as networking with parishes, with other religious institutes and non-government agencies. One section is devoted to 'good news' stories – marriages, births, new jobs, new accommodation, family reunions, working

6 For more information, see www.brigidineasp.org.au. The stated aims of the project are to provide hospitality and practical support for asylum seekers, to actively network with like-minded individuals and groups who are working for justice for asylum seekers and to promote advocacy for the rights of asylum seekers.

bees and celebration meals. Another section focuses on the difficulties asylum seekers face, and in many cases, overcome. Finally, there are always examples of the way in which people support them through fund-raisers, sponsoring 'nuns on the run', donating goods and helping at working bees.

On the advocacy side, their ten or twelve page newsletter is a quintessential example of employing the see, judge and act principles. The majority of its space is given over to analysis of government policies, critiques of these and the programmes government runs, up-to-date financial analysis of the cost of mandatory detention and reports on the latest findings of the preeminent researchers and commentators on refugee policy. Of greater importance is the constant call for readers to continue to lobby government.

Reading of their activities provokes a strong sense that the Brigidines and their supporters have moved well beyond traditional notions of 'charity', even though they maintain a very practical approach to meeting everyday needs as they arise. The central focus is on justice, and how to achieve it through all the means available in a modern democratic country. This includes appearing in the High Court on behalf of detainees, as Brigid has done. It includes a fearless approach to politicians, to those in the public service and in the courts with whom the sisters have constant contact.

Brigid's passion for justice for asylum seekers surfaced strongly when she started speaking about the bureaucratic hurdles the people themselves and their advocates face:

> I can't believe how bad the system is. Bureaucracies are capable of anything. Institutions are capable of anything. Don't tell me that it must be right because we've got policies and safeguards and we've had umpteen dozen reviews. Don't tell me that, because I can tell you that in any organisation you can get terrible outcomes…So, any sort of soft thoughts I've ever had [that] it's got to be right because someone in authority said it, (I don't think I ever had that too much)… I've got none now!

She had particularly harsh words for many of the companies which supply migration agents, some of whom may not speak English, and who are given totally inadequate time to prepare applications.

> They're so bad that the people are destined to fail at their review…[the courts] know, they absolutely know, that some of these firms are shockers. We name them…We name them, and they still use them. They know that there are a number of reviewers who fail almost everyone and they're still there – why?

She is equally critical of government ministers:

> But who can actually make any difference? It seems almost everything that you go to do, they say, 'Oh, it's on the Minister's desk'. I say, 'God, that must be a big desk! When is he going to get around to looking at his desk?' But so often individual people can't get out of detention on any sort of scheme because it's on the Minister's desk.

Brigid raised the important point that women religious have a unique opportunity to act as advocates for justice:

> People say to me, 'Oh you are brave'. I say 'Why?' They say, 'Well you know things might happen to you'. Well what can they do with me? I will always have a bed and a meal. No one is going to throw me out of thc Brigidines. Even if I go to goal, I am luckier than most; somebody would probably get me a lawyer. Whereas some of the people that I work with won't even get a lawyer when they are accused of something that is absolutely stupid, that they didn't do. So I mean, I haven't got anything to lose.

One of the things that sustains and inspires Brigid is the resilience of many of the refugees and asylum seekers with whom she has worked:

> The people have changed my life…When I see how the system is so devastatingly cruel to them and how they can then regain resilience and in most cases reclaim their lives, I think the human spirit is extraordinarily strong. There's been long-term damage to a lot of people, and I feel both angry and sad about that… there's very few of them that just sit there in a corner saying, 'Somebody had better help me'. They got on with it and try to rescue their families - most of them have families overseas. They don't go backwards. They don't spend a lot of time talking about how bad it was to be in detention for two years or whatever. They're on to, 'My kids are now in, we've got as far, we've got them from this country to this country and I'm getting them here'. And they're working at stuff that no Australians will work in. I'm amazed at them.

Brigid believes she is at her most effective in helping individuals and raising the important questions. 'I am a bit of a thorn in the side of some of the authorities,' she admitted, 'I don't know how much that makes a difference but I felt obliged to do it'.

Brigid is driven by her strong sense that she is living the life she is meant to be living:

> Some of the best teaching in the Church [relates to] the common good, [which] really impresses me, as does the whole sacramentality bit: that whoever you think God is, God is present in a whole variety of places and things and

> occurrences. If you believe in some way that the sacred is present and that's where you experience the sacred and that's where you experience good, that's where you should be and that's what you should be trying to do. Being pretty weak and a bit stupid at times, you are not always doing what you should do, but to the extent to which you can, you should.

Her capacity to annoy authority figures has not diminished over the years. 'We put in a couple of submissions to the Wealth Enquiry, I think one was on women and the other on education,' she recalled. 'Three or four of us went to present and George Pell, then Archbishop of Melbourne, was one of the people we presented to. George made some comment afterwards that Catholic schools should be helping people to become upwardly mobile. I said to him I thought the gospel was probably helping people to go in the opposite direction. People still quote that at me! It killed the conversation!'

'On another occasion, I gave a talk at an event and the current Archbishop of Melbourne, Denis Hart, was in the audience. He later asked the organisers he be consulted about future speakers because I was not a person in whom he had any confidence. I am not really sure what that quite meant. So the next time I did something, I just went, they didn't put it on the agenda.'

Brigid may have difficulty with the institutional Church but finds great comfort in her local parish:

> I like the fact that we sit in the church behind Mary and Ray and that we have a talk each week about what's happened to them. I like the fact that Maria, who works within the parish, is just such a human and decent person, I like the fact that the parish priest…is decent and he is ready to acknowledge that things are not too good but we are all sticking together. I like that fact that I can meet some young Irish people who lost a couple of their mates in an accident and that we are there together, even though we don't have much else in common, but at that moment we share. So the little local church is sort of a symptom of some of the good things I see in life. The wider church, the diocesan church - I just despair so much about that I don't have anything to do with it really.

She sees the only hope for the Church being in its ability to call on its long tradition of rationality:

> There's a rational approach within the Catholic tradition that is to be embraced. We ought to be able to say when any church leader is being at his most irrational, 'You're not in line with the Catholic Church that does take a rational approach. We believe in reason. We're not the Pentecostals or whatever who believe that if you stand there and you pray in tongues you'll know what to do.' That's not our

> tradition. Our tradition is that we have lots of teaching and principles we can go back to, and you are outside of it.

She still stands by a statement she made at the reforming chapter of the Brigidines' Victorian province in 1982: 'We are between churches. The present Church has been rejected by many. The emerging Church may not be for a lot of people unless we create something more credible than the present model.' It is a situation that concerns her greatly:

> Because our identity is inextricably tied to Church no matter what you think about church, and the official church is in such disarray. It has lost the plot. We need to talk together. I think we need help in talking about such issues as what is the church that we believe in? To what extent is it ok to distance myself from this other church? Some people still feel uneasy, probably guilty when they criticise the Church. I don't. I believe in taking a much more proactive role in saying what we think.

There are now about 90 women in the Victorian Province of the Brigidines, raising the question of their future survival, but this is not something that concerns Brigid, because when she was asked whether the congregation would in fact survive, she said 'No - I think it won't, I think there will always be specific expressions of Christianity around. Probably there won't be nuns as we know them, but things come and go in history and we will have been in existence 200 and something years; that's ok, that's a fair lifetime for anyone'.

Brigid felt that active religious orders are at the end of an era but would like to see them end with a bang rather than a whimper. Being passive when things are not right, she believed, will not change anything either in secular society or within the church.

> There's a failure of leadership everywhere I think, especially politically. Nobody's game to be truly a leader without toeing the party line. If you're in a party – whether it's a political party, a congregation, a church or whatever – there are some things you do all hold but you ought to be able to say, hang on - on that one I differ. If you can't do that there will never be any way forward.

Sisters of Charity

After she spent three years at the Bar Convent in York preparing herself for religious life, a young Cork woman, Mary Aikenhead, founded the Sisters of Charity in Dublin in 1815. It was an active congregation based on the spirituality of St Ignatius and the constitutions of the Institute of the Blessed Virgin Mary. In addition to the three vows of poverty, chastity and obedience, sisters took a fourth vow to devote their lives to the service of the poor. Their immediate work involved running a women's refuge, caring for orphans, visiting the sick, poor and imprisoned and setting up schools for the poor. In 1834 Mary Aikenhead fulfilled a long held dream of opening a free hospital for the poor regardless of race or faith. The first hospital to be staffed by nuns in the English-speaking world, St Vincent's Dublin, was to be the model for numerous hospitals established by the Sisters of Charity.

In a brief trip to Ireland before taking up his position as Vicar Apostolate of New Holland and Van Dieman's Land in 1835, John Bede Polding met Mary Aikenhead and spoke to her of the pressing needs of the convict colony. She agreed to the establishment of a foundation in New South Wales to be financed by the local church and four years later five Sisters of Charity arrived in Sydney on Christmas Eve 1838. They were the first women religious in Australia.[1] *The sisters began their work in Parramatta supporting the women in the Female Factory, opening a school for the poor and visiting the sick and indigent. They established St Vincent's Hospital, the first Catholic hospital in Australia, at Woolloomoloo in 1855. The order gradually expanded and opened schools and hospitals not only in New South Wales but also in Tasmania, Victoria and Queensland. They continue their mission through the Sisters of Charity Foundation and St Vincent's Health Australia.*

1 See M. R. MacGinley, *A Dynamic of Hope – Institutes of Women Religious in Australia*. Darlinghurst, Crossing Press, 2002, 66.

Maryanne Confoy rsc

Maryanne Confoy was born in 1939 and entered the Sisters of Charity in 1956. She took her final vows in 1959. Her name in religion was Sister Mary Laurent.

Maryanne Confoy is a warm, entertaining, intelligent and sympathetic woman who is clearly comfortable in her own skin. A member of the Jesuit Theological College, Maryanne's courses at the United Faculty of Theology (UFT) at the University of Divinity in Melbourne are less about researching and writing, she said, than they are about being authentic. Maryanne teaches, she said, 'according to the needs of the student. One student came to my leadership class and I spent two-and-a-half hours with him listening to him and letting him know where I thought he was at. I said to him, "You can do an academic paper if you want to but do you have the courage to do the paper you should do?" If students can walk away knowing who they are, that's what it's about.'

Those who enroll in Maryanne's courses do so because of her reputation as a teacher who has the capacity to engage with her students in such a way that they find the courage to go beyond the external self and face the vulnerability beneath. She finds students want to experience for themselves the undoubted benefits of self-knowledge and to find deeper meaning in their lives. She said:

> I look at the way we age, and how we choose, or don't choose, to face life's challenges. Our way of being in relationship with ourselves, with others, and with God, is either emerging and transforming, or embedded in an understanding of ourselves and others and God that will not be moved.

Maryanne is aware that students can find it difficult that their grades do not depend on scholarship but on evidence that they have wrestled with themselves and the material she has given them.

> I had one man who had been a missionary in Africa. He had had a tough time and hated my courses because they were so challenging and I wouldn't give him a grade. I told him, 'I know you can write papers but I know you don't know who you are so, after every session, I want you to go home and draw. I don't want you to write a single word. He said he hated me and I said, 'I know. You also hate yourself. You're the angriest man I've met for a long time so go home

> and do that. That's the only way you're going to get a grade from me'. That man eventually allowed himself to receive and is now a dear friend.

That Maryanne has the emotional, spiritual and intellectual resources to run classes such as this is not only because she has studied the theory of psychological and spiritual development, but also because she understands herself so well. 'People tell me that over the past several years, I've become mellower and easier to live with, but it was hard for me to live with me!'

Maryanne was born in Melbourne in 1939 into a family that loved going to movies. Wednesday, Friday and Saturday nights were spent at the Plaza, the Circle or the Regal theatres in Essendon. For her two films stand out – *Beau Geste* and *Joan of Arc*. Both are about heroic grandeur, heroic giving, and heroic loving. Over the years, Maryanne said she has often joked about finding her vocation from films, especially from *Joan of Arc*. 'I was a very receptive young person,' she said, 'I was moved by heroism. These films would have formed my consciousness in ways that I was not cognitively aware of but was deeply, affectively, touched by.'

While Maryanne describes her home life as one which had the ups and down familiar to most families, 'it was by no means a happy family', she said, 'but we all knew where we stood, there were never any pretences. My family gave me the gift of radical honesty. You knew exactly where you stood with mum and dad. There was no fooling around, so that radical honesty was such that I was facing things in myself'. As she has aged she treasures the growth in friendship with her sister and 'the life I received through my nieces and nephews and their families'.

Educated by the Sisters of Charity at St Columba's in Essendon, where for her 'sport was more important than schoolwork', Maryanne enjoyed the mentoring of her music teacher and the experience of playing the violin in the school orchestra. Fellow students remember her as being 'a real wag' and were astonished when she entered the convent straight from school in 1956 at the age of 17, rather than taking up the Commonwealth scholarship she had been offered. Her disappointed parents took some time to accept her decision, but became reconciled to her choice as the years passed.

Maryanne joined seven other women ranging in age from 16 to the mid-40s at the Sisters of Charity novitiate at Wahroonga in Sydney. There were over 500 nuns in the order then, most of them teaching and nursing. Given the name of the third-century Roman saint and martyr, Laurence, Maryanne was trained as a primary teacher while in the novitiate and for several years taught in parish primary schools in Sydney and Melbourne. In the 1960s she finally had the opportunity to take up her scholarship and complete a Bachelor of Arts degree at the University of Melbourne. This enabled her to move into teaching secondary teaching, first at St John's, Clifton Hill, then at Catholic Ladies College, Eltham, and finally at her old school, St Columba's, in Essendon.

Happy and fulfilled in her religious life and in the classroom, Maryanne would almost certainly have continued to teach in secondary schools for the rest of her working life had it not been for Vatican II. In the wake of the Council, the Sisters of Charity, like all religious orders, were wrestling with the implications of renewal, including the formation of novices. Their rigid monastic-based approach was not suited to an active apostolic life in the modern world and Maryanne was asked by her congregational leader if she would do some study to prepare her for work in the spiritual development of the young women joining them. This request came at a time when one of Maryanne's friends in the order told her she no longer believed in God. Although Maryanne was shocked and distressed by her friend's revelation, this conversation proved to be a turning point in her life.

She and her friend had been in the novitiate together and Maryanne recalled that it had been a time almost 'bereft of intelligent discussion at any level'. Always an avid reader, she was told that novels, as important to her as films, were too risqué for a novice to read. 'When I thought of reading people like John of the Cross and Teresa of Avila I was told no, they're too mature for someone of your age.' After leaving the novitiate, however, and moving into teacher education, reading, including novels, became an acceptable part of Maryanne's professional life. As a young nun, she found not only mental stimulation but also spiritual guidance and human understanding in novels, especially in C.P. Snow's *Strangers and Brothers* series published between 1940 and 1970. 'Snow examined all the issues of life and human reality at the time,' she said, 'he was so familiar and so wise about the ways our life choices shape our lives'.

Snow's *Homecomings*, a novel in which the main character comes to a painful realisation of the causes of his failure in his relationship with his first wife, led Maryanne to reflect on the significant relationships in her own life. The novel impressed on her the importance of knowing and understanding yourself and of having genuine relationships. 'I remember thinking I must examine all my relationships and engage clinically to think where I am coming from and not just get caught up in a pious flow of language and ideas and Christian thinking. You really need to know who you are.' She refers to C.P. Snow as her first 'spiritual director' with C.S. Lewis as another formative influence.

Concern for her friend as well as soul-searching about what she could contribute to the spiritual formation of others encouraged Maryanne to consider the limitations of her capacity to support fellow religious in their faith journey. 'I tried to understand what the issues were when people were going through crises of faith,' she said. 'Were they having breakdowns, breakthroughs, or what?' She also remembers wondering whether a crisis of faith such as her friend's was spiritual or psychological. 'Is it a lack of belief in God or is it a stage, because at that time Erikson was in vogue and people were experiencing identity crises and I felt I needed to know more about what was happening to them,' she said. 'What interested me was the question of what made people tick in terms of understanding who God is and who they are in the changing experiences of their own lives.'

The work of the psychologist Erik Erikson, whose research on psychosocial development and the stages of human life was arousing considerable interest at the time, helped to clarify her understanding. In the early 1970s she went to Boston to study faith development and psychology and their interconnectedness in spiritual formation. Such a trip, unthinkable in her congregation before Vatican II, opened the door to previously unimaginable possibilities for Maryanne and set her life on a new, stimulating, intellectual and personal growth trajectory. Some of the celebrated people in the field of psychology were teaching in Boston at the time, including Erikson himself. Other 'hot shots,' said Maryanne, included James Fowler, who specialised in faith development, Lawrence Kohlberg, working in the field of moral development, the ego developmental researcher Robert Kegan and educator Thomas Groome.

To make best use of her precious time in America, Maryanne enrolled for two degrees, a Master's in Pastoral Ministry at Boston College and a Master's in Education, majoring in developmental psychology at Harvard Graduate School of Education. She did this without informing either institution that she was studying at the other. Entering before Vatican II she was used to working long days, fitting in her religious obligations with teaching and studying. Basking in the joy of learning, Maryanne had no problem with finding the mental and physical energy necessary to undertaking a heavy study program.

Towards the completion of her Boston College Master's studies Maryanne was invited to apply for their doctoral programme and had to confess that she had also completed the Harvard degree course requirements. 'Boston College was furious with me,' she admitted. 'They said if I was doing the degree properly I would not be able to do two degrees at once and it's true. They were right. I thought I was only going to be there 12 or 18 months and wanted to maximise my time.' She was given a choice: take her Harvard degree or transfer her credits toward a Boston College interdisciplinary doctorate in theology and education. She chose the latter. Her dissertation was entitled 'Adult Faith Development and Christian Religious Education'. 'I did very well, one doesn't say that, but I did.'

While she was studying, Maryanne lived with the Columban Sisters, an international missionary congregation.[2] 'They were more important to me than my studies,' she said. 'I had originally thought quite seriously about being a missionary,' she said, 'and the Columban Sisters were working directly with the poor in third world countries'. Because Maryanne was living in the provincial house, she met sisters coming and going from the various countries where they worked and saw at first hand 'their dedication and obvious love of the people they cared for'.

The 1970s was a time of what Maryanne called 'ferment, real ferment' among women's religious orders in the United States.[3] Staying with the Columban Sisters, said Maryanne, gave her a different focus from the feminism that seemed to be gripping many women religious, to the horror of the bishops. 'The Columban Sisters gave me stability,' said Maryanne, 'they lived simply and their values constantly challenged my values. I'd like to say I was changed by living with them, but I wasn't. Deep down I was still carrying my familiar values. We pay a price for authentic change which

2 The Columban Sisters, founded in Ireland in 1924, had arrived in the United States in 1930, and thereafter ministered in poor parishes and hospitals as well as establishing and maintaining a missionary outreach in South America and Asia.

3 See Kenneth Briggs, *Double Crossed Uncovering the Catholic Church's Betrayal of American Nuns*. New York, Doubleday, 2006.

takes time, suffering and the experience of letting go attitudes that hold us bound'.

Both the Sisters of Charity and the Columban Sisters had been founded to serve the poor, yet in comparing her own life to theirs, Maryanne claims the Columbans were 'for real' in ways she wasn't. She seriously considered transferring, so impressed was she by the way they worked and lived with the poor. Their influence on her can be seen in a story she tells about the religious habit, which was a major issue with religious at the time. Adaptation of the habit was in flux and the subject of much debate in communities. Maryanne was overweight and she liked the fact that 'the habit hid a multitude of sins', as she put it.

One morning, Maryanne went to the local drugstore and was dismayed at the sight of the long queue. The chemist, a good Irish Catholic, immediately beckoned her forward: 'Come in, Sister, come in!' He served her ahead of all those waiting in line and she remembers thinking, 'Thank goodness I don't have to wait!' Walking out of the shop with her purchases, it suddenly struck her that the habit was a mark of privilege. She saw that she needed to work on changing both her attitude to life, to privilege and to the habit. The Sisters of Charity had been given the freedom after Vatican II to choose whether or not to keep wearing the habit. After this experience in Boston, Maryanne changed to ordinary clothes.

During the years she spent living with the Columbans, Maryanne visited their sisters in various countries and gained first-hand insight into their missionary work. Two key memories stay with her. In Lima she visited a parish of squatters, located on a hillside. Dust permeated the homes carved into the hill. On entering one family dwelling she noticed a faded blue plastic flower decorating a mud-brick wall. 'The image of the mother's efforts in home-making has never left me,' she said.

On another occasion Maryanne was in Santiago, Chile, in the post-Pinochet period when an urgent request arrived at the convent from a sister living alone in a village on the remote high plains. Sister Sylvia needed a drum for a national feast day liturgy to be celebrated by the community she ministered to. For the first time the congregation would include local police, soldiers and ex-guerrillas who had been enemies for years. This particular celebration would be the first time they would all come together as a parish community in peace and prayer. As none of the Columbans in Santiago was free to take the drum, Maryanne volunteered. Before setting off on the 36-hour trip carrying the drum and a small backpack, she was advised to eat and drink as little as possible 'because there were no amenities for women'.

She travelled in a series of vehicles from a local bus to an old van. It was dark when she finally arrived and all the people were waiting to begin the liturgy. When she walked into the church, however, Maryanne thought she was hallucinating. Jesus and the twelve Apostles were seated round the altar table. A longer, closer look revealed that they were in fact life-sized wax figures. There hadn't been a resident priest in the village for several decades, so these wax figures held the memory of the Last Supper and the Eucharist. The community was deprived of the Eucharist because no ordained minister was available, but the loving ministry of the sisters in this, and other outlying and poor communities continued. The situation this community faced, and others like it, has had a lifelong impact on Maryanne.

On the completion of her studies in 1980, Maryanne left the Columban Sisters, feeling privileged by what she had seen and learned during her four years with them. She maintains her close friendship with the sisters, and stays with the community when she is in America. 'Boston is as much of my life, or is more of my life, than parts of Melbourne, Adelaide and Sydney,' she said.

Back in Australia Maryanne began to teach theology and ministry at Yarra Theological Union (YTU). 'I taught courses on faith and the human life cycle and they used to call them the bicycle courses,' she said. Others had met her congregation's need for someone to work in formation and Maryanne was free to focus on teaching and other possibilities. She became part of an accrediting group visiting World Vision projects in India and Bangladesh, and led a university group studying Chinese culture and language in Nanjing. Travel to Fiji and Tonga for the South Pacific Association of Theological Schools opened Maryanne to aspects of life in Oceania that enabled her to see the particular difficulties faced by women who ministered in all Christian denominations.

In the 1980s at YTU Maryanne continued to use novels and films in her classes to explore theology and ministry through human drama. One of her favourite authors at this time was Morris West. To her surprise she received a phone call from the National Library in Canberra inviting her to write a monograph celebrating his work. When she asked why she had been approached, she was astonished to hear that Morris West had suggested her himself. 'Morris West drew me to him', she said. 'One of my former students, Kim Power, was West's niece and it seemed she had told him about my theology course in which I regularly quoted his writings'.

Maryanne's monograph, *Morris West: Wandering Scholar and Restless Spirit* was published in 1997. West later invited her to write his biography.[4] They got on 'well enough', she said. However, when Maryanne asked in a telephone call if, when quoting him, she might change his language so that it was non-exclusive, West hung up on her. Maryanne took it philosophically: 'That was fine, because we were both feisty'. *Morris West – Literary Maverick* appeared in 2005, six years after West died.[5]

Much as she enjoyed writing, teaching remained Maryanne's major focus. In 1991 she was invited to Boston College to teach Thomas Groome's courses while he was on sabbatical.[6] The following year Mary Boys, another distinguished Boston College professor, asked Maryanne to cover her courses.[7] Maryanne then continued as a member of the faculty. 'I think they forgot I was there,' she said.

After four years teaching in Boston, where she lived again with the Columban Sisters, Maryanne was invited by the Jesuits in Melbourne to teach in the United Faculty of Theology (UFT) and eventually to engage in Jesuit pastoral formation. She was the first woman to take up such a position, one that she still holds. The invitation was not only a compliment to her skills as a teacher but to the effectiveness of her work.

Where many sisters have moved out of convents to live either on their own or with one or two others in small apartments or units, Maryanne lives in the Sisters of Charity's convent in Fitzroy, in inner city Melbourne. Known as St Vincent's Convent, it is a fine Victorian villa five minutes walk from

---

4 Maryanne Confoy, *Morris West: Wandering Scholar and Restless Spirit.* Canberra, Friends of the National Library of Australia, 1992 and Maryanne Confoy, *Morris West: A Writer and a Spirituality*. North Blackburn,Vic, Harper Collins, 1997.

5 Maryanne Confoy, *Morris West: Literary Maverick,* Milton. Qld, John Wiley, 2005.

6 Irish-born Thomas Groome is Professor of Theology and Religious Education at Boston College's School of Theology and Ministry.

7 Mary Boys is the author of several books, including *Maps and Visions: Educating for Faith*, Harper & Row, 1989.

the hospital the Sisters of Charity founded in 1893.[8] She enjoys living with the sisters, believing that community in its various forms is the essence of Christian identity and vocation. 'I really love being part of the community of the Sisters of Charity and I really love being part of the community of religious women and men,' she said. Asked by her students after Vatican II why, when so many women were leaving religious life, she chose to stay, she thought deeply about her life as a religious. 'It's because of the significance of the lives I've seen lived…they are really altruistic, they are really self-transcending lives.'

The teaching of Vatican II, especially on the priesthood of all believers, confirmed her conviction that her married sister too was living a loving and self-transcending family life, 'but marriage and family life makes sense to people whereas the celibate religious life does not make sense,' she said. 'It's a paradox.'

> If the vowed religious life does make sense then we have to ask whether we are living it authentically: religious may just be living a comfortable single professional or ministerial life. Religious life and ministry has a deeper challenge than that – it offers a witness of faithfulness to service in the present and to belief in eternal life; it is a witness to the gospel message of Christ, to working on behalf of the mission of God in our world, now and to come.

Maryanne thinks of Vatican II as pivotal not only to expanding the possibilities in her own life but also to the way she teaches.

> It enabled people to understand the call to holiness for all people, in the ordinariness of their lives, as opposed to classes of elitist or privileged holiness. That's why my courses are directed in the way they are – to help us understand the Godliness of our ordinary life, the holiness of who we are in our limits as well as our strengths, in the fact that in our life journey we all limp a little and need each other's support and care. We're all trying to love a bit better and to live more authentically, and we need each other's support along the journey.

Religious women, Maryanne believes, work as a bridge between the laity and the institutional Church leaders: 'That's a contribution we can make because we are neither ordained nor lay,' she said. 'We can be bridge-builders because we're not members of the ecclesiastical system. If I were to be told that I could be ordained tomorrow I would say no thanks. That's not

8 St Vincent's Hospital is now managed by St Vincent's Health.

my calling. We have a lot of freedom for ministry in our lives as apostolic religious women.'

Maryanne's work with The Way, a community for homeless men in Fitzroy, is an important long-term commitment for her, something she experiences as keeping her 'real'. But being open to 'the new' in life is also important to Maryanne. She accepted an invitation by the Christian Brothers to be part of a new direction in educational leadership as a council member of Edmund Rice Education Australia in 2007.[9] In 2013, she was appointed to the national board of St Vincent's Health Australia, the largest not-for-profit Catholic health and aged care provider in the country: a considerable commitment.

To undertake this work she resigned from her position as director of Kilbride, a venture that had commenced in 2000 when Margaret Cassidy, then province leader of the Brigidine Sisters, asked Maryanne if she would do something with a property the Brigidines owned in Albert Park. It was a large, imposing but run-down building near the beach in the heart of one of Melbourne's bayside suburbs. Originally a school, then an adult education centre, it had not been used for two years. Maryanne gathered a strong team of helpers around her and slowly, organically, the centre evolved and within a short time was offering a range of courses and workshops that not only included practical spirituality for everyday and human development, but also creative arts, living skills, love of life, music, cooking, and yoga. Alcoholics Anonymous and Gamblers Anonymous groups have a home there. 'We wanted to be counter-cultural in every way,' she said. 'Kilbride wasn't about money but community. Anyone could come in off the street and know that they could sit in the library, read a book, have a cup of tea or use the loo - without any cost. In the ten years of our "open house" policy our trust was never abused'.

After about 30 years at Boston College, Maryanne resigned from her teaching commitments there, but kept her connection with friends and colleagues and anticipates going to America for conferences to keep up her academic life for several years ahead. Being open to the new in ministry does not mean letting go the familiar in her life. Her friendships continue to be important to her as she ages. 'I'm challenged by my friends,' she said,

9 Edmund Rice Education Australia is a PJP established by the Christian Brothers in 2007 to manage their schools in Australia.

'and that obviously seeps in to my relationship with God. My understanding of who God is changes and deepens as I understand better who I am and what my vocation is about: that's the journey into truth and the fullness of living and loving in the reality of our time.'

Maryanne is sought after as a spiritual director and giver of retreats and workshops. The first to approach her for spiritual direction many years ago was a Cistercian monk. She refused initially, but eventually agreed in response to his persistence. She has since worked with other religious and lay people although she does not see herself as a conventional spiritual director. 'If you want to talk to me,' she tells those who come to her, 'I am happy to be present, to listen and respond to you and we will journey together as companions in the presence of God, learning to listen and live more deeply'.

In the early 1990s, when she was giving a workshop in Grafton, Maryanne met a Mercy Sister whose cancer and diabetes had led to several amputations, yet in spite of her suffering she still found joy and purpose in life. After listening to her and observing her, Maryanne commented, 'You've got something and I want to know what it is'. The sister laughingly said she didn't know what Maryanne was talking about. Two weeks later the sister sent a card in which she wrote, 'there are two things we need in life, the courage to live and the courage to love'. 'This was a woman who was not afraid of living and loving,' said Maryanne. Neither is she.

Sisters of the Presentation of the Blessed Virgin Mary

Honoria Nagle, always known as Nano, founded the Presentation Sisters in Ireland in 1775. Born in County Cork in 1718, her family belonged to the Catholic gentry and she and her sister Ann were sent to France in secret to be educated. They returned in 1746 on their father's death and lived with their mother in Dublin. Shocked by the poverty of the city, Nano returned to Paris to enter the Ursulines to pray for the poor but her spiritual director encouraged her to return to Ireland and educate them instead. In defiance of the law and in complete secrecy, she opened a small school at Cove Lane in Cork in 1754. Within three years she had seven schools, five for girls and two for boys, with more than 200 children. She visited the sick and elderly after school and became known as the lady with the lantern. The lantern later became the symbol of the Presentation Sisters.

Realising she needed help, Nano invited the Ursulines from Paris to take over her work, using her wealth to provide them with a convent in Cork in 1771. The Ursulines were enclosed, so this solution could not work. In 1775 Nano, at the age of 57, formed the Society of Charitable Instruction of the Sacred Heart of Jesus in Cork with constitutions specially suited to the work of educating and supporting the poor; the name was later changed to Sisters of the Presentation of the Blessed Virgin Mary. By the time the Relief Bill of 1782 allowed Catholics to open schools, Nano Nagle had already laid the foundations of an education system on which other great founders such as Catherine McAuley, Edmund Rice and Mary Aikenhead would build. She used her not inconsiderable personal wealth to support her schools and works of charity but her vision of uncloistered women met with such opposition from the Irish hierarchy, that following her death in 1784, her sisters accepted enclosure and solemn vows, both of which they believed were necessary for their continued existence. In 2000 Nano Nagle was voted Irish Woman of the Millennium in recognition of her work as a pioneer of female education in Ireland.

The first Presentation Sisters to come to Australia from Ireland arrived in Tasmania in 1866, with further foundations following in St Kilda, Victoria in 1873, Wagga, New South Wales in 1874, Lismore, New South Wales in 1886, Western Australia in 1891 and Queensland 1900. From these nineteenth century foundations, the sisters spread across Australia, attracting large numbers of young women to join them. Membership peaked at 850 in the mid-1960s. The Presentations Sisters continue to be one of the four largest women's religious congregations in Australia in terms of their membership, and the number of schools and other institutions under their control.

In 1946 the major superiors of the seven Presentation congregations in Australia agreed to common constitutions that were approved by Pius XII in 1958 in the name of the Society of the Australian Congregations of the Presentation of the Blessed Virgin Mary. In 1966 five sisters from the Society went to Papua New Guinea and formed a community of Australian and Melanesian Presentation Sisters.

At the time of publication, the Australian Society of Presentation Sisters is a federation of six autonomous congregations across Australia and PNG. Through the International Presentation Association (IPA), the sisters have special consultative status at the United Nations via the UN Economic and Social Council and Department of Public Information, with one full-time staff member serving the Presentation Sisters based throughout the world.

Bernadette Keating pvbm

Bernadette Keating was born in 1946 and entered the Presentation Sisters Victoria in 1966. She made her final vows in 1974. Her name in religion was Sister Mary Edmund.

When Bernadette Keating was first elected congregational leader of Presentation Sisters Victoria in 2000 she found her main role was pastoral. Most of the sisters, of whom there were about 100, were actively engaged in some form of ministry. Bernadette kept in touch with them, visited them, and ensured they had all the resources they needed for their work and for their personal and spiritual wellbeing. When, in 2009, she was elected leader once more she found that there had been significant change. The main needs were not outside the congregation but within. The average age of the sisters, now numbering 69, was 75; the youngest was in her mid 50s. Many were still involved in ministries, but most were reducing their workload and a significant number needed care. However, all the sisters wanted to ensure that the Presentation charism of their schools and community ministries would survive.

After considerable prayer and reflection, Bernadette and her newly elected leadership team concluded that their task was two-fold: the ongoing care of the sisters as they aged and new governance structures for the congregation. The sisters' Identity Statement declares that 'Aware of both our gifts and vulnerability we Presentation women desire a deep communion with God, with one another, and with the whole of creation. Touched by the suffering of our world, we are called to be women of hope, nurturing the flame of life wherever we are'.

The challenge was daunting: how to prepare a blueprint for the future of Presentation Sisters Victoria which respected their vision and identity, and took account of the likelihood that within 40 years they would be no more. 'We understand it will come to an end in Victoria,' said Bernadette, 'but currently we have people resources, we have a voice, we're educated women. How do we set this up for the future so that we are still enabling life--because that's where we come from?'

Bernadette sparkles when she talks about her time as congregational leader. It has its challenges and involves a great deal of work, but the satisfaction of putting dialogue and discernment into practice has been profound. A positive and enthusiastic person by nature, she grew up in Dandenong in the 1950s when it was a small country town where everybody knew her father, Tom, 'the stalwart of the church' and her remarkable mother, Mary. Mary had her six children in ten years, coped with the loss of her third child at eighteen months, and cared for her brother-in-law who, having broken his back in an accident, was paralysed.

When Bernadette told her mother at sixteen she wanted to enter religious life, she insisted she wait. Bernadette worked as a student teacher in a primary school, spent one year training and another year teaching. Later, as a young nun, when others were leaving in the post-Vatican II years, she realised how important the period before entering had been. 'I was glad that I had those years where I made my own money, and went out with boys and went to the dances, to the YCW, and all of the things we did,' she laughed. 'I had the experience of living independently and running my own life and from that place I was able to enter much more freely and sensibly.' Throughout this time she never lost the conviction that she wanted to give her life to God, but she was unsure of the how and the where. 'I felt quite a call to the missionary vocation,' she said, 'and I also felt a call to the contemplative vocation, and I thought, how do I work this out?'

A conversation with a priest helped Bernadette to decide. He suggested that most people enter a congregation they know, adding, 'You don't have to stay, you can always change'. Bernadette knew neither missionaries, nor any contemplatives, but she did know the Presentation Sisters from her years at St Mary's in Dandenong and O'Neill College in Elsternwick (later absorbed into Star of the Sea, Gardenvale). With hindsight, Bernadette believes she would have been happy taking up any of the three options: active, contemplative or missionary, as each to a degree incorporates the other. 'We're all missionary wherever we are,' she said, 'and we in Australia have started a mission in New Guinea which involves education, pastoral and medical work'. Contemplation was always an important part of the Presentation sisters' religious lives, she added, and has observed that as the community in Victoria ages, it is becoming more so. 'We were active for so long and certainly always took time for prayer, but we now recognise that prayer is the storehouse of the richness of our faith and our spirituality,' she said.

Bernadette entered religious life in 1966, the year after Vatican II ended, but changes in formation were yet to come. 'Our novice mistress was of the old school,' said Bernadette, 'and we couldn't understand a lot of what she said and I remember thinking the whole premise of the novitiate was to test our intention'. Bernadette and her contemporaries have often since talked about the impact the novitiate regime had on them, and why they stayed.

> We concluded that one of the most important aspects about it for us was the way we looked after each other. We were going through this together and it created very strong bonds. Yes it was difficult but it also forced us to strengthen our faith. For example, we spent long periods in the chapel wondering what we were supposed to be doing but it actually gave us enough reflection time to really ask ourselves, 'Is this for me?'

A year into Bernadette's novitiate, Mother Eymard Temby, a famous educator who once taught Germaine Greer at Star of the Sea College, became mother general. She often gave talks to the novices and in fact was one of four women religious in Australia who were then travelling in Australia and New Zealand talking to religious congregations about Vatican II. 'They spearheaded the acceptance of Vatican II and developed a new vision of where religious life could be going,' said Bernadette.

Under Mother Eymard's guidance, a great shift was happening in the congregation. 'We read the Council documents and it was exciting,' recalled Bernadette. 'Life was just opening up and we could see the possibilities. We were able to experiment with the liturgy and ministry, and religious education was changing from learning the catechism to really looking at what faith means, how to live and relate to others.' Mother Eymard read widely, said Bernadette, 'and had a real sense of where the Church needed to be moving'. Outside the congregation, she spoke to groups of Catholic laywomen about the importance of Vatican II, urging them to embrace change. 'The Holy Spirit is revealing some very significant truths here,' she reportedly told them.[1]

For religious women, explained Bernadette, one of the big changes was getting to know other religious at the year long course at Assumption Institute coordinated by Mercy sister Mary Duffy in 1969. The course was designed for newly professed religious who had been formed in old style novitiates. 'We had top people from the seminary and theological college

---

1 Christine Wallace, *Germaine Greer, Untamed Shrew, New York*. Faber & Faber, 1999, 13.

including Jim Scullion on scripture, Wally Black on moral theology and Greg Manly on liturgy,' said Bernadette. 'It was fantastic, but more than anything it started to break down barriers between congregations.' The breaking down of these barriers paved the way to the friendships that exist now between different congregations. 'Would we 100 years or even 50 years ago have considered doing anything with the Brigidines as we are now? No, we would have said, because they're not us!'

The Vatican Council brought a renewed understanding of their founder, Nano Nagle, who put herself and her own family at risk by setting up small schools in eighteenth century Ireland. 'She was a can-do woman,' said Bernadette. 'She saw the need to work among people rather than be in a convent with people coming in. The sad thing is that after her death, her sisters decided to accept enclosure.' They lived enclosed lives up till the time Bernadette entered. 'The spirit gets through,' she said. 'Vatican II blew the doors open and we're out with the people again.'

A revolution in her spiritual life took place for Bernadette just before she made her final vows.[2]

> When we came up for final vows we were offered a directed retreat. This was something new. Before we had always had preached retreats. I refused to do it but was promptly put in my place and I did it with great internal resistance. It was six days of total silence but for one daily meeting with the director. He would ask me how I was going. 'Fine.' How was my prayer life? 'Fine.' When I went back to the classroom the next week I was astonished to find myself on another planet. The fact of having that much time of silent prayer alone with God took me to a beautiful deep place. It said to me that, given the time, you do move to a deeper place in relation to God.

Working in Presentation primary schools in the 1970s as a teacher and later as a school principal, Bernadette saw the changes brought about by the Whitlam Government; the introduction of more lay teachers, and the shift in focus among the sisters to religious education. At the same time she did an arts degree part-time at Monash University, finally being given a year to study full time in 1982.

The move to alternative ministries 'among the people' happened slowly and Bernadette was one of the first to move out of teaching. 'I went on what we called the frontier group out to Melton South,' she said. 'It was a new

2 Between five and nine years after first profession, final vows are taken for life, after discernment and acceptance by the congregational leadership.

suburb with no infrastructure at all except a school and a new parish priest. Three of us offered our services. I stayed two years and loved working with families and taking Rite of Christian Initiation (RCIA) groups.' Bernadette gave up the possibility of an honours year at university to go to Melton but didn't hesitate to do so, since she wanted 'to give my whole self to that new part of my life'.

From Melton, Bernadette went to Clayton in what proved to be another pioneering move. When principal of the Presentation school in North Dandenong, she had helped Corpus Christi Seminary with its pastoral programme. This was clearly successful because in 1986, after two years in Melton, she was invited to meet the rector, George Pell, with a view to joining the staff. The Melbourne diocesan hierarchy felt that Vatican II required more input from the rest of the Church in the formation of young men for the priesthood, she explained. She told George Pell that while she had some skills she could bring to the work 'if you don't want me, I'll be thrilled because I'm perfectly happy working in a parish'. Bernadette was the first woman in Victoria to be appointed to the staff, the only woman in the seminary among about 70 men.

> The thing that amazed me when I first went in was how nervous the students were. I'm thinking, how can they be nervous of me? But after a while I could see why, because I changed the culture. As a woman I would interact with them and expect straight communication and it wasn't like that in their male boys-club environment with its jostling for supremacy and dominance.

Teaching had given Bernadette confidence, she acknowledged. 'I could speak up for myself and say what I thought and that was the value of having a female voice on the staff,' she said. Her confidence led Bernadette to go to George Pell when, on two occasions, she realised things were not right. 'I can't remember what the issues were but they were important enough for me to approach him. He was surprised and asked how it was that I knew this and he didn't. I pointed out that the students would hide it from him. George was very respectful of my opinion.'

While working as a pastoral formator at Corpus Christi, a challenge in itself, Bernadette had her first experience of leadership within her congregation when she was elected as one of the team.[3] 'Both these roles were totally new

3 A pastoral formator in the seminary prepares young men to offer the spiritual, emotional and practical support, care and guidance required for parish work.

to me and I felt played out in the end,' she said. Fulfilling another post-Vatican II possibility, when her four-year term was over in 1991, she went to the University of Loyola in Chicago to undertake a Masters of Pastoral Studies and a Masters of Religious Education for Adults. 'The advantage of being part of a religious group,' she acknowledges, 'is that they were able to then keep me for two years overseas while I did that study and it was absolutely wonderful'. For the first time in her religious life, Bernadette had no responsibilities and took full advantage of the time; well aware of the privilege she had been given. 'It's often occurred me to that if I had kept going as a lay teacher I either would have married and had a family or been single and looked after myself,' she said. 'Where would I ever have had the resources to study overseas with others keeping everything going in my absence?'

While studying full time during the week, her weekends were often spent doing workshops on RCIA, or formation for the priesthood and family ministry. 'The Irish sisters and priests were great,' she said. 'We'd hire a car and head off, four or five of us, and do our weekend workshop and then back for classes the next week. It was an opening, refreshing sort of time.'

As part of her pastoral studies, Bernadette undertook a preaching course, making herself a promise that if ever she was asked to preach, she would say yes. The opportunity has arisen several times within the congregation and at paraliturgies, but only once in church when she was invited to give the homily at Easter. 'A number of women approached me afterwards and said it was wonderful to hear a woman speaking.' Bernadette is philosophical about what Pope Francis is saying about the place of women within the church. 'It's early days in his pontificate and that will be a very hard one to shift,' she said. She believes there is a lot of fear still among many churchmen faced with strong, assured religious women such as Sandra Schneiders, Joan Chittister and Elizabeth Johnson. 'Really these are mighty women,' she said.

> We are sometimes concerned when we hear that the great majority of young men entering seminaries in recent years have a distinct tendency towards a pre-Vatican II mindset which focuses on formal liturgical styles, old fashioned clerical attire and hierarchical titles rather than accentuating a pastoral approach to people. It will be interesting to note the effect of Pope Francis' emphasis on mercy and pastoral sensitivity.

Being in Chicago was transformational for Bernadette. She felt 'psychologically strengthened' and with the depth of knowledge and assurance her studies had given her, 'felt I was really able to offer more'.

After many years of happily living in what were sometimes quite large communities of women, she had also learned to live alone. She was not sure how she would readapt to community life on returning to Melbourne but, to her delight, she was asked to help run the Presentation Sisters' Family Centre in Balnarring, where she, Genevieve Jeffery and the dog formed a very happy community. At the same time she lectured part-time on pastoral ministry and homilies at the Catholic Theological College and was on the pastoral coordination team at Corpus Christi College.

In 1995 Bernadette's life once more changed direction, when she was elected deputy leader of Presentation Sisters Victoria, during which time she also worked as a facilitator. Her term ended in 2004. Apart from a year or so after 2004, she has held leadership roles ever since. She was president of Presentation leaders in Victoria for two years, president of Presentation leaders in Australia for two years, and president of the Australian Society of Presentations for five years, including president of the International Presentation Association. In many ways she epitomises the significant shifts that have taken place in religious congregations since Vatican II. Her deputy, Patricia Tully, described Bernadette's style as 'open and inclusive'. 'Leadership in the past would have been authoritative and hierarchical,' she said. 'Bernadette is a strong leader, able to make the hard decisions. She listens to ideas and will change if need be.'

Patricia, a previous congregational leader herself, has found it a privilege being one of Bernadette's team and admires her level of preparation for meetings, her inclusion of lay people, where once only sisters would have been employed, and her strong sense of justice. 'Leadership is now a totally different way of looking at things and being,' she said. Joan Chittister, one of Bernadette's 'mighty women', captures the essence of this 'different way': 'Authority functions best when it brings direction and unity to a group, when it raises the questions that the group needs to face. Authority does not exist to give orders. It exists to facilitate the group's ability to facilitate itself'.[4]

The people resources of Presentation Sisters Victoria cover a range of ministries. One sister is a trained psychotherapist who sees people professionally at a sum they can afford. One works with the Smith Family, another works in the educational arm of Foundation House, two are

4 Joan Chittister in Diarmuid O'Murchu, *Consecrated Religious Life – The Changing Paradigms*. New York, Orbis, 2005, 139.

chaplains in schools and one is a prison chaplain.[5] One sister, who began an art programme for the homeless in St Kilda in the late 1980s is now in her 80s, and continues with the programme in nursing homes. Others work in the two major Presentation community missions in Victoria, the Family Centre in Balnarring and Wellsprings for Women in Dandenong, while a further two sisters work in Papua New Guinea alongside about 30 local Presentation Sisters in schools, hospitals and parishes.

Open to everyone, not only Catholics, the Balnarring Family Centre comprises six houses near the beach and offers respite for families. The waiting list is long and consists of people who are, in general, referred by agencies such as social worker groups or the Catholic Education Office. Wellsprings for Women in Dandenong was begun by Sister Ann Halpin in 1994 as a drop-in centre for women dealing with issues such as domestic violence, marriage breakdown, mental illness or unemployment. A holistic programme, addressing the physical, emotional, spiritual, recreational, educational and skill-based needs of the women is in operation, and the Centre now opens five days a week catering for around 300 women, including many from refugee and asylum-seeker families.

In addition to these two ministries, Presentation Sisters Victoria own two schools – Star of the Sea College in Gardenvale and Presentation College Windsor. While the school campuses occupy very valuable land, the sisters, who receive a small rent from each school, are unwilling to part with them. 'We could have given our schools to the Catholic Education Office,' said Bernadette. 'We talked to the principals and board chairpersons, and they begged us not to do that. They wanted to keep the unique character and spirit of the schools, and felt that if they were handed over to the CEO they would just be one among many.' Since entrusting their schools to the lay staff and Boards, the Presentation Sisters have watched the growing interest displayed among staff and students in the Presentation charism and in the founder, Nano Nagle. 'It is even stronger in our schools now than when we were there,' Bernadette admitted.

5 The Smith Family is an independent children's charity helping disadvantaged Australian children to get the most out of their education so that they can create a better future for themselves. Foundation House is the home of the Victorian Foundation for the Survivors of Torture established in 1987 in Melbourne, and is a world leader in supporting people who have been subjected to torture or trauma in their country of origin.

The members of Bernadette's elected leadership team of four each have their own area of responsibility and, from the outset of their term, have met weekly. At the beginning of each meeting they pray. 'It's a sharing of faith and is extraordinarily rich,' said Bernadette. 'We are responsible for where this congregation is going from now on, so we need to be able to develop the spirit and principles on which what we do will rest. In addition to our meetings we have times of reflection away together four times each year. We support each other.'

One of the first things that Bernadette did as congregational leader was to appoint an advisory group with legal and financial expertise to help the sisters through the complex changes facing them. This group comprises four laypeople that know the Presentation sisters well. Part of the strategy involves providing 'for the ongoing needs for wellbeing and quality of life of each sister'. To achieve this continued planning 'for appropriate housing and accommodation for the future' as well as 'maintaining suitable holiday accommodation' is required. The implementation of this strategy involves rationalising the congregation's many properties, some of which are rundown and unsuited to smaller communities of ageing women, although several of them, like their historic convent in St Kilda, are places to which many sisters are attached.

The first goal of the strategic plan looked at the life and mission of Presentation Sisters Victoria, the second was a bold call to 'develop a process and structure to manage the change from PBVM authority to authority by other persons of trust'.[6] This meant 'developing a collaborative model of governance that will encompass each of our heritage ministries' and the involvement of people outside the congregation to ensure that its work did not die'. What Bernadette and her team had in mind, though not set out in the plan, was setting up a Public Juridic Person (PJP), a separate and autonomous legal entity established under Canon Law that 'provides the authority and status for specific works or organisations to operate in the name of the Catholic Church'.[7]

A PJP is an aggregate of persons or things. In 2011 the congregation responded to an invitation from the Brigidine Sisters to join with them in setting up Kildare Ministries as a PJP. The Brigidines, like the Presentations,

6 Presentation of the Blessed Virgin Mary is the formal name of the congregation.

7 Michael Doyle, 'PJPs Explained: A Question and Answer Guide to Public Juridic Persons'. Catholic Religious Victoria Education Committee.

had long been aware that declining numbers would mean that they had to prepare for a future when one of three possibilities had to be faced, as Louise Cleary, current provincial leader of the Brigidines, put it: 'One – do we close our schools? Two – do we give our schools to the Diocese? Three – do we set up a new PJP?'

Until recently, PJPs within the Catholic Church consisted of parishes, dioceses or religious congregations. Since they required to be registered by local bishops, a conference of bishops, or the Vatican, national and international congregations founded under the authority of Rome tend to seek registration with Rome while congregations founded under the authority of a local bishop tend to seek registration locally. The Good Samaritans, for example, established a PJP in 2012 under the authority of Cardinal George Pell in Sydney since their founder John Bede Polding, had been Sydney's first archbishop.[8] However, setting up PJPs has become more widespread: 'There are now 17 or 18 worldwide,' Louise Cleary said, 'mostly clusters of health care facilities.' In Australia, two, the Mary Aikenhead Ministries and Mercy Partners, also include schools. This diversity complicates the process. The Brigidine and Presentation Sisters undertook at least two years of full time work before they were ready to launch Kildare Ministries in March 2014, which involved both congregations relinquishing the governance and their separate assets to Kildare Ministries and forming a board of trustees with full responsibility to act in their names within the terms of its statutes. Once established, a PJP operates independently of its founding body and can only be closed down by its registering authority.

As Mary Wright, a canon lawyer and Loreto sister explained, 'the Church doesn't often have something innovative like this happening and it is making the bishops nervous. A bishop only has authority in his own diocese and no one bishop has authority over every diocese. A big PJP can operate across a number of diocese and may well have a greater income than that of most bishops, which makes it powerful.'

A significant aspect of PJPs is the role played in them by the laity. With its emphasis on the priesthood of all believers, Vatican II invited lay people to participate more fully in the life of the Church. This has been marked in the years since the Council, especially in the past decade. Pope Benedict XVI was supportive of this change, arguing that the laity 'must no longer be

8 See brief history of the Good Samaritan Sisters on page 37.

viewed as 'collaborators' of the clergy but truly recognised as 'co-responsible' for the Church's being and action, thereby fostering the consolidation of a mature and committed laity'.[9] New PJPs such as Kildare Ministries offer lay trustees just such an opportunity. Currently, added Mary Wright, trustees on the boards of PJPs have been appointed by the members of the religious congregations that set them up. Only time will tell how boards will perform when the religious are no more.

'This venture is a leap of faith,' said Louise Cleary. 'It is an exercise in letting go of the past and of trust and belief in the future.' She has found it an interesting process working with Bernadette and the trustees. 'We've been looking at the deep story of our congregations, the story behind the facts,' she said, 'and have found remarkable similarities in our heritage. There is a 30 year gap between the founding of both congregations, both were founded in Ireland, both in the country and both for education – so we have a lot in common and a lot of distinct differences too, but this PJP will develop its own charism, its own identity'. Both Presentation and Brigidine Sisters have historic links to Kildare in Ireland; they found the name Kildare Ministries- Kildare meaning 'church of the oak' in Irish, thus reflecting strength, spirit and longevity - appropriate for their new venture.

Ever practical, Bernadette adds that one of the reasons for setting up the new governance structures was that the sisters wanted to do it 'while we still have choices and not when we are forced to do it'. When they felt the time was right, they held a gathering of all the sisters, presenting each one with a copy of the strategic plan. The response was overwhelmingly positive. 'Nobody objected or complained,' said Bernadette. 'It's been wonderful.'

Being part of the evolution these changes within Presentation Sisters Victoria has affirmed Bernadette, her team, and her community, in their understanding of themselves. Every now and then, they have the opportunity to acknowledge and celebrate this, such as the occasion in mid-March 2014 when eight of the sisters celebrated jubilees of 50, 60 and 70 years in religious life. 'One of my great privileges as congregational leader,' said Bernadette, 'was to reflect on these extraordinary women…who have shown us Presentation life, and to say to them…you have been the way, the truth and the light, inspiring and encouraging all of us'.

9 'PJPs Explained'.

The Contemplative Orders

Benedictines

Jamberoo Abbey is a Benedictine monastery that traces its origins to the way of life established by St Benedict in sixth century Italy. Influenced by the Desert Fathers and Mothers and monks such as Caesarius of Arle and Cassian, and selectively by the anonymous writer of The Rule of the Master, Benedict's method for living the monastic life is widely accepted as the cornerstone of western monasticism. From the beginning, women as well as men separately lived the contemplative life according to the Rule of St Benedict. The first group of female Benedictines lived in a monastery a short distance from Benedict's own at Monte Cassino. The Abbess was Scholastica, thought to have been Benedict's twin sister. Foundational to Benedict's Rule is prayer, work and lectio divina *or spiritual reading. The Rule encourages mutual respect and kindness to those within the monastic community and hospitality to those without.*

Benedictine nuns came to Australia in 1848 at the invitation of Archbishop John Bede Polding, himself a Benedictine monk from Downside Abbey near Bath in Somerset. Polding arrived in Sydney in 1835 with a vision of the colony as an Abbey-Diocese with Benedictine monks and nuns as its praying heart, himself as their Abbot. It was an unrealistic dream, not least because attracting monastic recruits from England was difficult and colonial Catholics were predominantly Irish and unsympathetic to English Catholicism. Nonetheless Polding persisted and with a small group of monks established the monastery and cathedral of St Mary's in Sydney. After his return visit to Europe in 1847, two English Benedictine nuns accompanied Polding to the colony for the purpose of founding a monastery for women. Scholastica (Jane) Gregory, was born in 1817, and had entered the Princethorpe Priory in Warwickshire to be prepared to give her life to the Australian mission; her brother Henry was Prior of St Mary's, Sydney. Magdalen (Constancia) le Clerc was born in 1798, and had been a member of the community at Stanbrook Abbey, Yorkshire, for more than 20 years. She had been Jane Gregory's teacher.

A year after arriving in Australia, and while they lived at St Mary's Monastery, Polding acquired a property for them on the banks of the Parramatta River. They called the residence Subiaco, the name given to the cave in Italy where Benedict once lived as a hermit. They soon opened a school for girls. Although the nuns at Subiaco and monks at St Mary's were regarded by Polding as 'members of one family' with himself as the head, in reality the nuns were disadvantaged: their revenue went to St Mary's while they lived on a small stipend in addition to doing the monks' sewing and washing.[1] *The school was closed in 1921 when papal enclosure was imposed on the community. The nuns survived by selling off portions of land and, during the Second World War, by making altar breads for army chaplains with the Australian and American forces.*

When the land around Subiaco was claimed for industry, the nuns built a new monastery in West Pennant Hills on the edges of Sydney where they lived until encroaching suburbia adversely affected their way of life.[2] *With the proceeds of the sale of their property, the community bought 80 hectares of rainforest on the Jamberoo Mountain Pass on the eastern slopes of the Great Dividing Range, about 20 minutes drive from Kiama on the south coast of New South Wales. Here they built a new monastery with accommodation for guests, men as well as women, who, irrespective of their religious faith, are seeking spiritual renewal. As well as offering group and individual retreats and spiritual direction, the nuns make a range of hand-decorated candles that are sold in the Abbey shop or on line. They also sell spiritual books.*

1 See R.M. MacGinley, *A Dynamic of Hope Institutes of Women Religious in Australia.* Crossing Press, 2002, 75-80.

2 See the Jamberoo website www.jamberooabbey.org.au.

Joanna Bagot osb

Felicity Bagot was born in 1952 and entered the Benedictines in 1995. She took her solemn vows in 2001. Her name in religion is Sister Joanna.

In late 2006, the Benedictines of Jamberoo Abbey, Australia's oldest enclosed order of nuns, gave ABC television's religious programme, *Compass*, unprecedented access to their enclosed, contemplative monastic way of life. In October the following year, five women of different ages, circumstances and beliefs, plus a small film crew, lived with the nuns for 33 days. For the first time in the history of the Abbey the world was able to look into its cloisters and to experience something of the lives of the nuns within the enclosure.

When the ABC sent out a general invitation for women to apply to take part in the programme, to be called simply *The Abbey*, nearly one thousand responded from all over Australia. Of the five who were chosen only one was a Catholic, and she had not been to church for years. The women, who slept in the largest of the Abbey's guest cottages, each in their own room or 'cell' - for the duration of the filming, there were no other guests - had no access to the outside world and followed the nuns' routine of work and prayer. They were embarking on a search for meaning, for self and for God.

The journey the five women undertook required them to renounce many of the things that were taken for granted in everyday life, but it also demanded that they deal with thoughts and emotions that were more easily repressed or denied in the bustle of their lives at home. Their greatest struggle was not with rising at 4am in time for Vigils, or living so closely with one another, but with keeping the silence, which is general outside times of recreation. As one woman commented, 'There's something here, I don't know what it is. I know I'm going to find out and it's scary.' *The Abbey* not only followed the personal journeys of the women who took part but also revealed the nuns' humanity. What each of the five women visitors found at Jamberoo bore witness to the lives of the sisters, as much as to their own, a witness that reached far beyond the five to a viewing public of many thousands.

Making a programme such as *The Abbey* would have been unthinkable before Vatican II. Strictly enclosed contemplative nuns remain separate from the world to devote themselves to prayer and contemplation. At the time of filming there were 32 in the community of diverse nationalities, backgrounds and ages, living together, 'bearing each other's different personalities and annoying habits with the greatest of patience', as the rule of St Benedict said. The nuns at Jamberoo reflect the eternal religious paradox; in losing your life you find it.

When Sister Joanna Bagot first came to Jamberoo in 1994 to visit the Benedictine nuns, she too was scared. For the previous few years something had been drawing her away from her full and satisfying life as a Lacanian psychoanalyst in Melbourne. Struggling to understand whether what she sensed was of God, whether it was some physical change such as an early menopause (she was 40) or neurosis, she said that 'Freud would have a field day'. Joanna (then called Felicity) contacted the Abbess, explaining that she was on a quest to discover what God wanted her to do with her life: she wanted to know whether the answer was joining the community at Jamberoo. 'I'd been in Sydney for Christmas and New Year's Eve, and I was driving back to Melbourne and had arranged with the Abbess to stay for a few days, and actually, it was at a time when the cottages were closed, but they were happy to have me stay,' she said.

Welcomed to the Abbey by two of the nuns, Joanna lay down on the guest cottage bed and slept. 'I had a dream that afternoon and somehow, something of that dream said to me, this is it,' she said. She dreamt about changing her clothes, which, as she remarked, was a pointed symbol in the circumstances. She felt relief that she had finally found not what she was looking for, but rather where God was leading her. But then, she said, the real struggle began in terms of what was it all about, what next?

Most people, not least a mature women with the depth of understanding of herself and others that Joanna had acquired in her studies and professional life, would have found such a situation difficult, if not actually disquieting. As part of her training, she had been in analysis for years and had a formidable reputation as a practitioner. She was co-director of the Freudian School of Melbourne, was in demand to give papers at international conferences, and had worked with clients in a busy practice. Exchanging this, and a life of cherished independence, friendships, music and travel, for a life lived with 30 other women in an enclosed community dedicated to prayer, was a prospect both daunting and difficult to explain. With hindsight, Joanna believes she must have been quite a challenge for the nuns on that first visit to Jamberoo.

'I was fairly direct and confrontational, fairly assertive,' she recalled, 'and I wasn't very passive with God. Some time later an old friend talked with me about the importance of being "docile with God" in the sense of the Latin origin "being teachable". This was a help in approaching a new life.'

It is not unusual for visitors to Jamberoo to mistake their response to the peace of the place, the beauty of its setting, and the lives of the sisters as it can be observed in chapel as a call to leave the world and become part of what they are experiencing. Joanna explained that 'sometimes people come in too much of a hurry with stars in their eyes, and it's also very common, and I think I've suffered from it myself, for people to come in and have expectations of the community. You want them to be a certain way...but when you arrive you think they're not like that at all.'

Although Joanna saw her first visit to Jamberoo as the beginning step towards the fulfilment of her own vocation, her preparation had in fact been years in the making. Growing up in the Sydney suburb of Northwood, the fourth of six children, Joanna's father was a barrister and Crown Prosecutor, while before marriage her mother was a gifted and experienced journalist. They were thoughtful, enquiring and devout Catholics. Born with a congenital dislocation of the hip, Joanna spent long periods in hospital in plaster from her armpits to her ankles. Often alone, either in a hospital bed or at home propped up in a cot on the front veranda, she learned to watch and listen. 'I'm still a person who can enjoy small things,' she said, 'and my focus can be very small'. She also developed the art of getting people to come to her and talk, she adds. Among the neighbours who regularly stopped and chatted was Lloyd Rees, one of several artists living nearby.

Eventually her bones healed and Joanna was able to go to school. She and her sister Verity travelled together from Northwood to Kirribilli, the Loreto convent by the water at Milsons Point. Joanna remembered being regarded as frail and was 'absolutely hell-bent on trying to be like everybody else... so I'd run pretty wild'. She did not see herself as bright like her sister but was angry when she did badly in a science test and was told by her teacher that she was capable of better work. 'I'll show her,' she thought, and was quite taken aback when, on topping the class, the only comment from Sister was, 'That's the least I'd expect from you'. Joanna claims that remark 'freed me to become who I was going to be from the age of 15'.

Born in 1952, Joanna took the changes of Vatican II for granted and never suffered from 'the emphasis on sin and guilt that predominated in the Catholic world. I remember at about 14 responding to the question of a retreat director about what was sin, saying that it was a failure to love. This was very clear to me at the time'. Joanna credits her Loreto teachers for this insight. 'I watched the development of the nuns who taught me post Vatican II from the standpoint of an adolescent,' she said. 'They were totally in tune with Mary Ward's understanding of the Gospel…ironically centuries past,' she said.

On leaving school, Joanna studied for an honours degree in psychology at the University of New South Wales. She did not enjoy the experimentally based studies of rats and mice and said she learned more about the human psyche in a year with the School of Drama. 'It was absolutely clear that a good dramatist understood more about human beings than any psychologist ever did,' she said. She also studied philosophy, sociology and English and 'earned my living through university playing the organ for weddings and washing dishes in an after-care hospital'. On completing her degree in 1974, she applied to various universities to do a clinical master's degree and took up an offer from the University of Melbourne where the Department of Psychology also offered her a tutorship. She moved into St Mary's College, also run by the Loreto Sisters, and was offered a tutorship there too. The Principal at that time was a Loreto nun she had known from Kirribilli and a great favourite, Sister Angela Quill.

> The 1970s were an exciting and idealistic time to be coming to spiritual awareness. (Not unlike the present times of hope with the election of Pope Francis.) The Post Vatican II Church was full of promise for lay people. In the university chaplaincy we all studied the Vatican II documents in depth and saw a future for ourselves with a new dignity in our contribution to the life of our Church. At the chaplaincy we were also privileged at daily mass to have the scriptures opened for us by the great scholar Michael Fallon.[3] He brought the scriptures to life for us every day. Later on at St Mary's College mass was often celebrated with us by the Jesuit poet and Professor in the English Department, Peter Steele.[4] No wonder I was a 'God wrestler'!

---

3 Michael Fallon is a Missionary of the Sacred Heart priest. He is a scripture scholar who has published commentaries on all the books in the Old and New Testament.

4 Peter Steele was a Jesuit priest who died in 2012 at the age of 72. He was a much-published poet and distinguished academic. A few months before his death he was awarded the Order of Australia for 'service to literature and higher education as a poet, author, scholar and

Life in the senior common room at St Mary's was stimulating and enjoyable and Joanna had valued access to the beautiful college chapel. 'You could wander down there any time of the day or night and sit. Something in me was searching there as well. Another Loreto friend, Sister Noni Mitchell, had schooled me in Gerard Manley Hopkins *Thou mastering me God*, and Francis Thompson's *The Hound of Heaven* over many years. We frequently shared the poets' articulation of their search, so much so, that I realise I had always been a "God wrestler" but I didn't for one minute think I was going to head towards a religious life.'

Again Joanna found the course work disappointing. 'Cognitive Behaviourism and Rational-Emotive Therapy were all the rage in those days, and I hated the implied model of the human person limited to behavioural terms,' she said, 'it's so empty. I think I was ripe for discovering that there was another way of thinking about it.' That other way came to her in the form of a lecture arranged by the Department of Psychology given by Argentinian Lacanian Psychoanalyst, Oscar Zentner.[5] Zentner's English was almost incomprehensible but good enough for Joanna to realise he had something important to say and that she wanted to hear it. 'He spoke of Lacan's rereading of Descartes' "I think therefore I am" in terms of the psychoanalytic understanding "I think where I am not" and the *méconnaissance* of the unconscious. At last, I was set on fire by these questions.'

Oscar Zentner and his wife María-Inés Rotmiler de Zentner, both Lacanian psychoanalysts, had fled the regime of the generals in Argentina and come to Melbourne where they hoped they could bring their children up in peace. Through meeting the Zentners and joining their Freudian School of Melbourne, Joanna found the passion she had been missing in her psychology work.[6] She and other analysts, psychiatrists and psychologists, immersed themselves in the study of Freud and Lacan. They had reading seminars late into the night, following texts in the original German or French, often finding serious corruption of Freudian texts in standard English translations. Work would start early the following mornings, with the first analysands usually arriving at 7.30am.

---

teacher, and to the Catholic Church'.

5 Jacques Lacan, a French psychoanalyst, famously re-reads Freud.

6 The Freudian School of Melbourne, founded in 1977, was the first English Language school of Lacanian psychoanalysis in the world.

After some years working in psychiatric hospitals with both children and adults, Joanna had set up in private practice in rooms in the inner city Melbourne suburb of Carlton and found the work intensely satisfying. Psychology had given her the skills to listen to people but her study of Lacan taught her about the 'unconscious structured as a language', that 'it's a matter of hearing that the unconscious can and does speak, unwittingly most of the time,' she said.

Joanna's professional and personal life was happy, stimulating and rewarding. She lived in a flat in Brunswick, drove a red MG and went to every production of both the Australian and Victorian State opera companies. 'With the Freudian School I had a very full, exciting and challenging life and a fairly clear trajectory of where things were going, and it all really just fell into my lap. I always had a sense of the sacred in my work with people. It is a privileged place, to be a listener. When my vocation eventually emerged into the light of day, Noni Mitchell said she wasn't surprised, she had thought something was brewing there in my spirit but had thought it might have been Carmelite.'

After some years, the Zentners resigned from the Freudian School in Melbourne, believing Australians should take charge of their own school. In this, Joanna explained, they took their lead from Lacan's own dissolution of his École Freudienne de Paris. She became co-director with two colleagues and took responsibility for running seminars, supervision of younger practitioners, conferences and publications. This involved national and international travel and often an opportunity to visit her sister Verity who, married to a Frenchman, lived near Cannes. On one of these visits Verity took Joanna to Saint-Honorat, one of the two islands of Lérins off the coast of Cannes, where a monastery had been built in the fifth century. The current Cistercian community at Lérins Abbey dates from 1869.

The sisters walked through the monastery museum looking at artefacts dating back to Roman times. A number of photographs covering the island's more recent history hung on the walls and Joanna remembers glimpsing out of the corner of her eye an image of nuns in habits and noting, with some surprise, an inner resistance.

The monks of Lérins Abbey were known for their Slavic chant and Joanna went alone to mass in the Abbey to hear the singing the following Sunday.[7]

7 The Monks at Lérins Abbey derive their music from the Abbey of Chevetogne in Belgium,

'It was incredibly beautiful,' she recalled. To catch the ferry back to Cannes in time for lunch, Joanna needed to leave before mass was ended. When she tried to slip quietly out of the chapel she was surprised to find the door locked. 'I realised that I had misread the sign advising this - even though my French was easily good enough to grasp it: a classic Freudian slip!' She later discovered it was to keep tourists away until the mass was over. The next ferry wasn't for some hours and Joanna was trapped. When the small congregation had dispersed, the chapel, monastery museum and shop all closed for lunch and, apart from sitting looking at the rocks and the sea and walking round the tiny island, there was nothing to do. 'I was absolutely bored out of my brain,' she said, 'it felt like forever'. When the shop finally reopened, she wandered in where 'something made me pick up a pamphlet on the monastery and a little booklet on the life of the monks'.

Some weeks later, back in Australia, she started to read the book and pamphlet. 'In some way I felt connected with them, that I was addressed by them. On the back of the pamphlet I found the details of Cistercian nuns living in a sister community to Lérins Abbey just beyond Nice at a place called Notre Dame de la Paix. Something made me feel that I needed to find out more about this but I was scared witless.' Clarity came with a dream a year later on New Year's Eve. 'I woke thinking it's time I did something about this.'

She telephoned the Cistercians in Nice and asked for someone who could speak English. She told her story (coincidentally to a Sister Johanna), who advised her to write to the Abbess. She wrote and asked if she could stay with the nuns for Easter but the Abbess, Sister Marie Christiane, suggested July. 'It was a very good idea, in terms of discernment, as you would, I think, instinctively want to slow someone down who's in too much of a hurry,' said Joanna. 'So I went in July, and stayed a couple of weeks there, full of fear and trepidation, absolutely terrified of what I was going to find, or what was happening to me…and I met this wonderful Abbess, a woman full of wisdom.' Joanna felt very much at home in the monastery.

Looking back she realises her first impressions were similar to those experienced by people who feel euphoric after a few days at Jamberoo. When she told Sister Marie Christiane that she felt God was attracting her to Notre Dame de la Paix, the Abbess exclaimed, 'Oh, I hope not!' 'It was

---

in turn derived from Kiev.

exactly the right thing to say to me,' laughed Joanna. 'She thought it would be too painful for me to leave my home and country and it was the absolute honesty of that, that appealed to me.' Joanna said that, in retrospect, she believes that being drawn to explore the idea of a vocation to contemplative life in France was God's way of getting her attention. 'It was appealing to all of my pretensions,' she said, 'French liturgy's absolutely gorgeous and the beauty of the whole thing was alluring…If I had pursued it, Marie Christiane would have had me back, if that was actually what God was asking of me, but I think it would've all been over by lunchtime, because at that stage it was all about superficial things.'

The Abbess sent Joanna home with three pieces of advice. Firstly, to make a retreat of discernment with a Jesuit, in her mother tongue; secondly, to cultivate 'holy indifference' – that is, 'Let God do it, don't try to do it yourself. If it's to be, God will bring it about.' And, thirdly, she advised Joanna to see the Benedictines in Australia 'just as part of a spiritual courtesy'. Joanna was keen to speed things up but events conspired to slow them down. She arrived back from France in July, quickly found a Jesuit who, while he was prepared to guide her in a retreat, suggested she wait three months. 'I ran around trying to understand "holy indifference" - I was sort of paddling around in waters I didn't know very well,' she recalled. It was some time before she realised she simply had to get out of God's way. She was not particularly keen to meet the Benedictines; her Franciscan spiritual director steered her in the direction of the Poor Clares, but her every attempt to visit them was thwarted by unexpected circumstances and when her Jesuit director suggested that she go to mass at the Carmelite convent in Melbourne, she felt no connection there, either.

The story of Joanna's vocation unfolds like a cliffhanger but, at the time, the long-drawn out uncertainty about the direction of her life was frustrating. 'I wanted to know was this something to do with God or was it something I'd dreamed up?' she said. 'Was I having an exotic midlife crisis? Marie Christiane thought it entirely possible.' She was plagued by thoughts such as these, even as she ran her fulltime private practice and bore other professional responsibilities.

In October 1993 Joanna spent several weeks at Campion Hall, the Jesuit retreat centre in Melbourne. She found it one of the hardest things she had done in her life. She was undertaking a retreat of discernment, but had no idea what that was, and expected clear guidance and instruction from her Jesuit director. He stood back, which was what she needed. By the end of the retreat Joanna said, 'there was one thing I was very sure of, and it has stood me in good stead for a long time since, was that it was something of God, not something of me. My only remaining problem was where should I test my vocation?' Two months later Joanna drove up the mountain to make her first visit to Jamberoo, as the French Abbess had advised her.

When a person presents themselves at the Abbey with a view to entering the community, discernment for both the individual and the community is a long, slow process but for Joanna, 'I knew that something was drawing me very deeply'. She was invited to come to live within the community for three weeks so that they could get to know her and she them.[8] Once the decision was made, things fitted into place easily. Extricating herself from her life in Melbourne was far less complicated than she had imagined. 'I didn't have to make it happen,' she said. A colleague took over her lease at the practice, Joanna slowly concluded work with her remaining clients, sold her flat and car and in March 1995, at the age of 42, began her new life.

> I spent a year as a postulant, with my own name, Felicity, living within the community following the daily cycle and rhythm of prayer and work and studying the rule of St Benedict. At the end of that time the solemnly professed members of the community voted to accept me. I was given the habit and a white veil and asked to choose a 'religious' name. I think I'm one of the very few people here who's actually said, 'no, you give it to me'. I was given Joanna.
>
> The novitiate marks the beginning of monastic life and lasts for two years. During that time I worked within the community and continued my studies of the Rule and of the vows of stability, conversion of life and obedience. At the end of my novitiate, again with the agreement of the community, I took temporary vows for three years. I was then a junior member of the community. I made my solemn profession six years after entering, in 2001.

For years people had paid Joanna to listen to them. Ironically, in joining a Benedictine community, she was committing herself to live by a Rule written 1500 years earlier which begins with the plea: 'Listen with the ear of the heart'. The Rule does not outline a way of perfection but a practical approach to what the Trappist monk Thomas Keating calls, 'awakening to the divine within us'. The key is the daily rhythm of work and prayer: the

8 Today prospective candidates spend three periods of three weeks at the Abbey before making a final decision.

Divine Office is chanted in the Abbey church seven times a day, beginning with Vigils at 4.30 in the morning and ending with Compline at 7.00pm. Practicing silence, *lectio divina* or the reading of sacred texts, and tending to the activities every monastery undertakes in order to survive financially and domestically, makes up the remainder of the day.

To illustrate the spirit of the Rule Joanna told the story of two monks at the time of the Desert Fathers praying together. When one of the monks dozed off, the other, far from admonishing him, gently rested his head in his lap. The story, she said, is an example of the generosity and kindness Benedict wished his monks to show each other. Joanna testified to having been the recipient of great kindness from the community since she entered. She finds Benedict reassuring in the way he understands people - their frailties and their strengths. 'He has a wise piece of advice in the Rule, that you've got to give the strong something to strive for but you mustn't, with the weak, give them anything to flee from, so you've got to cater for different talents and personalities,' she said.[9]

> When you first come to a community you make all sorts of efforts to fit in and try to do everything the right way. But you haven't a clue. I can remember the first time I sat in the refectory (where we eat in silence while someone reads from the Rule or a spiritual book) thinking what on earth are these people doing? It didn't make any sense to me. It's a completely different world, but it must be different, it needs to be different…and one of the most formative experiences is actually failure and that you don't live up to your ideals. This is the life experience to be mined. You ask yourself how you are going to grow through this, and it's hard. The community's not full of perfect people. They're ordinary frail human beings. Somebody might have this or that problem; what matters is how you deal with it inside yourself. How can you really live the Gospel of Love in response to each situation? This is a constant challenge. Moving away from expectations of other people to get more in touch with what are your own frailties rather than looking at everybody else's faults is a really important process.

One of the most important aspects of contemplative community life is silence, that deep silence that is not the absence of words but the presence of prayer. Such silence, Joanna pointed out, takes a long time to learn. The Great Silence begins at 6.30pm, half an hour before Compline, and continues until after Lauds (morning prayer) at 7.30am. During the day the nuns take their main meals in silence, and try to avoid talking in

9 Rule of St Benedict, Ch 64: v 19.

the cloisters and when working. Silence encourages a predisposition to reflection and mindfulness. Common sense, however, is also a Benedictine value and there are times when talking is important, said Joanna, 'because for St Benedict the Rule of Love comes before all else'.

Silence, Joanna added, prepares the ground for prayer – 'the prayer of listening, the prayer of praise, the prayer of being God-centered rather than self-centered'. Prayer is the real work of a Benedictine community, and people write to Jamberoo from all over Australia and overseas asking for prayer. Every request receives a response and is acted upon. At the time of publication Joanna is the community person who writes back. 'I find it incredibly humbling and inspiring answering these prayer requests,' she said. 'They cover the full range of life's experiences and I'm moved by the faith of these people. Their requests are not addressed to us personally but to these strange people called nuns who pray. It's somewhere to send the cry of the heart.'

Another current work for Joanna is the care of a frail 90-year-old sister. It is, she said, more a pleasure and privilege than work. 'To care for such a noble soul represents everything I believe makes life worth living,' she said.[10] When she first entered the community she found watching the current Abbess's care of a sister with premature Alzheimer's deeply formative. It was truly inspiring, she said, to see love and prayer lived in action in that relationship in 1995. 'Eventually we were all involved in small ways in the care of that sister. It helped me make the transition from one life to another.' She continued:

> Overall the big difference between our life and that of apostolic communities is that our apostolate in the Church is primarily prayer and worship on behalf of a suffering evolving world. We play our small part in the world wide continuous cycle of prayer. When we go to bed another Benedictine community somewhere in the world is rising to take up that cry of prayer for the world. And so on, from community to community, following the path of the sun around the globe. St Benedict speaks of the monastery as 'the School of the Lord's Service'. His Rule is basically a distillation of the gospel for actual daily life. We are on a life-long journey of learning to live the gospel with each other. Mostly this will be learning through our own failures. We are both agents of grace and challenge to

10 Sr Carmen Ruiz osb died on 15 August 2014, the feast of the Assumption. Her Abbess and her carer Sr Joanna were with her when she took her last breath. Sr Carmen came to Australia from Spain as a 25-year-old missionary to the New Norcia Benedictine Mission in WA. She joined the Benedictine community in NSW in the early 80s.

> each other. So our lives are interrelated in a very intensive way. We don't have the distractions and satisfactions that are available to communities involved in apostolic works outside their communities. Ultimately we seek to go to God together, not as individuals. 'Where is your sister/brother?' asks God of Cain and of us.

The nuns at Jamberoo Abbey, said Joanna, 'are a signpost, in spite of ourselves, towards another way of living, a living from the depths of the gospel of Jesus Christ'.

Servants of the Blessed Sacrament

Peter Julian Eymard founded the Servants of the Blessed Sacrament, a contemplative order for women, in Angers, France, in 1859. Three years earlier he had founded an active order for men, the Congregation of the Blessed Sacrament. In establishing his women's congregation, Eymard enlisted the support of Marguerite Guillot who had worked with him in the Third Order of St Mary at Lyons. As Mother Marguerite of the Blessed Sacrament, she remained Superior until her death in 1885.

Born in Grenoble in 1811, Eymard was ordained a diocesan priest in 1839 and after some years of intense pastoral work, joined the Marist Fathers in Lyon and became highly regarded for his spiritual direction of seminarians and priests. One of his directees was Julian Tenison Woods who years later became spiritual director to Mary MacKillop in Australia. Eymard's decision to found his own religious order emerged from a profound spiritual experience during prayer in 1851 during which he was haunted by the current state of the Church, in particular lack of spiritual support for priests, spiritual direction for the laity and respect for and devotion to the Eucharist. His vision was that both the male and female congregations render 'a solemn and perpetual service of adoration to Our Lord Jesus Christ, ever dwelling in the Blessed Sacrament of the altar for the love of mankind'.[1] *Eymard died in 1868 and was canonised by John XXIII in 1962 at the end of the first session of the Second Vatican Council. He was named Apostle of the Eucharist.*

1 Excerpt from the Constitutions written by Eymard for the sisters and approved by the Vatican in 1885.

Carol Hogan sss

Carol Hogan was born in 1931 and entered the Servants of the Blessed Sacrament in 1953. She made her final vows in 1958. Her name in religion was Sister Mary Frances.

Residents of Hampden Road in the quiet middle-class Melbourne suburb of Armadale were startled on one winter's day by a crescendo of crashing and banging coming from inside the convent at number 50. It was August 1968 and the Servants of the Blessed Sacrament had been living silently, almost invisibly, in the street for 18 years. Carol Hogan, a member of the community for most of that time, vividly remembers the commotion. The nuns in their long white robes, herself included, were attacking the convent grille with hammers and saws, literally demolishing it.

The sisters were in the midst of a month of intense study of the teachings of Vatican II, led by a French diocesan priest, Marius Garail. Chaplain to their mother house in Paris, he had been sent by the superior general to explain how these teachings would affect them. Carol later wrote that,

> Drawing on the documents of the council, he presented the community with the Church's renewed theology of Eucharist, liturgy, revelation, church, religious life, social justice, the primacy of conscience and the call to listen to the poor of the world. For perhaps the very first time the sisters were being exposed to theology – the renewed theology of Vatican II – and the possibility of psychological and theological growth. [2]

The destruction of the grille dramatically demonstrated Father Gerail's impact on the community. 'Our time-honoured ideas of religious life were crashing around us,' said Carol.

> We thought revelation was locked in a safe never to be changed. Because of Father Gerail we saw it happening in our lives now. He opened our eyes to a new theology that was freer and more enlightened, one that gave Christianity bigger possibilities. Before his visit the attitude of our leaders had been that Vatican II was not for us – not for enclosed nuns. Father Gerail broke open the bonds.

2 For Carol Hogan's description of these events see 'Eucharistic Metamorphosis: Changing Symbol, Changing Lives' in Anne Elvey, Carol Hogan, Kim Power and Claire Renkin (eds). *Reinterpreting the Eucharist: Explorations in Feminist Theology and Ethics*, London, Equinox, 2013.

The grille symbolised the nuns' retreat from the world so as to spend their lives in perpetual adoration of Jesus Christ in the consecrated host held in the large, ornate monstrance in their chapel. 'Quite simply', explained Carol, 'we believed in the presence of the historical Jesus in the host. All our thoughts, words and actions were focused on deepening our mystical union with Christ'.

Father Gerail asked the sisters to rethink Eucharist (as the mass was now called) and to explore what this might mean for their spirituality, their way of life and their ministry. 'He was brilliant,' said Carol.

> He had all the nuns in different groups talking and praying and getting in touch with the world again. We had many intense and prolonged discussions and we had never discussed anything before. He turned the convent upside-down and we embarked on a journey that brought us from being Servants of the Blessed Sacrament to Eucharistic women.

Carol recalled a sense of newfound freedom. She had been happy living behind the grille in Hampden Road but, looking back, realises her happiness was limited by the narrowness of her understanding of God, and her restricted way of being in community. She said:

> It was always that I loved Jesus, and God, and Jesus loved me, and everything I did was for love, just like Thérèse of the Child Jesus, and I remember sometimes just crying, I think with the stress of it all, and particularly in those times when we were under the first Australian superior, and there was no outlet for anything, really. You saw your family once a month, apart from Lent when we didn't see them at all, though we did have an extra visit later on. There was no outlet whatsoever, so you just lived that.

Father Gerail held out the possibility of continuing to live contemplative lives but incorporating the transformative thinking of Vatican II, so that the community's spirituality was integrated with an openness and interaction, both with each other and with their environment.

Carol was 37 when she helped demolish the grill at 50 Hampden Road. She had lived in Melbourne all her life, growing up in the northern suburb of Essendon, where her father had a business as a retail dairyman. Milkmen would arrive at 1am, load their horse-drawn carts with cans and bottles of milk and cream and set off on their deliveries. Before she married, Carol's mother was a secretary and afterwards kept the books for the dairy business. The eldest of three girls, Carol was educated by the Sisters of

Charity at St Therese's Primary School in Essendon and at their secondary school, St Columba's College. Receiving her First Holy Communion at the age of seven was a profound experience: 'I felt very special, very happy and somewhat angelic'.

A deeply pious little girl, for some years Carol regularly made her way alone, in the dark, to early morning mass at the parish church. 'The parish church was fairly modern for those days and I was totally rapt by the sense of awe and mystery,' she said. 'I think I felt a kind of heavenly otherness about the ritual in Latin, of being caught into a mysterious and kindly environment, even into God. I remember thinking I was very much loved by God.'

Carol's parents were not especially religious though her father, who would not accept payment for the milk he delivered to the nuns 'here and there', had fond memories of Sister Josephine, a Charity sister who had taught him at St Monica's parish school in Moonee Ponds. Carol grew up in an era in which the majority of Catholics were not encouraged to question or explore their faith, when nuns were respected for their higher calling, and everyone deferred to priests. 'No one knew much about Catholicism, really. Most Catholics didn't,' said Carol. 'It was the priest who knew everything.'

At St Columba's Carol joined the Young Christian Students and learned about Catholic Action. Key elements, Carol recalled, were considering questions such as: 'Who is Jesus in the gospels? How can I be like him? How can I make the world a better place?' Looking back she realises that the focus on action 'tipped [my] Christianity into the following of Jesus, and not so many rules and regulations, although I was still totally bound by them, and totally submissive'. The only action she could bring to mind was when she and her friends 'as good Catholic girls' wrote to the Jantzen factory objecting to their new two-piece bathing costumes, reflecting a pious preoccupation with the body rather than a concern about the social justice issues its founders had in mind.

On leaving school, Carol went to the University of Melbourne where she completed an arts degree. 'I was going to have a good time and do all the things the nuns had told me not to do, which I didn't, of course.' In her first year she fell in love with a young man who subsequently became a priest. At the end of her second year, her future uncertain – all she knew was that she didn't want to teach – she went hitch-hiking round Tasmania with a couple of girlfriends, one of whom was her best friend Marcia. 'We were the most unlikely bushwalkers you can imagine,' she laughed. She took the opportunity, while in Hobart, to see Sister Catherine, who had prepared her for First Communion at St Therese's in Essendon. 'She said to me, "What are you going to do when you finish your degree?" I said, "I think I'll be a nun." The words just popped out which I found really odd. It was the first time I thought about it'.

Although these words came as a shock to Carol, her friend Marcia, who was about to enter the Blessed Sacrament Sisters, was not surprised. She later told Carol that she had always known she had a vocation. Carol's mother, on the other hand, burst into tears when she heard about her daughter's conversation with Sister Catherine, and begged her not to do it. She was reassured by Carol's final flourish at university, when she attended seven balls in seven weeks, with seven different young men. After having such a good time, Carol's mother could not believe that her daughter could consider life as a religious. However, while Carol 'fell into a job as a librarian' at the university, she began tentatively considering different orders. She knew she would not be happy teaching or nursing, and decided to join Marcia in entering the enclosed contemplative order of the Blessed Sacrament Sisters in Armadale. 'I went to a talk somewhere on the dreadful state of the world…and thought the best thing I can do for the world is pray for it,' she recalled. 'That's why I entered – and all the sisters who entered with me would say the same thing. We went to be with Jesus in the Blessed Sacrament because the real presence was very real to us.'

Looking back, Carol recognised that she had an attraction to the contemplative life. At the time she recalled being powerfully influenced by Thomas Merton's *Elected Silence*.[3] The book describes Merton's spiritual journey as a young man in his early 20s - Carol's age - his conversion to Catholicism and entry into the contemplative Trappist order. Carol shared his yearning to be closer to God in a life of prayer and silence, which was considered the highest ideal in religious life by the Church. It was a form of life, Carol insisted, for which she was utterly unprepared.

Unlike their male counterparts, the Blessed Sacrament Fathers, to whom the church of St Francis in central Melbourne had been entrusted by

3 Thomas Merton, *Elected Silence*. London, Hollis & Carter, 1949 is the British edition of Thomas Merton's autobiography, *The Seven Storey Mountain*. San Diego, Calif., Harcourt Brace, 1948. It was published seven years after Merton entered Gethsemani Abbey in Kentucky.

Archbishop Mannix, the Blessed Sacrament Sisters were new to Australia when Carol entered in 1953.[4] They had been persuaded by the French Canadian Blessed Sacrament Fathers to make a foundation in Melbourne. A suitable property was acquired in Hampden Road, Armadale and seven sisters arrived in September 1950. All but one, an Australian, were from the Cenacle in Quebec.[5] According to Carol, the French Canadians knew nothing about Australia, and the community was very poor. Several of the nuns did not speak English. They had a fine superior in Sister Berthe, but most were uneducated and had entered very young. Accustomed to central heating in Quebec, they found the Armadale house desperately cold, despite their heavy woollen habits. One sister couldn't cope and went back to the Mother House in Quebec almost immediately.

By the time Carol entered three years later, the community in Hampden Road had expanded its numbers to 14. The sisters' lives, she explained, followed a rigorous pattern of prayer and silence. They chanted the divine office in Latin together every day beginning with lauds at 4.30am, followed by prime at 6.30, Terce at 9.30, and Sext at midday. The afternoon office, none, was at 3pm, Vespers at 6, and finally Compline at 9pm. The sisters also attended mass each morning, said the rosary together in the early afternoon and later celebrated Benediction. Each day every sister was engaged in three periods of personal prayer before the Blessed Sacrament, with an examination of conscience. The latter, Carol commented wryly, 'was rather excessive given the atmosphere of the convent'.

According to their Rule, the sisters were obliged to practice perpetual adoration of the blessed sacrament. However, because their numbers were insufficient, the community in Hampden Road was only able to sustain three days and nights of continual prayer before the elaborate golden monstrance in the chapel.

Carol described the convent as a bleak, cold and unfriendly place in contrast to the chapel with its 'masses of flowers, rich vestments, sacred vessels and

4 St Francis' Church was built between 1841 and 1845 in Lonsdale St, Melbourne. It is one of the oldest Catholic churches in Australia and from 1848 until the late 1860s was Melbourne's Catholic cathedral. Archbishop Mannix entrusted the church to five Blessed Sacrament priests and two brothers from North America in 1929.

5 French sisters had established the Canadian foundation in 1903. The convents of the Blessed Sacrament Sisters were known as Cenacles – a word used to describe the room where the Last Supper took place.

brass candelabra' surrounding the glowing monstrance which only a priest was allowed to touch. It was the still heart of the house. As Carol wrote:

> Central to their [the sisters] understanding was the conviction that somehow in the Blessed Sacrament, Jesus was more present, more real than anywhere else in the world. It was this sense of loving presence, together with a spirituality of sacrifice, which enabled the sisters to negotiate the very hard and demanding life of a Blessed Sacrament Sister.[6]

The sisters survived financially by making and selling altar breads which, said Carol, provided an appropriate and contemplative form of paid labour. Previously the Good Shepherd Sisters in Abbotsford had made altar breads for the diocese, but they had generously handed this work over to the Blessed Sacrament Sisters.

In their twice-daily recreation periods, one lasting an hour, the other half an hour, the sisters engaged in general, not personal, conversation. Since they never saw newspapers, watched television or listened to the radio, and their reading was limited to religious books for a half hour each day, conversation tended to be stultifying. 'We used to talk about the chooks and the cat until one day I said, "I've had enough of the chooks and the cat,"' Carol recalled.

An aspect of convent life that Carol had accepted without question, but nevertheless found difficult, was the custom that limited them to having only one bath a week. It is not hard to imagine the discomfort of wearing ankle-length woollen habits in the heat of the Australian summer:

> Maureen and Vianney, two of the sisters who entered four years after me, started kicking up. They were smart; Vianney was a physio, Maureen had done some nursing. They were articulate, thinking women. I'd never been trained to think. They asked for a bath every day, which was agreed to when they were postulants. I hadn't done that. I just sweated away in my woollen habit and got rashes and stuff, but it was all for love. Once they were professed, Maureen and Vianney had to put up with one bath a week like everyone else.

When their superior, Sister Berthe, was appointed superior general of the Blessed Sacrament Sisters in Paris, her successor in Melbourne, a practical Australian, introduced cotton habits.

Carol found the novitiate hard. 'I didn't get my period for 18 months, which is pretty indicative of how tough it was,' she said. But she persevered,

6 Anne Elvey, op.cit, 12.

convinced of the value of the way of life she was assuming. She was completely immersed in God's love for her and her love for God. Only many years later did she come to understand the cost entailed in the lack of outlet for ordinary human needs such as friendship, personal and intellectual development and contact with family. A grille separated the sisters from their families on monthly visits, and in common with other enclosed and semi-enclosed orders, sisters did not leave the enclosure other than for medical appointments, nor did they attend family funerals.

When the Jesuit Charles Mayne, rector of the Melbourne diocesan seminary at Werribee visited the convent in the 1960s, he caused something of a stir.[7] He was an influential figure among young Catholics in Melbourne and a good friend of Maureen and Vianney. 'He gave them the *Je Sais, Je Crois* series,' said Carol, 'one of which, by a French priest, was on Eurcharist. The series was seminal to the changes introduced by Vatican II. He also gave them the catechetical series taught by Johannes Hofinger S.J. at the East Asian Pastoral Institute in Manila and Francis Xavier Durwell's *In the Redeeming Christ – Toward a Theology of Spirituality*. Of special significance to Blessed Sacrament Sisters in these writings, explained Carol, was 'new eucharistic imagining' with its shift from presenting the Eucharist as a crucifixion memorial 'to being inclusive of death and resurrection'.

According to Carol, when Maureen and Vianney showed some of this 'subversive' material to the superior she took it from them, after which they hid books under their scapulars when Father Mayne had been to visit. Some months before the smashing of the grille at 50 Hampden Road, Mayne had given Maureen and Vianney each a copy of *The Documents of Vatican II* edited by the Jesuit Walter M. Abbott. The superior took the books, convinced that, since theirs was an enclosed order, Vatican II did not apply to them. She returned them after three weeks, telling the sisters that the books must be kept wrapped in brown paper in front of the other nuns.

Judging that she was not the right person to handle the challenges the sisters would face with the implementation of Vatican II, Sister Berthe transferred the superior to the generalate, now in Rome, and appointed someone new. In addition, Sister Berthe sent Marius Garail to teach the sisters the critical importance of Vatican II not only to the Church, but also in their lives.

7 Charles Mayne SJ (1906-1990) was rector at Werribee Seminary from 1947-58 and of the Glen Waverley Seminary from 1959-67. He was a reformer and promoter of new ideas, with an emphasis on lay initiative and social justice.

The convent divided into factions; there were those who wanted change and those who didn't. Like Carol, there were nuns who had wielded hammers in the front parlour with a sense of exhilaration and excitement, while there were others anxious about what change might mean. They had taken part in smashing the grill with mixed emotions. Not long after, Carol was shocked when one of the sisters she felt close to said that she was leaving the convent. 'We were in the room where the paste to bake the altar bread was made, sitting on the flour bags, when she told me. I was really upset. She said, "Carol, the system is not producing women of charity, maturity and prayer".'

Carol believed her friend was right, and that the culture of the system did not give the sisters the opportunity to develop as adults. For the first time since entering, Carol had serious doubts about her life with the Blessed Sacrament Sisters. 'I can remember once being in a particular part of the convent between the newer building and the old house, and thinking, my God, here I am, I've devoted the best years of my life to this. I could've married, and the thing to which I devoted my life is falling apart.'

At about this time Carol read an article in *The Advocate* about psychotherapist Ronald Fogarty, a Marist Brother, and the remarkable work he was doing in helping religious communities come to terms with the changes involved in the Vatican II call for renewal. She sought and gained permission to see him. The first thing he asked her was, 'Who are you?' 'I'm Sister Mary Frances in a long white dress,' she answered without thinking. 'I felt Carol had died and become this cut-out nun,' she added.

Brother Fogarty had worked with women in enclosed communities in America and Australia and explained to Carol that careful counselling was required by anyone attempting to lead a contemplative life; Carol embarked on a course of counselling. 'At the time I thought I was going mad,' she said. 'He was a lifesaver and put me on the way to recovery. He gave me confidence in myself.'

The new superior at Armadale had been matron of a hospital and was 'tough but fair', said Carol. 'She knew we had to change. She understood that some of the sisters were psychologically unwell because only the mentally strong can take the contemplative lifestyle, especially the total rejection of any relationship except with Jesus, the lack of opportunities for growth, except through prayer.'

The Superior brought in experts to teach the sisters ways of adapting to changes such as relating to each other more freely, and dressing and grooming themselves when they discarded the habit. The sisters were given instruction in catechetics and a priest came to talk to them about sacramental theology. During the first dramatic year of change, ten sisters left in twelve months. 'It was a terrible shock to the system especially as they included one of my best friends,' recalled Carol.

Carol decided to remain committed to the Blessed Sacrament Sisters, even though breaking the grille had signalled the beginning of personal transformation. It was not an easy process, and involved wrestling with the challenges of her spiritual and personal development work with Ronald Fogarty, with the upheavals involved in a serious study of the Vatican Council documents, and the impact of change on the convent itself.

'After a slow and somewhat reluctant beginning,' said Carol, 'our community began to explore what a renewed theology of Eucharist might mean for our spirituality, our lifestyle, and our ministry. It was also a journey that involved new ways of praying and new insights into Peter Eymard's ideas'.

Don Cave, a Blessed Sacrament priest and a friend of Carol's, who taught at the University of Melbourne, did some extensive work on Peter Eymard.

> He discovered that Eymard said that the Eucharist was for the life of the spirit in us. It was not so much to be adored. That was a huge insight, that the Eucharist was to be lived, was to nourish us so that we could live a eucharistic life.

Carol struggled to understand the implications of this spirituality but remembers what a strong influence Don Cave had on the sisters. From being an inwardly focussed group of women cocooned in a world of silence and contemplation, they opened their doors and welcomed dozens of people to their chapel every Sunday to share with them a Eucharist in English that was creative, prayerful, and experimental, involving of adults and children alike, celebrated with music and dance. 'We were a bit of a showcase for good liturgy,' recalled Carol.

In 1973 Carol was given permission to study theology at the United Faculty of Theology (UFT) at the University of Melbourne. This took her into a world previously denied women in the Catholic Church. When a Jesuit priest gave an informal presentation arguing that no biblical or theological reason to prevent women from being ordained existed, Carol, who had grown up without questioning her faith or the teachings of the church, was shocked. Although she lived at a time when equality for women was a major issue in society, no such ideas had entered the enclosed world in Hampden Road. The Jesuit's presentation played a major part in Carol's questioning of the infallibility of Catholic teaching.

The dismantling of Carol's internal grille began in earnest in 1978. 'I was invited out of the blue, God knows why, to this ecumenical women's conference in Adelaide and I met up with three Uniting Church women – Coralie Ling, Roz Terry and Anne Drummond Gowers – two of whom were feminist theologians.' For a number of years after returning to Melbourne from the conference, Carol met monthly with them and other Uniting Church women to read and reflect on feminist psychology, theology and spirituality. 'We used to have a lot of fun on those Saturday afternoons,' she said. Key authors for them were Letty Russell, Rosemary Radford Ruether, Elizabeth Johnson and Elisabeth Schüssler Fiorenza. 'My feminist friends and I devoured them, and began to feel a deep sense of freedom, excitement, affirmation and sometimes anger. It is to these women that I owe my lasting commitment to feminist theology'.

At about the same time as she encountered feminist theology, Carol was appointed one of the chaplains at the University of Melbourne, a position she held for 24 years. She made the support of international students of all faiths her main focus. Her role at the university also gave her the opportunity to establish a further feminist theology group among older students. Their founding principle was Rosemary Radford Ruether's defining words: 'the critical principle of feminist theology is the promotion of the full humanity of women. Whatever denies, diminishes, or distorts the full humanity of women is, therefore, appraised as not redemptive'.

'In other words,' said Carol, 'Jesus was not about the oppression of women, in fact, quite the reverse'. Carol knew she had embarked on a journey from which there was no turning back. Her mother had died in 1993, and Carol had been working for years at the university and knew she needed a break. In 1994, then in her mid-60s, she spent a year in Boston. 'I realised I would never understand feminist theology, and free myself of the pervasive patriarchal ideology and culture of the church unless I went away and studied it,' she said. 'A whole new world began to fascinate me and opened up new and infinite possibilities of the mystery of God and women's identity and place in the church.' It was a further transformative experience. Carol was not, however, the first Blessed Sacrament Sister to go overseas to study: her friend Vianney had gone to Berkeley to study theology in 1974, the year Carol started her degree at UFT.

In Boston Carol picked up every feminist subject she could and found it exhilarating and transformative. 'I did a summer programme with Elizabeth Johnson, author of *She Who Is*,' she said, 'and another on Biblical Studies with Elisabeth Schüssler Fiorenza at Harvard. I also did a semester with someone else on ministry, another on feminist psychology and spirituality, and one on China because of my work with international students. I did everything I could and came back to Melbourne on fire'.

Although feminist theologians had written on theology, scripture, creation, pneumatology and liturgy, Carol believes that until Susan Ross published *Extravagant Affections: A Feminist Sacramental Theology* in 1998, nothing significant had been written on feminism and eucharistic theology other than Caroline Walker-Bynum's book on the religious significance of food to medieval women.[8] 'I started thinking well, we're eucharistic women, nobody does any serious work on eucharistic women so I'm going to do it myself.'

Carol already had a number of study units to her credit, and in 2002 left her job at the university in order to commit full-time to a doctorate under the supervision of Kim Power on the Eucharist. 'As a eucharistic sister, I felt it was an urgent need,' she said. She took as her title, 'Eucharistic Metamorphosis: Changing Symbols – Changing Lives':

> It was very hard going, very lonely. I couldn't have done it without Kim Power because she was so generous with her time. Coralie Ling found Susan Ross's *Extravagant Affection* for me, and that really kick-started me. I interviewed most of the Australian Blessed Sacrament Sisters, and then I began to read whatever I could find on feminist psychology and spirituality, then theology of Eucharist and sacramental theology. There's very little written by women.

Carol described her focus on the Eucharist as her life story:

> First it was the Blessed Sacrament, then it became eucharistic celebration, which was community building and was about social justice and we did our amazingly vibrant liturgies. Then Vianney came back from Berkeley talking about the way we use language, but until I started seriously reading feminist

8 Rosemary Radford Ruether, *Sexism and God-Talk: Towards a Feminist Theology*. Boston, Beacon Press, 1983. Susan Ross, *Extravagant Affections: A Feminist Sacramental Theology.* London, Bloomsbury Academic, 2001. Caroline Walker Bynum, *Holy Feast and Holy Fast: the Religious Significance of Food to Medieval Women.* Oakland,UC Press, 1987.

> theologians, I didn't connect it with Eucharist…Then I read Luce Irigary and her understanding of how we're all equal but different, and I thought about God as father and us as soldiers of Christ and I started looking for a new model. Elizabeth Johnson said as your symbol is, and as your God is, so is your life. If you have a God who's a warrior then you're going to live a warrior kind of life and my thesis is about how the core symbol of Eucharist changed, how it affected our spirituality, our lifestyle, and our ministry, and mine in particular.

While she was writing her doctorate, Carol established two new feminist theology groups, one with a group of women from Women and the Australian Catholic Church (WATAC), of which she was a member until it was disbanded in Melbourne, and the other in the parish of St Carthage's opposite the University of Melbourne in Parkville.

After Carol was awarded her doctorate in 2007, she began to pray and reflect on what she might do with the last years of her life. With Rosemary Radford Ruether's words in mind, she asked herself who are the most denigrated, diminished people of our world today. 'I decided that it was women and children who were living - existing - in sexual slavery or were trafficked.'

Through considering what impact she could possibly have in fighting such a lucrative industry, Carol learned that in 2001 women's congregations round the world had decided to put their resources into fighting trafficking and that the Australian congregations' response to this call for action was to set up Australian Catholic Religious Against Trafficking of Humans (ACRATH) in 2004.

ACRATH raises awareness about trafficking. 'We go to schools, we go to parishes, we go to groups all over the country and give presentations,' said Carol. 'People are horrified to think that today approximately 23 million people are enslaved worldwide of whom 80 per cent are women and 50 per cent are children, and there are an estimated 1,000 trafficked people in Australia at the moment.' As well as being an informational resource ACRATH is actively involved in working against trafficking and assisting those who have experienced it. It also spends a great deal of time in lobbying both federal and state parliaments.

Carol admires Project Respect, a feminist, community-based organisation founded by Kathleen Maltzahn. It aims to empower and support women in the sex industry, including women trafficked to Australia. 'I would have joined them and I still sometimes feel tempted, but I can't add any more to my life,' she said, 'but I have a lot of sympathy with them and go to their meetings and meet with some of their members'.

At the time of our interview in 2012, Carol, then in her early 80s, lived alone in a unit in Kensington. Overlooking grass and greenery in a quiet tree-lined street, her home was full of light and colour. Her car was parked in the garage at street level, and her living area was on the first floor, with her bedroom, study and bathroom on the floor above. Her walls were covered with pictures, surfaces with papers and books, and chairs with cushions. It was a warm and welcoming space. When the convent in Hampden Road was sold, she was given the option of either living with others or on her own. 'I always thought that I'd love to live in a community of women who'd pray in a feminist way and do this work together,' Carol said. 'I'm not going to get that'. Not all the sisters accept Carol's theology, but they accept her and she accepts them. Her loyalty is still to her own sisters. 'We are in constant contact with each other and are committed to caring for each other in any way that is needed.'

Including Carol, there are eight Blessed Sacrament Sisters remaining in Australia, where the order is clearly coming to an end. 'We're very aware of that and have been for years,' she said. 'We are setting up a trusteeship and all our finances are managed by the Blessed Sacrament office, so we're well prepared.' She finds the hierarchical Church more difficult. 'I don't have any truck with it. It can't hurt me and I am at peace with it. I am waiting with interest to see what Pope Francis does about the enquiry into the Leaders Conference of Women Religious CWR and the American sisters.' [9]

Carol finds there to be no separation between the spiritual and the secular in her life. 'Because we're imbued with the spirit, everything we do is hopefully done in love,' she said. 'I don't pray formally as much as I used to. Sometimes I just relax on my "prayer" chair, or lie on the couch and space out and let Sophia Spirit take over or I'll read Elizabeth Johnson again and write a liturgy on it or I'll be preparing for our feminist theology meeting, I spend a day or two on that. It is also in my encounters with other people that I find yet another presence of the Spirit.' Of course there are times of grief, pain, doubts, questions and anger. When that happens Carol stops and reflects. 'I place myself in my loving God's embrace and trust in her

9 In 2012 the Vatican condemned the Leaders Conference of Women Religious for its radical feminist views. The LCWR was founded in 1956 and represents 80 per cent of Catholic Sisters in the US.

love for me. Sometimes it takes a few hours, sometimes weeks, but I know that there is always resurrection.'

In December 2013, Carol Hogan was diagnosed with pancreatic cancer. In January she emailed her friends explaining that she was packing up her life in Kensington and moving into palliative care. 'I am at peace,' she wrote, 'and hopefully will live this last stage of my journey with integrity and trust in my loving Sophia God Mother who holds me in her embrace.' Carol died on 2 June 2014.